Postprint

THE WELLEK LIBRARY LECTURES

THE WELLEK LIBRARY LECTURES

The Wellek Library Lectures in Critical Theory are given annually at the University of California, Irvine, under the auspices of UCI Critical Theory. The following lectures were given in May 2016.

UCI Critical Theory

James A. Steintrager, Director

For a complete list of titles, see page 231

N. Katherine Hayles

Postprint

Books and Becoming Computational

Columbia University Press *New York*

Columbia University Press
Publishers Since 1893
New York   Chichester, West Sussex
cup.columbia.edu
Copyright © 2021 Columbia University Press
All rights reserved

Library of Congress Cataloging-in-Publication Data
Names: Hayles, N. Katherine, 1943– author.
Title: Postprint : books and becoming computational /
N. Katherine Hayles.
Description: New York : Columbia University Press, [2020] |
Series: The Wellek Library lectures | Includes bibliographical
references and index.
Identifiers: LCCN 2020022410 (print) | LCCN 2020022411 (ebook)
| ISBN 9780231198240 (hardcover) | ISBN 9780231198257
(trade paperback) | ISBN 9780231552554 (ebook)
Subjects: LCSH: Book industries and trade—Technological
innovations. | Book industries and trade—Social aspects. | Digital
media—Social aspects. | Cognition. | Communication and
technology.
Classification: LCC Z278 .H39 2020 (print) | LCC Z278 (ebook) |
DDC 302.23/1—dc23
LC record available at https://lccn.loc.gov/2020022410
LC ebook record available at https://lccn.loc.gov/2020022411

Cover image: Digital composite
Cover design: Lisa Hamm

Contents

LIST OF ILLUSTRATIONS VII

ACKNOWLEDGMENTS IX

1 Introducing Postprint 1

2 Print Into Postprint 41

3 The Mixed Ecologies of University Presses 87

4 Postprint and Cognitive Contagion 133

5 Bookishness at the Limits: Resiting the Human 171

Epilogue: Picturing the Asemic 189

NOTES 191

BIBLIOGRAPHY 211

INDEX 219

Illustrations

2.1a and 2.1b. Jacquard cards used to produce the "Coquette" label and the label   45

2.2. Pages from *Livre de prières*   46

2.3. Front view of the Paige Compositor   47

2.4. Rear view of the Paige Compositor   48

2.5. Side view of the Paige Compositor   48

2.6. Reproduction of a page from Paige's patent application   51

2.7. Section of type disc, Lumitype phototypesetter   56

2.8. Commercial version of Lumitype/Photon   59

2.9a. Top view, fiber-optic bundle   63

2.9b, 2.9c. View of fiber-optic bundle input and output   63

2.10a, 2.10b. Page and image from *The Wonderful World of Insects*   65

2.11. Xerox DocuTech 128HLC   69

5.1. Cover image of *Between Page and Screen*   173

5.2a, 5.2b. Composite screen shot from *Between Page and Screen*   173

5.3. Screen shot showing "spinto" projection from *Between Page and Screen*   176

5.4. Mirtha Dermisache, plate 1 in *Selected Writings*   181

5.5. Mirtha Dermisache, plate 5 in *Selected Writings*   184

5.6. Mirtha Dermisache, plate 12 in *Selected Writings*   185

6.1. Nick Sergeant, "The Human Stain"   190

Acknowledgments

This book has been catalyzed by two major forces: my lifelong love of books and my intellectual engagement with the concept of cognitive assemblages. Growing up in very small town in northeast Missouri (population 1,014), I had few resources to satisfy my curiosity about the world, nature, and science—no theater, no symphonies, no scientific instruments at home and barely any at school, no stimulating lectures by public intellectuals. In this preinternet era, the one resource I did have was print books. I devoured those at home before I was ten and then turned to the minuscule town library, which lasted until I was twelve or so. Then puberty struck, and my interests turned elsewhere for a while. Leaving that small town for college sparked my curiosity and widened my horizons; I would often read far into the night until the letters blurred on the page and dawn began to break. Books for me were objects of veneration, doors that opened onto vistas much broader, stranger, and more enticing than I could experience in person. So it was inevitable, I suppose, that I would one day write a book about print books.

It was not until I had developed the concept of cognitive assemblages, however, that I was able to bring together my affection for print with my intellectual interests in computation. I was fortunate to witness firsthand the enormous technological changes as computation came of age, from the first mainframe

Acknowledgments

I worked on in college (fed by IBM cards and large enough to fill a room with all four kilobytes of memory) to microcomputers, word processing, desktop publishing, and then the amazing growth of the web. Through it all, I was fascinated by the technical devices themselves and even more by their implications for what it means to be human. Print books, too, in all their variety have also affected not only our ideas about the human but also the neuronal and synaptic pathways by which we understand the world and ourselves. The conjunction of print and computation, a configuration that I call "postprint," thus presents a potent opportunity to explore through multiple registers, diverse historical events, and resonant metaphoric clusters our contemporary condition in developed societies.

On this journey, I have benefitted from many fellow travelers who have offered insights, stimulations, responses, and corrections. I am grateful to Matthew Kirschenbaum and John Maxwell for reading a draft of chapter 2 and offering comments as well as for their own excellent publications on print and computation. My colleagues at Duke University, including Rey Chow, Markos Hadjioannou, Mark Hansen, Mark Kruse, Carlos Rojas, Victoria Szabo, and Priscilla Wald generously shared ideas and initiated collaborative projects. Many former students, who have now become well-known scholars in their own right, have continued to challenge me to up my game, especially Zach Blas, Nathan Brown, Melody Jue, Kate Marshall, and Jessica Pressman. Francesca Farrando, Danuta Fjellestad, Patrick Jagoda, Todd Presner, and Rita Raley have been valuable sources of inspiration and collaboration, as have the research and books by Amarath Borsuk, Lisa Gitelman, Frank Romano, Garrett Stewart, Ted Striphas, and Edward Webster. I am grateful to the Literature Department of Duke University for support and help and to the English Department of the University of California, Los Angeles, for office space and computing support.

A version of chapter 2 was published as "Human and Machine Cultures of Reading: A Cognitive Assemblage Approach,"

Acknowledgments

PMLA 133, no. 5 (October 2018), and I am pleased to acknowledge *PMLA*'s permission to publish it here. I am very grateful to the Estate of Mirtha Dermisache and to Sigilio Press for permission to reproduce in chapter 5 three plates from Martha Dermisache, *Selected Writings*, ed. Daniel Owen and Lisa Pearson (New York: Siglio/Ugly Duckling Press, 2017), © Estate of Mirtha Dermisache, Buenos Aires, 2020, images courtesy of Siglio/Ugly Duckling Press, New York. I also appreciate Amaranth Borsuk and Brad Bouse's cooperation in reproducing images from their collaborative project *Between Page and Screen*.

Finally, I am very grateful to the editors and professionals at Columbia University Press for their invaluable help in preparing the manuscript for publication. This book originated as a series of three René Wellek lectures at the University of California, Irvine, in the spring of 2016, and I am grateful to the Department of Comparative Literature and UCI for sponsoring my visit. Wendy Lochner has been a supportive and patient interlocutor as the book gradually took form from this early venture. Annie Barva made many improvements in her copyediting, and Lowell Frye gently and persistently shepherded the manuscript along. Special thanks are due to Michael Haskell and designer Lisa Hamm for their generosity and willingness to help me create the "X-ray" pages, even though it meant considerable extra work for them to do so. I hope that my readers will agree it was worth the effort.

These acknowledgments would not be complete without recognizing Nicholas Gessler's contributions to the book. His name appears explicitly on several pages, but his influence and vast technical knowledge are subtexts for many more. Not everyone is fortunate enough to have a technical genius for a spouse; the only downside is that he is (almost always) right whenever we disagree!

Postprint

1

Introducing Postprint

Musing, you hold two books, one in your left hand, the other in your right. The left-hand book is a first edition of William Faulkner's classic novel *The Sound and the Fury* (1929), for which you paid a staggeringly extravagant sum at a rare-book dealer.[1] The right-hand book is a copy of the same novel that you bought on Amazon for a tiny fraction of that cost. Although you may not know it, the right-hand book was printed by CreateSpace, a digital publishing platform, at a nearby location to ensure you would receive it the next day. The bindings of course are different, but other than the colophon and publication date, all the words in both texts are the same. What do the differences matter, you think, except to a bibliophile like you, who prizes the aura of a first edition? Both are print books, aren't they?

The contradictory perceptions articulated here express the conundrum at the heart of contemporary print books. On the one hand, as Alexander Starre puts it, "the printed book as it is sold in bookstores or shelved in university libraries is essentially the same as it has been since Gutenberg invented moveable printing."[2] As Starre's careful qualification of shelved books hints, this illusion can be maintained only if the print book is regarded as an object in isolation. As soon as contexts are brought into view, the picture changes dramatically, represented in my example by noting the "aura" of the pricey first edition versus the print-on-demand knock-off. These contexts reveal that every aspect of print has been utterly transformed from Gutenberg's (or Virginia Woolf's) time, including how print books are composed, edited, designed, manufactured, warehoused, distributed, inventoried, sold, and read. This book argues that it is time—indeed, past time—to create a vocabulary and conceptual framework acknowledging the sea change that occurred when computational media permeated the printing industry. Like the slow accretion of chemicals on objects submerged in ocean water, this change took a half century or more to be fully realized, beginning roughly around 1950 and reaching full penetration with the new millennium. The term I propose to designate this new state of affairs is *postprint*.

"Oh no," I hear you groan, "not another 'post-'!" Yes, I know, it's a drag, but it honestly seems the most appropriate term to describe where we are now with respect to the contemporary production and consumption of bound books. *Post-*, as always, implies both succession and displacement, continuation and rupture. For clarity, I use *print* to refer to the long reign of bound books produced by printing presses from the fifteenth century to the mid–twentieth century and *postprint* for books produced after roughly 2000. The half century of innovation between 1950 and 2000 marks the decades when computational technologies transformed the printing industry. Of course, many innovations preceded this period, including lithography (1796), chromolithography (1837), rotary presses (1843), and offset printing (1875). But these changes were incremental, affecting only a small portion of the print regime. The period from 1950 to 2000 represents a difference in scale so dramatic that it amounts to a qualitative, not merely quantitative transformation. It is no exaggeration to say it constitutes a rupture in the genealogy of printed books—the rupture denoted by the term *postprint*. To find a transformation of comparable import, we would need to reference the invention of moveable type and the Gutenberg printing

Introducing Postprint

press. Although numerous studies have explored the implications of the printing press and the massive economic, social, cultural, and religious changes it brought about (including studies by Elizabeth Eisenstein and Adrian Johns, among others[3]), the full story of postprint is only beginning to be written. This book aspires to contribute to that effort.

What elements make postprint distinctively different from print? One approach would be to reference the differences that code makes in the material production of texts. The book artist and theorist Amaranth Borsuk captures this aspect of the computational transformation when she notes that "a text's digital life untethers it from any specific material support, making it accessible through a variety of interfaces (including the computer, cell phone, tablet, and dedicated e-reader), each of which influences our reading." The codes underlying digital texts position print in a profoundly different way than it was positioned in the previous epochs, for in the postprint era hard copy becomes merely one kind of output among many possible displays. As Borsuk concisely observes, "When books become content to be marketed and sold this way [as e-books], the historic relationship between materiality and text is severed."[4] I would modify her observation by adding that although the specificity of display varies, as she notes, it is important to realize that digital forms are also instantiated in specific platforms, operating systems, coding protocols, and display mechanisms. The difference is emphatically not between the materiality of print and the immateriality of digital forms, as is sometimes proclaimed, but rather between different kinds of material instantiations and diverse kinds of textual bodies.

To enhance the reader's awareness of the code layers essential for generating the print page in the postprint era, this book features ten black pages with white ink that display one or more of the code layers necessary for producing the facing white page. By analogy with X-rays that reveal the body's otherwise visually inaccessible skeletal frame, these pages may be considered

A computer manipulates BINARY codes of ONES and ZEROS.						
Data View						
Add...	Text (ASCII)			Binary			
000	A	c	o	01000001	00100000	01100011	01101111
004	m	p	u	t	01101101	01110000	01110101	01110100
008	e	r		m	01100101	01110010	00100000	01101101
012	a	n	i	p	01100001	01101110	01101001	01110000
016	u	l	a	t	01110101	01101100	01100001	01110100
020	e	s		B	01100101	01110011	00100000	01000010
024	I	N	A	R	01001001	01001110	01000001	01010010
028	Y		c	o	01011001	00100000	01100011	01101111
032	d	e	s		01100100	01100101	01110011	00100000
036	o	f		O	01101111	01100110	00100000	01001111
040	N	E	S		01001110	01000101	01010011	00100000
044	a	n	d		01100001	01101110	01100100	00100000
048	Z	E	R	O	01011010	01000101	01010010	01001111
052	S	.			01010011	00101110		

Here is the binary code for the sentence "A computer manipulates binary codes of ones and zeros," shown in the first table. The other table correlates binary code with the ASCII symbols. For example, "A" has the binary "0001" in the left column, with "100" across the top. Filling from the right, this makes the string 1000001. It takes seven bits to encode the letter; the eighth bit is reserved for special characters, here coded with 0 as null value, giving the final string as 01000001. Note that every symbol, including spaces and carriage returns, must be encoded. The "Control" column codes for these; carriage return is CR, or 1101000.

"X-ray" versions of the print page, revealing the code architectures hidden from the print reader's view but essential for the (post)print reading experience. Captions identify the relation of the displayed code to the print page, and readers are invited to read across the page spread, correlating black with white, code with output.

Moreover, this design alludes to the phenomenon that Jessica Pressman calls the "aesthetic of bookishness." She argues that the advent of the digital has had the paradoxical effect of stimulating widespread interest in the history of the book, with a flowering of scholarship in this area that is truly remarkable.[5] Our collaboratively coedited essay collection *Comparative Textual*

Introducing Postprint

Media: Transforming the Humanities in the Postprint Era, which was among the first to put the term *postprint* into circulation, brought together some of this research to demonstrate that digitality has not endangered print books, as Jeff Gomez asserts in *Print Is Dead*, but rather has opened possibilities to compare different forms of textual media by engaging in what I have elsewhere called "media-specific analysis."[6] Here media-specific analysis takes the form of visual presentations of code along with print pages, suggesting that traditional forms of reading print may now be augmented to include reading the underlying code as well. The idea of media-specific analysis grew out of my long interest in the materiality of texts, shown perhaps most extensively in my artist's book collaboration with designer Anne Burdick, *Writing Machines*.[7] Almost a decade ago, then, I was already experimenting with the idea of "postprint," but it has taken the intervening years for me to have the time and framework through which I could make this more than a rhetorical assertion. Now, with this book, I present a fully fleshed-out argument based on archival research, interviews, and, perhaps most importantly, an encompassing conceptual framework within which to position postprint as part of larger social, economic, and cognitive transformations. I see these transformations as analogous to other world-changing and species-defining cognitive developments such as the inventions of language and literacy. Borsuk makes much the same point when she succinctly observes, "It bears emphasizing that writing itself fundamentally changed human consciousness, much as our reliance on networked and digital devices has altered us at the core."[8]

Why Cognition?

How to capture the essence of these transformations? Although the interjection of code into textuality captures limited aspects of the change, the transformation's full scope is much broader.

My approach has been to scale up (and down) to what I see as the catalyst for all of postprint's diverse aspects—namely, the emergence of cognition in artificial media. Just as the advent of the digital has catalyzed the history of the book by bringing the codex back into visibility, shattering its taken-for-granted quality acquired through centuries of habituation, so the emergence of cognition in artificial media has stimulated a reconceptualization of cognition in general, including biological cognition. Through several books, including *How We Became Posthuman: Virtual Bodies in Cybernetics, Literature, and Informatics*; *My Mother Was a Computer: Digital Subjects and Literary Texts*; *How We Think: Digital Media and Contemporary Technogenesis*; and especially *Unthought: The Power of the Cognitive Nonconscious*,[9] I have explored the relationship of human cognition to computational media and to cognition generally. This journey has also involved reexamining the role of cognition in human life, for which I drew on recent work in neuroscience, cognitive science, and related fields demonstrating that cognition is much broader and deeper than consciousness. To make the argument effectively, I obviously needed to define *cognition*. To emphasize that cognition includes consciousness but is not limited to it, I wanted to position it so it would include affective responses, internal and external sensory systems, nonconscious cognition, and other embodied, enactive, and embedded bodily capacities. I also wanted it to connect with contexts that include internal and external milieu. After considerable deliberation, here is what I came up with: "Cognition is a process of interpreting information in contexts that connect it with meaning." This definition has the advantage of conciseness; it also invokes two terms especially potent within the humanities, *interpretation* and *meaning*, which also require more explication.

Starting from this foundation, I argued that all biological lifeforms have some cognitive capacities, even those without brains, such as nematode worms and plants. To reposition the terms *meaning* and *interpretation*, I drew from biosemiotics, a field that studies sign creation, interpretation, and dissemination among nonhuman species. For biosemioticians such as Jesper Hoffmeyer, Terrence Deacon, and Wendy Wheeler, meaning-making practices are essentially behaviors evoked by environmental changes, such as a deciduous tree losing its leaves in winter.[10] In this minimal sense, all life-forms perform interpretations on information coming from their environments (for multicellular organisms, also coming from their internal sensory systems), which are meaningful to them within their world horizons (or *Umwelten*, as Jacob von Uexküll puts it[11]).

This framework radically shifts the position of humans in relation to other life-forms. Rather than emphasizing human uniqueness (along with the inevitable corresponding denigration of other species), it emphasizes continuities of cognition across the biological spectrum while still acknowledging the specificities of each species' capacities. At the same time, it also recognizes humans' special ability to take responsibility for those attributes associated with symbolic reasoning and higher consciousness, such as the ability to formulate complex plans, implement them, and recognize large-scale patterns and significances. Taking responsibility positions humans not as dominators of the planet but as caretakers of it for their own benefit, for other species, and for the planet-wide systems of material processes on which all life depends.

In addition to recontextualizing human cognition in relation to other life-forms, this approach also enables a different understanding of computational media relative to human cognition. Although many biosemioticians argue that computers cannot create meanings because they are not autonomous, this objection is an arbitrary limitation belied by what computers actually do. As far I know, no computational media are conscious. Nevertheless, like nonconscious organisms, computers have internal and external milieus: they process and interpret information, including information from sensors and actuators when these things are present, and they create meanings in the sense of performing behaviors that have efficacy within their environments. Because cognition is inherently embodied, making these claims does not obscure or avoid the fact that computational media have profoundly different instantiations—that is, bodies—than do biological organisms, nor does it imply that computers operate like brains or vice versa.

Thus repositioned, cognition spans all three domains—humans, nonhumans, and computational media—while foregrounding the importance of specific embodiments and embeddings across the domains. Moreover, the extension of human cognition through computational media has been and in all likelihood will continue to be a major driver in human evolution now and in the foreseeable future. Human cognition no longer relies solely on the glacial pace of biological evolution but now proceeds through the exponentially faster processes of cyber-bio-evolution, where evolution through generational change is measured in months rather than in hundreds of thousands of years. Wherever cognitive processes take place—in humans, nonhumans, and technical devices—they bestow the advantages of flexibility, adaptability, and evolvability. At the same time, all cognitive processes depend on material processes, such as chemical reactions, that are not cognitive in themselves because they do not perform interpretations, make choices or selections, or create meanings. It took the spark of life to activate those possibilities, and it took millions of years more for that spark to evolve into life-forms capable of creating similar cognitive possibilities in artificial media.

Although my definition of cognition focuses primarily on individual cognizers, I also want to emphasize that interpretations and meaning-making practices circulate through transindividual collectivities created by fluctuating and dynamic interconnections between humans and computational media, interconnections that I call *cognitive assemblages*. Much of the world's work in developed societies is increasingly done through cognitive assemblages. You may not think about it in these terms, but when you activate your car's starter motor by means of a key with an embedded chip, you are participating in a cognitive assemblage. That sequence can be described as follows: the embedded key chip links up with your vehicle's computer and allows the ignition button to activate and complete an electrical circuit, initiating a chain of events in which a current is fed to the solenoid, which turns on an electromagnet, attracting an iron rod, whose movement closes two heavy contacts, thus completing the circuit from the battery to the starter, which then turns the shaft so that the pinion (or gear wheel) engages with a large gear ring around the rim of the engine flywheel, which begins to turn at increasing speeds, and voilà!—your car starts. This sequence used to be purely electromechanical, but now virtually all contemporary cars have keys with embedded chips and vehicle computers, which typically work to control, disseminate, and modulate information. Similarly, you are participating in cognitive assemblages when you talk on your cell phone, turn on a light switch, fly on a plane, take the subway, order groceries on Amazon, use your credit card to pay a restaurant bill—each of these everyday activities is interfaced with computational media such that it will not work without them. As different entities, human and nonhuman, enter into communication and information circuits, the assemblage fluctuates in its groupings and functions. The cognitive-assemblage framework aims to be flexible enough to accommodate these differences while still being specific enough to be useful.

If we ask why computational media deserve primary emphasis in the framework developed here, the answer may not be immediately obvious. They are not, for example, the most impactful for ordinary human lives; that honor might go to transportation networks, from dirt paths to jet aircraft. Nor are they the most important for human well-being; sanitation facilities and water-treatment plants would be better candidates for that nomination. But transportation networks, sewage-disposal systems, and water-treatment plants are nowadays likely to have computational components as controllers, communicators, distributors, and interpreters of information flows. As with an automobile starter circuit, these computational components intervene in previously developed technologies to make them more flexible and adaptive to changing circumstances. It is precisely their cognitive capabilities—their ability to interpret information flows in ways that connect them to contexts of meaning—that account for their deep penetration into virtually every aspect of contemporary life and for the enormous effects they are having on how we humans live our lives and the kind of creatures we understand ourselves to be.

In (very) broad outline, then, the situation looks like this: It took a few million years for biological evolution to result in *Homo sapiens*, the first species to engage extensively in abstract thought and symbolic reasoning. Humans are the cognitive species par excellence, and we have used these abilities to instantiate symbolic reasoning and logic in artificial media, which now have their own evolutionary dynamics. In suggesting a parallel between biological and artificial evolution, I do not intend to minimize the significant differences between them. These differences can be understood through what I call the two great inversions.[12] The first inversion replaced the biological mandate "survive and reproduce," the process through which biological evolution proceeds, with the computational mandate "design and purpose." Computational systems, unlike biological organisms, are designed for specific purposes, so their evolution in this sense proceeds in top-down fashion.

The second great inversion concerns the directionality of evolutionary trajectories. From day one, biological organisms had to be able to cope with fluctuating and unpredictable environments; if they could not, they did not survive. From this foundation, a cognitive trajectory toward increasing complexity eventually led to the capability for abstract thought. Computational media, by contrast, instantiate abstract thought at a foundational level in the logic gates, which are almost completely deterministic. From this base, layers of software increasingly enable computational media to deal with uncertain and ambiguous information. When sensors and actuators are added, computational systems may also be able to deal with environmental ambiguities and fluctuations. In addition, developments beyond von Neumann architectures, such as neural nets and neuromorphic chips, further advance in the direction of fault-tolerant systems able to draw inferences from unruly data and to operate successfully even with contradictory information.[13] In this sense, then, the trajectory of computational evolution proceeds in the opposite direction from biological evolution. The biological progression is from uncertainties up to abstraction, which the computational progression inverts so that it proceeds from abstraction up to uncertainties.

In summary, my focus on cognition is intended to capture the aspects of computational media that make them not just another technology but a *cognitive* technology able to interpret, disseminate, and contextualize flows of information so they become meaningful within specific contexts. This is why these media are able to impart to a huge variety of other technologies the advantages that cognition bestows—flexibility, adaptability, and evolvability. Once mechanical processes are interpenetrated by computational components able to interpret information and create meaning from it, they are able to carry out tasks impossible for machines without cognitive abilities.

For example, mobile robots stacking boxes in a warehouse are able to do tasks that would be impossible for a forklift lacking a human driver.[14] The forklift by itself cannot navigate around obstacles; it is unable to judge properly how to lift and stack boxes, nor does it know when to start and stop. The forklift can operate *only* when human cognition comes to the rescue and provides the cognitive abilities that it lacks. But as the box-stacking robots demonstrate, incorporating computational components into machines now enables machines to take on tasks that formerly could be done only by humans.

Of course, humans create, program, implement, and maintain these cognitive devices (by operating within the relevant cognitive assemblages). Nevertheless, the intervals in which cognitive technologies operate autonomously are becoming both more numerous and longer in duration. Self-driving cars, already in use, are an obvious example, but they are the tip of the iceberg. Much of the infrastructure of developed societies already incorporates and completely depends on cognitive technologies, including electrical grids, communication networks, currency and monetary exchanges, transportation vehicles in all their forms, and so forth. In fact, I will make the bold claim that daily life in developed societies can proceed in normal fashion *only* because of the incorporation of cognitive assemblages, without which crucial infrastructural systems simply would not function.

Cognitive Assemblages and Becoming Computational

As a phrase, *cognitive assemblage*, like Janus, faces in two directions at once. One face turns toward the embodied, embedded, and enactive processes of cognition, which are always species specific, related to specific contexts and circumstances, circumscribed by the sensory and cognitive capacities of organisms that create distinctive world horizons, and performed by individual entities. The other turns toward fluctuating collectivities through which information, interpretations, and meanings circulate. It foregrounds connections between entities, circuits of stores and flows, resistances and affordances that they inflect and direct, and the diverse meanings partially shared and partially obscured that emerge through those connections and circuits. Although each of the connections can be specified through the materialities creating them, the flow allows information to travel among different substrates and diverse interpretation media. In this sense, the cognitive-assemblage framework enables two different kinds of discourses: one that focuses on the materialities of individual participants and another that focuses on the more abstract flows that bind entities together into a collectivity.

It is worth emphasizing that a cognitive assemblage may include conscious participants, but its functionality does not require it to do so. It can also operate through nonconscious cognition and with nonhuman entities as well as with humans. A cell phone call, for example, means one thing to the person receiving it, another thing to the phone receiving/producing it, and still something else to the repeating tower used to help transmit it. If the human is cut out of the loop, for example, when a user does not answer and the call goes to voicemail, then all of the participants receiving and interpreting the call are nonhuman computational cognitive entities.

In appropriating the term *assemblage*, I draw on the work of both Bruno Latour and Gilles Deleuze and Félix Guattari, with some differences. In Latour's invocation of *assemblage*, often used as a synonym for *network*, objects with no cognitive capacities, such as a hammer or pulley, are agents just as much as cognitive entities are (although, in fact, Latour rarely instances cognitive technologies such as computers, preferring to remain in the realm of mechanical devices).[15] In contrast, my view of assemblage makes a clear distinction between cognitive entities and noncognitive ones. In Deleuze and Guattari's texts, "assemblage" is often how the term *agencement* is translated. The French term better captures the dynamism they envision for an assemblage, in which components are always on their way to becoming something else. In contrast to their usage, I assume that entities may be relatively stable and preexist the assemblage in which they participate. Another inspiration for me is Deleuze and Guattari's notion of "becoming" (as in "becoming-animal" or "becoming-woman"), which for them is a result of seeing entities as more or less temporary arrangements, with special emphasis on movements from majoritarian configurations to minoritarian ones.[16] Of course, Deleuze was highly influenced by the work of Gilbert

Simondon, another powerful thinker about the way transindividuation (movements beyond the individual that form a consistent aggregation) takes place, as well as by Alfred North Whitehead, whose processural philosophy also heads in this direction.[17] My hesitation about adopting such philosophical positions wholesale has to do with what I see in Deleuze and Guattari as their neglect—indeed, almost complete erasure—of the mechanisms that work toward preserving the stability of entities, from the skin that for mammals is the body's largest organ to the fundamental role of DNA in conserving information across the generations of biological life-forms to the systemic dynamics that make computational media distinct as well as interconnected. Such stabilizing mechanisms are always in dynamic tension with destabilizing ones, but to emphasize only destabilization is as distorting as to emphasize only stabilization (for example, the mistaken focus on DNA as the sole arbiter of how inheritance works even though it is now recognized to be in dynamic interaction with epigenetics and other mechanisms). These reservations are expressed typographically in my subtitle by the absence of the Deleuzian hyphen in "becoming computational."

The idea that the evolution of computational media is now completely entwined with human evolution strikes me as a conclusion as inescapable as it is potent with implications for the future of humans and the planet. In my work in progress, "Cyberbio-evolution: A General Ecology of Cognitive Assemblages," I explore this idea in depth, which I call *cybersymbiosis*. We (humans) are becoming computational in one way or another, just as computational systems are edging toward the biologically fundamental processes of dealing with uncertainties and ambiguities. If we are to believe the intimations of our science fiction writers, perhaps computational systems are also evolving toward the biological mandate of survival and reproduction (as in films such as *Terminator*, *Ex Machina*, etc.). It follows that books in all their diversity, as facilitators of and interactors with human cognitions, are also in the process of becoming computational. My focus is not only books by themselves, however, but also books in the context of encompassing cognitive transformations. The conjunctive *and* in my subtitle is meant to position their becoming computational as one aspect of a much larger picture: the becoming computational of humans and, indeed, of the entire planet.[18]

Cognitive Assemblages and Postprint

What kind of work can the cognitive-assemblage framework do in relation to postprint? It provides a way to conceptualize innovations in print technology as redistributions of cognitive capabilities between humans and machines. Such an approach enables new questions to be asked about the benefits and limitations of the emerging assemblages—a crucial point, for example, in chapter 2 in explaining why the Paige Compositor was rendered obsolete by the Mergenthaler Linotype typesetting machine. **It also provides a way for transformations in printing machines to be linked to corresponding changes in editing, designing, producing, selling, and consuming books because at a foundational level all of these changes have resulted from the introduction of computational media. Many branches grow from this trunk, and although they may appear different in function, form, and placement along the production cycle, tracing them back to the root transformation enables us to understand them as related effects and not simply as different kinds of phenomena. Postprint reveals this convergence by locating print within the computational-media ecology in which it currently exists.**

In addition, postprint suggests new kinds of connections with existing fields of inquiry. The area centrally concerned with print technologies in relation to books is of course the history of the book. The recent flourishing of scholarship in this area has made

```
30    <H1>Cognitive Assemblages and Postprint</H1>
31 ▼  <NOP>What kind of work can the cognitive-
      assemblage framework do in relation
      to postprint? It provides a way to
      conceptualize innovations in print
      technology as redistributions of cognitive
      capabilities between humans and machines.
      Such an approach enables new questions to be
      asked about the benefits and limitations of
      the emerging assemblages—a crucial point,
      for example, in chapter 2 in explaining why
      the Paige Compositor was rendered obsolete
      by the Mergenthaler Linotype typesetting
      machine. <B>It also provides a way for
      transformations in printing machines to
      be linked to corresponding changes in
      editing, designing, producing, selling, and
      consuming books because at a foundational
      level all of these changes have resulted
      from the introduction of computational
      media. Many branches grow from this trunk,
      and although they may appear different
      in function, form, and placement along
      the production cycle, tracing them back
      to the root transformation enables us to
      understand them as related effects and not
      simply as different kinds of phenomena.
      Postprint reveals this convergence by
      locating print within the computational-
      media ecology in which it currently
      exists.</B></NOP>
32    <X>In addition, postprint suggests new
      kinds of connections with
```

XML code facilitates communication between humans and machines as well as between computational devices, thus enabling cognitive assemblages to function.

many important contributions, especially in its attention to the materiality of texts and the everyday practices of literary production and consumption. Nevertheless, the kind of wide-ranging yet coherent approach I advocate here is still underdeveloped and underappreciated within the discipline as a whole, perhaps because of a lingering distrust of and ignorance about computational technologies and their relation to literary enterprises. Only in the past few years have studies emerged that link the history of the book with computational media, such as Johanna Drucker's *SpecLab: Digital Aesthetics and Projects in Speculative Computing*; Matthew Kirschenbaum's meticulously researched *Track Changes: A Literary History of Word Processing*; Dennis Tenen's *Plain Text: The Poetics of Computation*; and Amaranth Borsuk's *The Book*, among others.[19] To my knowledge, my focus on cognition here pursues the link between the history of print and computational technologies along lines not previously explored. It brings to light new archival resources in the history of technology not generally acknowledged within studies of the history of the book; through interviews, it also develops connections with scholarly publishing practices that illuminate the complex ways in which humans respond when they find themselves having to deal with technologies they did not invent and may not completely understand but that they also cannot avoid.

The focus on cognition also serves as a springboard to further understand cultural phenomena: the ways that print has been enmeshed in what it means to be human in literate, developed societies and how these ways are changing as some of the cognitive tasks that once were performed exclusively by humans are now carried out by computational media. Such a change in the distribution of cognitive capabilities carries important and, indeed, momentous implications about the future of the human species as well as about the everyday practices of writing, editing, and producing books, a throughline that connects all the chapters.[20]

Finally, my exploration of this subject has a personal motivation as well. Like many academics in the humanities, I live a significant portion of my everyday life through and amid print books. They are my teachers, collaborators, companions, friends, and opponents urging me to up my game. Embarking on this book has thus for me been a way to ground theoretical ideas in an area crucial to my professional practice and central to my sense of self. In a word, I am deeply *invested* in print culture and in the transformations it is undergoing as it morphs into postprint. At the same time, this book also serves as a test bed to put on trial general ideas about cognition, evolution, cybersymbiosis, ethics in/as innovation, and human futurity to see which of them hold up and which don't.

Postprint as Equivocal Figure

In a sense, the marriage I am proposing under the rubric of postprint is much stranger than that of a Montague and Capulet who have fallen madly in love because it joins not just two estranged lineages but multiple ones. Consider, for example, the relation between book studies and the history of technology. One would think the two should be closely related because the book, as book historians rightly delight in pointing out, is a result of complex technological processes. Yet they have much fewer crossovers than might be imagined, in part, I suspect, because of the aura and cultural capital of books compared, say, to a ball-bearing factory. Or think of the history of computing in relation to book studies. As mentioned earlier, only recently have studies appeared that link the two, even though, as I show in chapter 2, their fates have been entwined since the 1950s. Or, again, consider the cognitive studies of literature, an emerging field with several landmark studies and collections, and of electronic literature, the area of literary creation, discussion, and criticism that most directly connects to computation. With few exceptions, the two fields proceed along divergent tracks and have almost completely different archives of reference, principally because "cognition" in cognitive studies is invariably taken to mean human cognition without extending the idea to computational media.

Yet the seemingly unconnected threads sticking out from these multiple fields cross one another all the time, and it takes only a shift in perception to bring the linkages between them into view. I think here of equivocal figures, such as the vase that suddenly is perceived as the profile of a young woman. I hope that the idea of machine cognition and the related concept of cognitive assemblages will stimulate a shift in perception that brings a new configuration into view for my readers, the result of a marriage between multiple partners with several different lineages. In my experience with equivocal figures, once both possibilities are perceived, it is possible to switch from one to the other by focusing on a point of connection—say, a pedestal indentation that becomes a projecting chin. Perhaps the term *postprint* may function as the verbal cue, akin to the pedestal indentation, that allows folks to see how the new configuration emerges from yet interacts with older perceptions, creating a rich sense of dynamic interaction between them. My intent is thus not simply to negate older configurations that assume that only humans have cognition but also to enhance them by putting them in different contexts of meaning and interpretation, processes central to my framework of cognitive assemblages but also operating within readers in relation to the new picture I hope to bring into visibility.

Recent Book Scholarship in Relation to Postprint

One of the lineages contributing to this new configuration is the history of the book. In the profusion of recent book studies, three trends have special relevance to bringing the postprint configuration into view: the impulse to synthesize multiple aspects of the book into a single picture; an emerging emphasis on everyday practices within the print world; and the appearance of narrative strategies specifically catalyzed by the conjunction of digital technologies with the print codex. Together, these trends reveal how the present study overlaps with published scholarship yet also how it opens new possibilities for continuing research.

In the first category of enlarging the scope, Amaranth Borsuk's *The Book* is exemplary. Its very existence in MIT's Essential Knowledge series testifies to the resurgence of interest in the history of the book and the growing scholarly attention to the codex form and its predecessors. The large scope becomes apparent when Borsuk writes that her aim is to consider the book as object, content, idea, and interface. An especially attractive feature is the confident way she handles the advent of digital technologies and the possibilities they present for new kinds of experimentation. Confronting the claim that digital texts will result in the death of books, she brushes aside the looming anxiety booklovers might feel by causally remarking, "That question isn't as interesting, though, as the question of how each of these technologies [from the invention of moveable type to e-books] has been, and will continue to be, part of the book's development."[21] Her chapter on artists' books makes good on this perspective by including many hybrid print–digital productions as well as works of electronic literature. Although attentive to technological innovations and forms, Borsuk nevertheless locates the moment when literature happens in a reader's mind: "Books are always a negotiation, a performance, an event: even a Dickens novel remains inert until a reader opens it up, engaging its language and imaginative world." She even concludes her study by reinforcing the message: "All books, I hope this volume suggests, arise in the moment of reception, in the hands, eyes, ears, and mind of the reader."[22]

This is a comforting thought for those who want to see the history of the book as a continuing engagement between the artifact and the reader's mind that stretches unbroken across the centuries. It is also typical of older formations in putting sole emphasis on *human* cognition. Yet Borsuk knows as well as anyone that this is not the complete story and that in the contemporary era cognitive machine operations often intercede between book and (human) mind. We need go no further than her own creative work to have this key insight confirmed. Her innovative book *Between Page and Screen* (2016), coauthored with Brad Bouse, presents as a print codex but contains no words, only optical codes that when held up to a digital optical reader project word poems that chronicle a difficult and challenging love affair between P and S (discussed at length in chapter 5).[23] In the arrangement that Borsuk and Bouse have set up, machine interpretations and meaning-making practices are the necessary antecedents for a human reader to perceive any words at all. The result is a book that instantiates itself as a cognitive assemblage, a dynamically interacting coproduction between machine and human cognition. What crucial clue can bring this changed perception into view? I like to think it is "cognition"—the realization that the machine performs not just any operations but specifically cognitive ones. Once this realization has crystallized, it becomes necessary to modify Borsuk's closing claim that literature is an event that happens in a reader's mind to a more precise formulation that literature is an event happening (sometimes) in a cognitive assemblage.

A different encompassing approach is pioneered by Garrett Stewart in *Book Text Medium: Cross Sectional Reading for a Digital Age*. He comments that "this is the first account to venture in a fully material sense . . . a sustained conjunction of book studies, textual studies, and media studies: or, better put, book history, textual analysis, and media theory."[24] Somewhat idiosyncratically, he understands the term *medium* to refer to language rather than to a particular delivery vehicle. This perspective is at once innovative and clever, for it defines *medium* in such a way that it largely insulates his analysis from having to deal much with technology, positioning it instead to play to his strengths in the areas of verbal ambiguities, language play, and the material properties of book objects. For my money, no one is better at this game than Garrett Stewart. He excels in excavating homophonic puns from linguistic structures as well as in understanding in deep terms how the material properties of the codex can be used to create meanings. He demonstrates this in his earlier publication *Bookwork: Medium to Concept to Object to Art*, a study devoted to what happens when a book is demediated or altered by an artist so that it literally cannot be read and functions instead as an artifactual object stimulating new realizations in the mind of a viewer.[25]

Yet even Stewart finds opportunities to draw connections between his typical interests and computer interpretations—for example, when in *Book Text Medium* he discusses Borsuk and Bouse's *Between Page and Screen*. His response is worth quoting at length for the connections it makes:

> Uploaded here is a whole new implementation of the "picture book" as "illuminated" text. A very long leap, then, and not just technological but aesthetic. Even political, as we'll see—since ceding to the computer the right to do our "book reading" for us, even when only a trope for exaggerated interactivity, has consequences not soon bottled up. A transhistorical leap, to be sure, is needed to move from one end of this long cultural spectrum to the other, from sacred painting to such interactive computer graphics. But recent phases of the intervening terrain have been variously occupied—and rigorously thought (as well as passed) through—by several decades of resistant conceptualist invention in the work of words.[26]

We see here the turn from direct consideration of the technology (having the computer do our reading for us) to more familiar territories of conceptual art and the "work of words," but not before Stewart acknowledges that having a computer read initiates "consequences not soon bottled up." Indeed! It would take only a gentle nudge, I think, for the new configuration I am limning here to appear from this vision of conceptual and verbal art as interventions in the way humans see ourselves and the objects we create. What's missing is a sense that computers are also capable of cognition and that they, too, produce interpretations and meanings that circulate within machine contexts as well as human ones. Like a seed crystal dropped into a supersaturated solution, "cognitive assemblages" might do the trick.

Another way in which this study aligns with book studies while nevertheless bringing a new configuration into view is in the emphasis on the everyday. Through interviews, archival research, and textual analyses, Amy Hungerford's *Making Literature Now* conveys a vivid impression of what it means to work as a writer and creator of literature in the contemporary moment.[27] Especially useful are her distinction between celebrity and subsistence writers (that is, writers who cannot make a living writing) and her insightful analysis of how each kind of writer depends on the other. The celebrity writer not only solicits work from subsistence writers but also uses their (usually underpaid and sometimes unpaid) labor to create an aura of "art for art's sake" that enhances the cultural capital of the celebrity writer's own (usually highly paid) work. Of course, it is not news that celebrity writers hand off certain writing tasks to subsistence writers (think ghostwriters), but Hungerford shows that the present configurations of digital technologies with print books enable new kinds of circular payoffs for both.

One of Hungerford's case studies is the digital version of *The Silent History* (discussed here in chapter 4 as the print codex published when the app version was completed), with Eli Horowitz as master creator enlisting app users to submit "Field Reports" that extend the narrative via Global Positioning System (GPS) technology into local habitats and local knowledge. Although she does not mention it, we might also think of *Ship of Theseus*, the collaborative project between celebrity media creator J. J. Abrams, who masterminded the concept, and Doug Dorst, whom Abrams enlisted to write the narratives. It is no accident that this codex, like *The Silent History*, is formally innovative, for both works are postprint productions completely interpenetrated by the digital technologies crucial for their physical instantiations.[28]

Although Hungerford emphasizes the personal connections between writers and publishers (especially McSweeney's), she is also alert to differences between digital instantiations and print books. Her chapter on *The Silent History* recognizes that the digital instantiation is actually quite different from the print version (see chapter 4 for an analysis of how the codex version's verbal text differs from the app version's). Moreover, she is quick to make the connection between users of the app and the silent protagonists of *The Silent History*, who are alienated from normal social relations by their inability to learn or understand verbal language. In both the app and codex versions, we learn that the "silents," as they are called, are subjected to mandatory computational implants that enable them to speak, but at the price of confining their articulations solely to the words and phrases in the computer's databases. In direct address to the reader, Hungerford makes the connection between the implanted silents and the app users (who may be hearing an audio version of the narrative through headphones): "You find yourself manipulated by a central processor that pipes language into your brain . . . [and that] makes us into the very figure of the wandering silent."[29] The recognition that the "central processor" is a cognitive actor trembles on the brink of visibility here. If brought into full view, it would enable a cascading series of realizations about what it means for humans to act within computational environments that are capable of performing interpretations and creating meaningful contexts, some of which are aimed at machine addressees rather than human ones. Here the new configuration, once perceived, would enlarge the scope of inquiry so that it pertains not just to a single digital work but to our contemporary condition as actors within cognitive assemblages.

In the field of book history, Ted Striphas perhaps comes closest to the interests of the present study in *The Late Age of Print* when he interrogates some of the technologies that made the contemporary codex into a mass-produced commodity integrated with digital technologies in its production, distribution, marketing, and consumption. It is interesting that in 2009 he still found it useful to pick up on Jay David Bolter's phrase "the late age of print" for his title, referring to Bolter's study published in 1990 in a preweb era that is now apt to seem quaintly old-fashioned. Striphas quotes Bolter's assertion that "just as late capitalism is still vigorous capitalism, so books and other printed materials in the late age of print are still common and enjoy considerable prestige."[30] Of course, printed books are still common, but whereas the phrase *late age* emphasizes continuities, the term *postprint* acknowledges both continuities *and* ruptures. Moreover, *postprint* denotes that far more than the physical artifact is involved, extending the transformation's scope into every aspect of book production and consumption. In addition, the cognitive-assemblage framework developed here links these artifactual and technological changes with large-scale cultural, economic, and psychological processes through the operations of hybrid human–technical collectivities crucial to contemporary developed societies. Striphas writes that his focus on the everyday has the advantage of concentrating on change "without presuming a full-blown crisis exists."[31] I agree with his strategy of avoiding an apocalyptic tone, although I would add that precisely because cognitive assemblages have become the everyday does not mean that they are not effecting transformations of massive scope and import. They are both banal and momentous, everyday and utterly transformative.

For my purposes, the clearest example of how digital technologies affect contemporary book production comes in Striphas's chapter on the history and implementation of the International Standard Book Number (ISBN). He cites a report from O. H. Cheney in 1932 asserting that the major chokepoint in the book industry's expansion was its lack of standardized distribution mechanisms, thus highlighting the importance of back-office operations for the entire trade. The solution, Striphas explains, included the development of standardized numbers that would uniquely characterize each volume. He makes the point that the "ISBN isn't merely a glorified stock number. Rather, it's a carefully conceived, highly significant, and mathematically exact *code* that contains detailed information about the identity of each book," including information about the book's language, region or nation, publisher, title, edition, and binding. "Corporate booksellers," he continues, "make books fungible, commensurable with one another. The ISBN was a crucial back office counterpart of these processes."[32]

So useful had ISBN codes become by 1980 that the International ISBN Agency contacted its counterpart, the European Article Number (EAN) International, to integrate the two systems in ways that would account for currency and national differences, which required that a prefix referring to the country of origin be added to the ISBN. Charmingly, the solution was to invent the fictious country of Bookland, denoted by the prefix 978. It was not until several years later, in the late 1980s, that the U.S. book industry finally agreed that all books sold in bookstores "would be imprinted exclusively with the Bookland EAN bar code."[33] It is no coincidence that this period was also the era when mainframes were being replaced by desktop computers, making computational functionalities accessible to every bookstore and book distributor. Although Striphas does not emphasize the point, the incorporation of ISBNs into computer databases via digital optical readers in the 1980s greatly expanded the ISBNs' utility, allowing them to be integrated with other information about books in ways that vastly improved not only distribution but also warehousing, inventory, shelving, and sales records. Striphas's account vividly demonstrates how important back-office operations are to the organization of the book industry. It follows that the penetration of computational processes into these operations also had enormous consequences for everyday practices that affected not only how books became mass-market commodities but also how they were—and are—produced, edited, formatted, warehoused, sold, and read: in brief, how books began to function within the cognitive assemblages crucial to contemporary developed societies.

Positioned somewhere between book studies and media studies is Alexander Starre's analysis of what he calls *metamedia*. He uses the term to demonstrate that the penetration of computational media into composing practices has affected the structures and meanings of literary texts. "Broadly speaking," he writes, "a literary work becomes a metamedium once it uses specific devices to reflexively engage with the specific material medium to which it is affixed or in which it is displayed."[34] As he acknowledges, in *Writing Machines* I developed a similar concept of "technotext," a literary work that reflects within itself the technological conditions of its composition and production. I have also discussed some of the texts he analyzes in terms of their self-reference to digital technologies, including Mark Danielewski's *House of Leaves* and Jonathan Safran Foer's *Extremely Loud and Incredibly Close* and *Tree of Codes*.[35] Starre is careful to delineate the ways in which his work diverges from mine, but the broader point, I think, is that we agree that digital technologies have deeply influenced not only how books are produced but also how they are conceived and written. "My argument about medial self-reference takes on its full significance when sketched out against the background of a different medium," he writes—that is, when seen in the context of digital technologies as distinct from paper-bound books.[36]

If I had to critique Starre's approach, I would focus on his claim that the term *metamedia* (which I like a lot) is broader than the term *technotext* because it corrects what he calls the "technological bias" of the latter.[37] Whether my approach consists of a "bias" toward technology or a focus on it depends on how important one considers technology, in particular computational media, in our contemporary moment. My argument here is that computational media, in addition to transforming everyday practices in innumerable ways, have also fundamentally altered the nature of cognition, repositioning human actions so that they increasingly operate within the contexts of cognitive assemblages. Of course, this repositioning affects how print books are conceived and written in the digital era, but the full scope of the transformation is much broader. Although the concepts of postprint and becoming computational include the phenomena that Starre references through metamedia, they also bring into view an emerging configuration in dynamic interplay with older formations associated with print culture, as we will witness, for example, in chapter 3, on how digital technologies are transforming scholarly publishing.

Media Archeology, Cultural Techniques, and Cognitive Assemblages

In addition to overlapping with history of the book and book studies, the cognitive-assemblage approach has commonalities with media archeology as well as some differences. According to Wolfgang Ernst, media archeology (in Ernst's spelling, "archaeology") proposes a countermethodology to a human-centered narrative approach, considering events from a nonhuman point of view, in particular the viewpoint of technical media. As Ernst puts it, "The media-archaeological method . . . is meant as an epistemologically alternative approach to the supremacy of media-historical narratives."[38] Focusing on technical media, Ernst characterizes them by pointing to the difference between painting and photography. Whereas the materials required by painting are always accessible to human senses, the active processes in photography (leaving aside setting the speed, aperture, and focus and clicking the shutter) are physiochemical reactions and are not generally directly accessible by human users. Today's camera, considered distinct from the human operator, has a cognitive viewpoint, and one of the goals of media archeology is to explore this viewpoint as fully as possible. Working from a different set of premises, Ian Bogost accomplishes a similar task in his discussion of the Foveon-equipped Sigma DP digital-image sensor.[39] As his analysis makes clear, media have bodies; that is, they are materially instantiated. And their bodies are increasingly equipped with sensors, actuators, and information processors. They perform interpretations and arrive at meanings specific to the contexts in which they operate and the functions they are designed to perform.

In practice, media archeology often focuses on legacy media such as early cinematic devices, telephones, telegraphs, and so forth. The tendency in media archeology is to promote, as Ernst describes it, an "awareness of moments when media themselves, not exclusively humans anymore, become active 'archaeologists' of knowledge." The differences between narrative and media archeology deepen when the devices are cognitive or, as Ernst writes, when "techno-epistemological configurations" underlie the "discursive surfaces"—that is, when software architectures generate the output that humans see.[40] If one focuses only on the (human-centered) display, the machine's viewpoint is lost, and one consequently has little or no idea of what is actually generating the display and the results it conveys.

Ernst's assertion that devices are "'archaeologists' of knowledge" claims more than his argument rightly earns, but in the present environment of networked and programmable machines it can be justified. For example, emulators (or virtual machines) are designed to mediate between an older operating system and a newer one, translating between legacy and newer code so that files can be read and commands can be executed that otherwise would be unreadable and inoperable. Such a machine can be considered an "archeologist" (whether it is an archeologist of knowledge would require a longer discussion about what "knowledge" means in a machine context). The media-archeology approach positions human subjectivity, especially its inclination toward narrative, as a limitation from which a machine viewpoint can liberate us. Such a perspective can wean us away, as Ernst says, from "wanting to tell stories," which only serves to "reinforce our subjectivity,"[41] and instead catalyze awareness of how machines actually work—that is, how they operate through nondiscursive methods.

The media-archeology approach has much to recommend it. It opens up explorations of machine capabilities in their own right and activates Foucauldian questions about such crucial matters as the nature of the archive beyond language, in which, as Jussi Parikka puts it, "power is no longer circulated and reproduced solely through . . . practices of language, but takes place in the switches and relays, software and hardware, protocols and circuits of which our technical media systems are made."[42] A limitation, apparent in Ernst but less true of media archeology in general, is a tendency to create an either/or binary between human and machine viewpoints. In the contemporary era, combinations of machine and human perspectives are far more typical, as theorists such as Parikka and Lori Emerson recognize and exploit in their analyses.[43]

The latter point has another aspect, too: in focusing only on the technical capabilities of media, salutary as that may be, the media-archeology approach sometimes leaves to the side the historical circumstances in which those devices were created, including why the inventors focused on certain functionalities rather than on others, why some devices were commercially successful and others were not, and how the devices transformed the media ecologies in which they were embedded. As Simondon writes in the introduction to *On the Mode of Existence of Technical Objects*, "In technical reality there is a human reality," though he also insists on the converse, that in human reality there is technical reality. He continues: "If [a focus on technical objects] is fully to play its role, culture must come to terms with technical entities as part of its body of knowledge and values."[44] Writing in the 1950s and 1960s, Simondon was ahead of the curve. The narrative approach that arguably dominated media history and theory through the 1980s received a shock to thought when in 1992 Friedrich A. Kittler's *Discourse Networks 1800/1900* burst upon the scene: thereafter, media theory took a decisive turn away from narrative and toward the materialities of media.[45]

In this sense, the media-archeology framework (along with the Kittlerian thrust of what is somewhat problematically called "German media theory") provides a useful corrective. As Ernst makes explicit, however, it does so at the expense of exploring the human reality entwined with the technical: "Media archaeology concentrates on the nondiscursive elements in dealing with the past: not on speakers but rather on the agency of the machine."[46] Because media archeology tends to obscure the human reality entwined with technical reality, it falls short of being a complete account of the cognitive operations of technical devices. Chapter 2 adopts a media-archelogy approach to the extent that it emphasizes the cognitive capabilities of the typesetting machines that evolved from the late nineteenth century to the end of the twentieth century. Throughout, however, it also attends to the humans who created the machines, discussing their motives, organizational contexts, and distinctive contributions. It thus benefits from media-archeology perspectives (a debt I am pleased to acknowledge) but combines them with historical-narrative approaches to present a fuller picture of how the human side of cognitive assemblages interact with the technical cognizers emerging within computational media.

Perspectives focusing on "cultural techniques" have recently emerged as contenders for the title "German media theory." Bernhard Siegert's excellent introduction to his book *Cultural Techniques* articulates the central ideas of this approach and locates it within media theory more generally. Siegert quotes Thomas Macho's argument that "cultural techniques—such as writing, reading, painting, counting, making music—are always older than the concepts that are generated from them. People wrote long before they conceptualized writing or alphabets; millennia passed before pictures and statues gave rise to the concept of the image; and to this day, people may sing or make music without knowing anything about notes or musical notation systems." The argument, then, is that culture "bubbles up" from the everyday use of objects and only retrospectively solidifies into concepts, rituals, and abstractions that, according to some, constitute what can be considered "cultural" beliefs or even "culture" as such. Expanding on this assumption, Siegert writes that "operations such as counting or writing always presuppose technical objects capable of performing—and to a considerable extent, determining—these operations."[47] By focusing on technical objects (construed quite broadly as including doors, filters, and grids, each the subject of one of Siegert's chapters), the cultural-techniques approach claims to have a view of culture at its source, uncontaminated by the biases and misperceptions lurking in accounts that start from the assumption that culture is what people say or think rather than what they do.[48]

Although sharing with media archeology a focus on objects, the cultural-techniques approach diverges from it in taking a keen interest in how objects are created, used, modified, and discarded, which necessarily expands the scope of the approach to human interactions with technical objects. Humans, in this view, are constituted through the objects they fabricate and the practices through which objects are put to use: "Humans *as such* do not exist independently of cultural techniques of hominization," Siegert asserts. The interest for Siegert is not so much on objects by themselves or humans by themselves but rather on the interactions that connect them. With a nod to Latour's actor-network theory, he writes, "When we speak of cultural techniques, therefore, we envisage a more or less complex actor-network that comprises technological objects as well as the operative chains they are part of and that configure or constitute them."[49]

The cognitive-assemblage approach travels along the same path as media archeology in affirming that objects may have viewpoints, and it shares with the cultural-techniques approach an intense interest in understanding the chains of connection and causality that enmesh humans and objects together into assemblages. The main point of difference lies in the emphasis on *cognitions* as processes central to understanding how cognitive assemblages are constituted, function, adapt and evolve, and have become pervasive in contemporary societies. The design of simple everyday objects such as the doors, grids, and filters that Siegert discusses now increasingly involve computational media (through computer-aided design and computer-aided manufacturing and other kinds of simulation software); in the case of automated factories, their fabrication also runs through computational devices (such as industrial robots). Hence, in the cognitive framework the emphasis falls not solely or even primarily on hominization as creating distinctions between humans and nonhuman animals (Siegert's "humans *as such*") but rather on the ways in which humans are now inextricably bound up with networks of intelligent devices, from jet aircraft to underground fiber-optic cables and almost everything else in between.

The subtitle of Siegert's book ends with *Articulations of the Real*, indicating that cultural techniques not only interact with and help to define the human but also interact with the world as it exists independent of human perceptions. "The analysis of cultural techniques observes and describes techniques involved in operationalizing distinctions in the real. They generate the forms in the shape of perceptible unities of distinctions. Operating a door by closing and opening it allows us to perform, observe, encode, address, and ultimately wire the difference between inside and outside."[50] Similarly, the cognitive-assemblage framework acknowledges that cognitive devices do more than interface with humans; they also interact with one another and through more or less complex networks of sensors, actuators, and transmitters perform actions independent of human interventions and in many instances removed from human knowledge of their actions. The emphasis on cognition implies that intelligent devices not only "articulate the real" but also, as my definition of cognition emphasizes, interpret it as well. Diverging from both media archeology and cultural techniques in this respect, the cognitive-assemblage framework raises large questions that emerge when meaning-making practices, not exclusively human anymore (if they ever were!), also extend to nonhuman life-forms and computational media.

Chapter 3, featuring interviews with personnel at five university presses, illustrates the specific questions that arise when the conscious assumptions and nonconscious intuitions of humans practicing cultural techniques interact with computational media. Directors, editors, and other staff involved in university book production bring to their tasks deeply held beliefs about what books are as well as about what scholarship is and should be. Their beliefs are rooted in years of experiencing books as intellectual projects scrutinized, interrogated, and evaluated for their intellectual contributions and as physical artifacts designed, handled, and appreciated for their aesthetic qualities. As computational media take over tasks formerly done solely by humans, such as designing from templates, these people face everyday consequential decisions about how much they want to rely on technical cognition and how much they want to preserve as enclaves in which human creativity and decisions are paramount. Nowhere is this clearer than with university presses that are developing online-publishing venues, such as the University of Minnesota's Manifold platform. The necessity to prepare a text so that it conforms to what computational media can process is in constant active tension with the desire to make the product express what its human creator envisioned. Of course, there are opportunities as well as constraints in this dance between human and technical cognition. The complexities of the situation require a new kind of approach that draws on media archeology and cultural techniques but goes beyond both in its attention to the kinds of interactions emerging from and constitutive of the cognitive assemblages so crucial in today's developed societies.

Introducing Postprint

What Lies Ahead

Books have long been recognized as devices that support and extend human cognition, from their earliest instantiation in the vertically inscribed reeds of Chinese *jiance* to classical scrolls, from medieval manuscripts to mass-produced modern print books. Only in the late twentieth century, however, did books begin to function as cognizers, capable of knowing where they are, how long their user has been reading a particular passage, who else has read and underlined that passage, along with any number of other interpretations and meaning-making practices. Coincident with the development of such e-readers were other machines with cognitive capabilities that fundamentally changed the nature of printing, completely transformed the book industry in its everyday practices, and critically altered the distribution of cognitive tasks among humans and machines. It would take many volumes to explore the full significance of these changes, and exploring the correlative transformations in how we understand the human would take exponentially more. Many studies investigating these questions have already appeared, from Manuel Castells's classic trilogy on the Network Society to, more recently, Mark Hansen's *Feed-Forward: On the Future of Twenty-First-Century Media*; Erich Hörl's *General Ecology: The New Ecological Paradigm*; and many others, including my own work from 1999 on.[51] The inquiries of this volume are more specifically focused on the typesetting and reprographic machines that became cognitive, the publishers who work with these machines, and the effects on human self-conceptions when code intervenes between textual displays and underlying algorithmic processes.

Chapter 2, "Print Into Postprint," explores five points at which printing technologies began to acquire cognitive capabilities. The theme of embodiment enters this chapter through the description of how the machines were designed and constructed (that is, how they were instantiated), beginning with the Paige Compositor. It is scarcely a new observation that the easiest way to imagine technological change is to start with what already exists and introduce a few modifications. Only gradually do design imperatives begin to assert themselves from what the new object is in itself, independent of the devices from which it descended. Early bathtubs looked a lot like the barrels from which they started, early cars resembled buggies, and so forth. The Paige Compositor was the first typesetting machine that might be said to have cognitive capabilities, and its antecedent was the human compositor. Inventor James Paige's idea was to duplicate in mechanical form all the motions that a human compositor used to compose a line of type. In this decision, he doomed his machine to the worst of two worlds: the machine lacked the robustness of mechanical devices as well as the self-repairing nature of human embodiment and cognition that would allow it to recover from error and breakdown. As a result, the Paige Compositor was a commercial failure, although one could argue it was a conceptual triumph.

Another nodal point is the invention of the optical typesetter, specifically the Lumitype. The histories of science and technology are replete with instances in which an outsider to a field is able to make a dramatic breakthrough precisely because he is positioned at the margins. The physicist Erwin Schrödinger influenced generations of molecular biologists with his little book *What Is Life?*; Harold Hidebrand, a petroleum engineer, invented AutoTune, a device that corrects a singer's voice in a recording so it always hits the right pitch, when he applied the digital-signal processing he used for oil exploration to the human voice; and so forth.[52] In the case of the Lumitype, the outsider influence came when an electrical engineer, Louis Moyraud, teamed up with René Higonnet, an amateur photographer, neither of whom had previous experience with printing. Once again, embodiment is crucial because the machine they invented fundamentally changed the typesetting process from metal type pieces inking paper to flashes of light exposing a photographic plate.

If we fast-forward to the 1990s, the invention of Xerox's DocuTech is perhaps most notable for its engagement with corporate politics and the light it casts on what it takes for new ideas to take hold in a corporate environment. It reveals the gap between the individual inventor working on his own in a basement (as Higonnet and Moyraud were) to teams of engineers headed by a project manager, whose job it is not only to bring the new product to market but also to navigate all the perils of corporate competition with rival teams and jealousies among those pursuing alternative solutions.

Whereas chapter 2 focuses on cognitive machines and the people who invented them, chapter 3, "The Mixed Ecologies of University Presses," changes the perspective to editors, publishers, designers, and scholars who do not invent the technologies but find them indispensable for their work after others have brought the machines to market. Thus, chapters 2 and 3 address the two kinds of entities involved in cognitive assemblages, respectively: machines with cognitive abilities and humans who utilize those machines. In chapter 3, the inertia of centuries of print traditions comes front and center, operating both within university presses and in the ways scholarly productivity is conceptualized and evaluated within the academy. Given the discussion at the end of chapter 2 of the difficulties of incorporating ethical considerations into technical innovations within capitalistic contexts, this inertia in humanities scholarship is not unequivocally a bad thing, although there are forceful arguments that university presses and tenure committees urgently need to update their worldviews more fully to take into account how scholarship is changing in the digital era. Nevertheless, even in these relatively traditional environments, changing practices within some presses and corresponding reforms within some tenure and promotion committees are demonstrating a movement toward postprint, resulting in the present situation of mixed ecologies. Among this chapter's noteworthy insights are the changing shapes of scholarly careers as researchers move toward websites rather than to print books and as younger scholars transition toward more public-facing discourses that the web enables.

Chapter 4, "Postprint and Cognitive Contagion," analyzes two fiction texts, *The Silent History* and *The Word Exchange*,[53] to explore the hopes and fears aroused by leaving the regime of print and entering into postprint. Because contemporary human cultures are heavily invested in writing and the written word, the sea changes initiated as signs became digital and thus deeply entwined with computational media are transforming the functionality and meaning of human cognition. As Dennis Tenen argues and as these texts explore, postprint insinuated a new condition of partial illiteracy into the heart of literate cultures. *The Silent History*, a text that bears the mark of the digital in its genesis and realization, depicts this new condition as both loss and gain. In contrast, *The Word Exchange* presents a darker vision of human cognition enfeebled and endangered by the advent of postprint, urging a return to traditional print as the only effective remedy.

Once the genie is out of the bottle (that is, once code generates the visible sign), however, language cannot so easily return to its former status as a production of human cognition alone. Chapter 5, "Bookishness at the Limits: Resiting the Human," follows this line of thought to its limits in two different directions: to the complete immersion of the human reader in a cognitive assemblage, on the one hand, and to books that could never be read by computers because they have no legible words, on the other. The former is explored through *Between Page and Screen* by Borsuk and Bouse, mentioned earlier as an example of a book that can be read only with a computer. Books that can be read only by humans are interrogated through the work of Mirtha Dermisache, an Argentinian artist specializing in creating asemic productions—that is, human mark making that escapes alphabetization. In the contemporary moment, asemic inscriptions are celebrated as resistant practices to algorithmic instrumentality, and so they also bear the mark of the digital but as a movement against rather than a motion forward into algorithmically enabled reading and writing. But this resistance also has an intrinsic ambivalence about it. Because the marks in Dermisache's books cannot be read in a conventional sense, her mark making can be seen as pointing toward the kind of conclusion Vilém Flusser advocates when he argues that the advent of code spells the end of alphabetic writing; from his point of view, alphabetic writing has no future.[54] Nevertheless, the fact that Dermisache is adamant that her work should appear as bound codices—that is, as books—suggests that the book as a cognitive and artistic form is endlessly resilient and will continue even if its contents no longer represent verbal language.

This book aspires to contribute to materialist studies of print, to media studies focusing on the interactions of print and computational media, and to cognitive-cultural studies of the influence of computational media on concepts of the human. Perhaps its greatest ambition is to present the cognitive-assemblage framework as a way to integrate all these areas into a coherent methodology and theoretical perspective. Whether it achieves some or all of these goals is, of course, not up to me but to the book's readers. Whatever its fate as an intellectual project, its very existence as a text composed, edited, designed, produced, marketed, and sold (and in some instances read) by computational media witnesses the advent of postprint. Print is dead; long live postprint!

2

Print Into Postprint

Chapter 1 discussed cognitive assemblages in general terms, emphasizing their two aspects, one focusing on contextual embodiment and organism/device specificity, the other on flows and connections between entities. This chapter provides specific examples of cognitive assemblages in the history of printing technologies as the machines increasingly incorporated computational components and interacted in different ways with the humans who invented, implemented, operated, and oversaw them. As the machines' cognitive capacities increased, so did their flexibility and their ability to take on tasks formerly done by humans. But the chapter also shows that the distribution of cognitive tasks between human and machine does not always mean that the more cognition the machine has, the more successful it will be. On the contrary, the Paige Compositor discussed here illustrates just the opposite; this case study indicates that if the cognitive load exceeds the technology's ability to implement it, fragility rather than flexibility will be the likely result.

A second theme articulated here shows that when machine cognition changes, so also does the media ecology in which humans as well as machines are immersed. As a consequence, changes in machine cognition affect how human cognition is understood and how it operates within the relevant cognitive assemblage. The chapter advances through a spreading circle of implications, starting with technicians directly involved in commercial printing operations, progressing to a broader public with the advent of desktop publishing and print-on-demand, and ending with the public at large using e-books and e-readers. As the circle widens, so too do the effects on cultures as humans' encounters with machine cognitions become routine occurrences in our experiences of reading and understanding books.

Any account of how computation changed printing technologies is bound to be partial and incomplete; the full story is simply too vast to be accommodated within a chapter, a book, or even several books. Also, there are many blurred boundaries and incremental developments, so what gets emphasized and what remains untold are somewhat arbitrary. These caveats notwithstanding, this chapter focuses on five nodal points that I chose in part because they were recognized even in their time as decisive turning points. They trace the transition from print to postprint from the late nineteenth century to the new millennium.

The first nodal point focuses on the shift from human to machine cognition in the Paige Compositor, invented by James Paige in the late nineteenth century. Although the machine failed commercially and famously bankrupted Mark Twain in the process, it nevertheless is noteworthy because it instantiated a vision of how print production could move from a craft largely dependent on human cognition to a hybrid human–machine assemblage.

The second node marks a rupture rather than a shift because it fundamentally altered the material basis for book production from metal type pieces to light bursts on photographic paper. This ontological break, understood as a tectonic movement from atoms to photons, was instantiated in the invention of the Lumitype phototypesetter in the middle of the twentieth century, leading to three or four decades of improvements and dissemination of this technology until in the mid-1980s the market was saturated and signs of obsolescence were already becoming apparent.

The third node is neither a shift nor a rupture but a digression of a kind, instantiated in the development of a coherent fiber-optic bundle that in effect enabled the light flashes of a phototypesetter to be digitized and thus addressable by a computer. The Computer Assisted Typesetter (C/A/T), developed by Graphic Systems Inc. in the early 1970s, opened possibilities that were cut short when phototypesetters gave way to more fully computerized devices such as laser printers and typesetters. Coherent fiber optics instead revolutionized the electronic transmission of information, exploding into massive infrastructure projects with the development of the internet and the web. To my knowledge, the C/A/T was the only typesetter to use fiber optics, so its importance lies not in its centrality to printing but in its pioneering of a technology whose massive influence was exercised in other areas.

The fourth node explores the moment when reprographic technologies merged with desktop publishing to create the technology that made print-on-demand possible, initiating a transformation in the media ecology of print production, with consequences for print books that continue to reverberate in the present. This node focuses on the invention and development of Xerox's DocuTech in the early 1990s, a machine that not only implemented machine cognition to a greater extent than previous devices but also transformed the ways in which human cognition interacted with the machine's cognitive capabilities.

The fifth node leaps into the twenty-first century with the development of e-books and e-readers, when for the first time the shifts, ruptures, and transformations in how print books were produced became obviously apparent to readers. The consequences of postprint spread beyond printing professionals to the general population, initiating changes in the media ecology that have profound consequences for what the act of reading means in legal, social, and neurological terms. Now at the end of the new millennium's second decade, the century-long transition from print to postprint has been largely completed, although we are still struggling to understand and cope with its myriad implications.

The Shift from Human to Machine Cognition

If we ask when text first became computational, we would have to go back to the early nineteenth century, when Joseph Marie Jacquard invented the card-controlled looms that bear his name. Although usually employed to create intricately patterned fabrics, the Jacquard loom was occasionally used to create woven texts. Figure 2.1.a and 2.1.b show the Jacquard cards needed to create the "Coquette" clothing label and the label itself; the stack's size emphasizes that the density of information contained in a Jacquard card, measured in bits of information per gram, was extremely low compared to today's electronic media. Figure 2.2 is a fabric "page," a one-off production extravagantly showing what Jacquard looms could do, excerpted from the *Livre de prières* (Book of Prayers) woven in Lyons, France, in 1883.

Machine Cognition in Typesetting: The Paige Compositor

If we confine ourselves to thinking of "print" as ink marks on paper, however, we can pick up the story of computation's infusion into print with the Paige Compositor invented by James Paige in the 1880s.[1] Begun in 1877 in the Franham Typesetter Company workshop located in the Colt Firearms Company, a working prototype was finished more than a decade later, in 1888. About this time, Dwight Buell, one of the machine's investors, visited Mark Twain in his home and invited him to see the machine in action. Albert Bigelow Paine quotes in his four-volume work *Mark Twain: A Biography* (1907) a memorandum Twain wrote ten years later:

> [Buelle] said it was at the Colt's Arms factory, and was about finished. I took $2,000 of the stock. I was always taking little

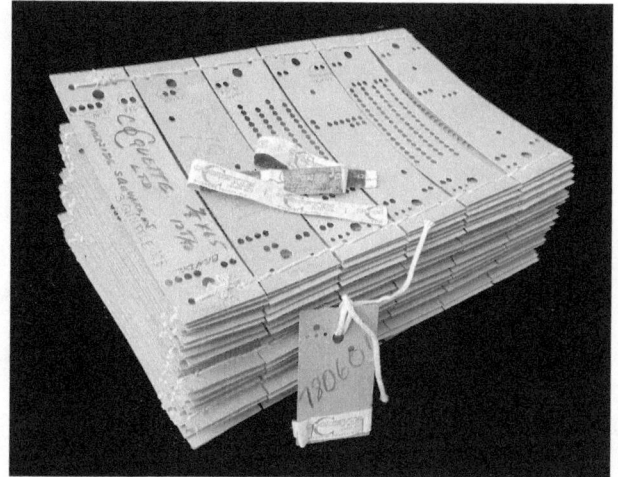

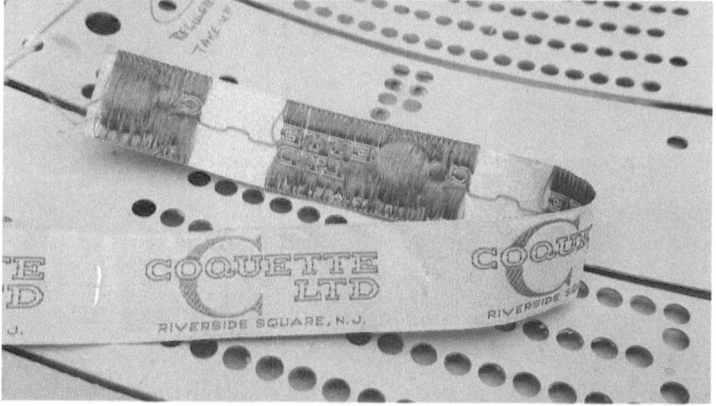

2.1a and 2.1b Stack of Jacquard cards used to produce the "Coquette" label and the finished label, n.d.

Source: From the Nicholas Gessler "Things That Think" Collection. Images courtesy of Nicholas Gessler.

chances like that, and almost always losing by it, too. Some time afterward I was invited to go down to the factory and see the machine. I went, promising myself nothing, for I knew all about type-setting by practical experience, and held the settled and solidified opinion that a successful type-setting

2.2 Pages from *Livre de prières* (Book of Prayers), woven in Lyon, France, in 1883.

Source: From the Nicholas Gessler "Things That Think" Collection. Image courtesy of Nicholas Gessler.

machine was an impossibility, for the reason that a machine cannot be made to think, and the thing that sets movable type must think or retire defeated. So, the performance I witnessed did most thoroughly amaze me. Here was a machine that was really setting type, and doing it with swiftness and accuracy, too. Moreover, it was distributing its case at the same time. The distribution was automatic; the machine fed itself from a galley of dead matter and without human help or suggestion, for it began its work of its own accord when the type channels needed filling, and stopped of its own accord when they were full enough. The machine was almost a complete compositor; it lacked but one feature—it did not "justify" the lines. This was done by the operator's assistant.[2]

Noting Twain's implication that the machine could "think," Paine comments on the inventor's perfectionism, which ultimately proved his (and Twain's) undoing. "Paige was never content short of absolute perfection—a machine that was not only partly human, but entirely so. Clemens' [sic] used to say later that the Paige type-setter would do everything that a human being could do except drink and swear and go on a strike."[3] Aiming for perfection, Paige added features that enabled justification, the only task that the machine could not do when Twain saw it. In the improved version, the machine notified the operator when no more type pieces could be inserted, calculated the amount of space left, and, using quadrats (pieces used to insert spaces) of eleven different dimensions, justified the lines to within five-thousandths of an inch.

What were the cognitive capacities of the Paige Compositor? It contained more than eighteen thousand components, using a complex arrangement of levers, cams, and other mechanisms to

2.3 Front view of the Paige Compositor, scanned from *Scientific American*, March 9, 1901, an issue featuring the machine with the caption "A Machine with 18,000 Elements—The Paige Typesetting Machine." The large case projecting above the machine contained the vertical channels in which the type pieces were set. The pieces thus sat edge to edge, unlike the Gutenberg model, in which the type pieces were mounted in flat, horizontal trays.

2.4 Rear view of the Paige Compositor, scanned from *Scientific American*, March 9, 1901.

2.5 Side view of the Paige Compositor with stool showing where the operator would sit, scanned from *Scientific American*, March 9, 1901.

typeset, justify, and distribute the type.[4] It was capable of recognizing individual type pieces through a series of nicks that uniquely identified each; moreover, it also was able to recognize broken or cracked type pieces as well as any foreign matter and remove them. The nicks were constructed so that the machine would not mistake the type pieces even if they were broken or stuck together. Perhaps most impressively, the machine could redistribute the "dead matter"—type pieces that had been used—back into the appropriate trays, ready for reuse.

How do these capacities square with Twain's implication that the machine could "think" and the comment that Paige wanted the machine to be completely, not only partially, "human"? In my book *Unthought* and in this project, I try to avoid the word *think* because it is loaded with anthropocentric implications; I instead turn to the more inclusive and less human-centered term *cognition*, as discussed in chapter 1. So I would not say that the machine could "think" but rather that it had certain cognitive capabilities. Phrasing it this way, I also want to avoid Paine's implication that a machine that can "think" is therefore human. From my point of view, this implication shows why the term *think* is not a good choice: it conflates "thinking" with being human. Obviously, there are profound differences between human embodiment and the mechanical instantiation of this (or any) intelligent device. Because cognition for humans is embodied, it involves many sensory and neural networks beyond the brain and is intimately related to environmental and evolutionary conditions. Moreover, cognition is not a uniquely human attribute. My position, central to *Unthought* and explained in the previous chapter, is that all nonhuman biological organisms can cognize, as can many technical devices.

Of course, Twain and Paine were speaking metaphorically, so it may not be fair to take them literally. Nevertheless, their comments illustrate that in a discursive field fraught with erroneous implications and long histories of misunderstanding, precision is essential. Focusing on cognitive capabilities instead of on a vague claim to "think" allows one to specify what cognitive capabilities are at issue, how they are physically instantiated in the machine, and how the machine responds to and processes the information available to it.

The Demise of the Paige Compositor

On August 25, 2016, I made a trip to the Mark Twain Museum in Hartford, Connecticut, to see the only extant Paige Compositor and examine the museum's archives.[5] The machine has never been operational at the museum, and no one on the staff knows exactly how it worked, although the archives contain some information in this regard. Most useful were excerpts from Paige's patent application of 1887, which included 275 drawing sheets, 123 specification sheets, and 613 claims and thus became known as "The Whale" in the U.S. Patent Office.

A document in the archives entitled "Notes on Typesetter" (author unknown) collected material from the Paine biography (volume 2) and other sources to compile a chronology of Twain's investments as Paige attempted to make progress on the machine. This document quotes Twain in January 1889 as claiming, "No typesetter could match it for accuracy & precision when it was in perfect order, but its point of perfection was apparently a vanishing point."[6] The point (in both senses) was painfully accurate, for when the *Chicago Herald* agreed to use the machine in September 1894, it broke down repeatedly, and only Paige knew enough to repair it. After two months, the *Herald* had had enough and discontinued its use; thereafter the machine was never used commercially.

How does the Paige Compositor compare to its successful competitor, the Linotype machine invented by Ottmar Mergenthaler? Following a line of thought that would reoccur in the late twentieth century, Paige conceived of the machine by considering the actions that a human performed within typesetting

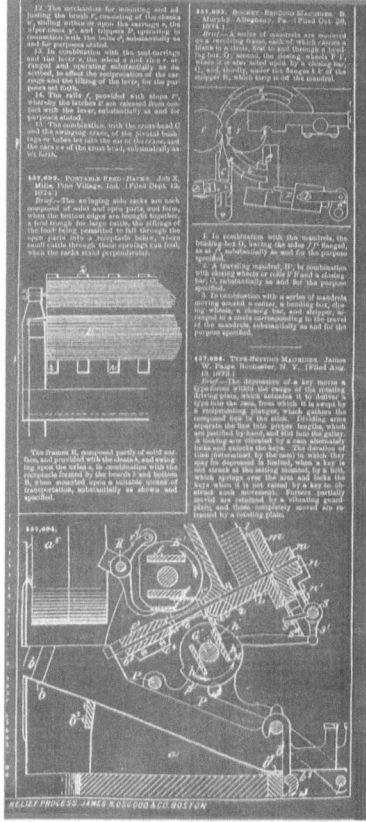

2.6 Reproduction of a page from Paige's patent application for the Compositor, 1887.

Source: From the archives of the Mark Twain Museum, Hartford, CT. Used with permission from the Mark Twain Museum.

and compositing and then duplicated each of these actions in mechanical fashion. As future inventors would come to realize, a better approach was to rethink the problem from the ground up. This was the path taken with the Linotype machine, which was first used commercially in June 1886 when it was installed at the *New York Tribune*.[7] Rather than duplicate human motions involved in hand-setting type using a compositor's stick, the Linotype cast an entire line of type at once, called a "slug," using molds called "matrices." The machine was controlled by a ninety-character keyboard, where the operator composed lines of text.

Each keystroke released a matrix from the magazine mounted above the keyboard; each matrix was specific for size and style of type and went through a channel to the assembler, where all the matrices were lined up in the order in which they were composed. As soon as a line was complete, the machine took over and cast the slug. When printing was completed, the matrices were returned to the magazine for reuse, and the slug was melted down. Whereas the Paige Compositor was designed to redistribute "dead matter" using cognition, the Linotype employed a method that distinguished between ephemeral "instances" and the brass molds used to create the individual letters. John M. Maxwell argues that this method can be seen as a "leveling up."[8] By preserving the rendering system but scrapping the renditions, the Linotype instantiated in its "hot-metal" casting technique a new way to instrumentalize the traditional spatial distinction between type pieces set in forms and type pieces ready for distribution. Precisely because this new way reconceptualized how a manual technique could be mechanized, it simplified the cognitive load on the machine.

In the cognitive framework, it is crucially important to consider how cognition is distributed in the cognitive assemblages constituted by the two machines and their operators. Whereas the Paige Compositor tried to re-create complex human interpretations through its levers, cams, and other mechanisms, the Linotype relied on the human operator for many decisions (for example, recognizing type pieces). For that reason, the Linotype was more robust, simpler to repair, and more economical to manufacture, resulting in a considerably lower purchase price. While the Paige Compositor was (literally) consigned to the scrap pile of history, the Mergenthaler Linotype went on to become the industry standard. From a perspective focusing on the distribution of cognition within a cognitive assemblage, we can say that Paige sought to give the machine too much cognition at a time when cognition could only be implemented electromechanically and so ended up with a machine of such complexity and fragility that it could not be made commercially viable.

Ironically, according to "Notes on Typesetter," in 1886 "the Mergenthaler people offered to exchange half their interests (machine they were working on) for ½ interest in Paige patent." Twain, apparently seduced by the Compositor's cognitive prowess and without paying adequate attention to the practicalities of its commercial operation, "turned them down," thus sealing his own financial fate as well as that of the machine.

From Atoms to Photons: Phototypesetting and Computation

Matthew Kirschenbaum tells in his extensively researched and beautifully crafted analytical history of literary word processing, *Track Changes*, the story of how writing became word processing,[9] a narrative that he dates to the late 1970s with the launch of Word Star (1979) and continuing into the early 1980s, when, as he wrote to me, word processing had "penetrated the home computing market" and thereby become "a commonplace."[10] A related history is the interpenetration of computational devices into typesetting and printing technologies, focusing on what happens once the writer has completed her task and turned her manuscript over to a publisher. Although this topic is somewhat to the side of Kirschenbaum's interests,[11] it is central to understanding how the processes of book production were transformed into human–machine cognitive assemblages. Over decades, the resulting redistribution of cognition fed forward into reading devices and consequently into reading practices, where it increasingly affects how (human) readers think of themselves in the mixed-media ecologies characteristic of contemporary society. In this sense, the story of how book production achieved cognitive capacities is complementary to the story of word processing in Kirschenbaum's work, enabling us to construct a fuller picture of the transformative effects of artificial cognition on human selfhood and subjectivity as they are formed through reading and writing practices, including (or especially) through literature.

Decisive for this story is the invention of phototypesetting, for it broke the link between metal type and printing by using light and images rather than cumbersome pieces of metal to produce printed texts. Moreover, as we will see, photographic images lent themselves to pixelization and consequently to computational representation. In his history of the phototypesetting era, Frank Romano vivifies the differences in materiality when he notes that the light-focusing disc on the Lumitype machine, the first commercially successful phototypesetter, "weighed one pound and a half, and was eight inches in diameter. It replaced 4,000 pounds of cold metal type that would cost $25,000 and would require 90 cubic feet of storage space. The disk would sell for $495."[12] Moreover, the Lumitype and similar machines could be used in a clean office environment, thus giving them much more flexibility than such "hot-metal" processes as the Linotype, which gave off considerable heat and particulates from the repeated casting and melting of metal type.

Phototypesetters gradually integrated more and more of the cognitive capabilities of computational media into their design, beginning with the interrelated problems of hyphenation and justification (where to divide words and how to fill out a line once no more words would fit, called "h&j" in the trade) and progressing to full-page formatting and typesetting. The story of the Lumitype's invention by René Higonnet and Louis Moyroud shows this transition with unusual clarity, thanks to Romano's history/memoir. He mentions in his foreword that his book "has taken 54 years to write."[13] It builds on his involvement in the phototypesetting industry, beginning in 1959, when as a twenty-something young man thinking about college he was hired by the Mergenthaler Linotype Company and then worked later at Photon and Compugraphic. On his thirtieth birthday, he went off on his own, founding the magazine *TypeWorld* a few years later. His industry connections, the material collected in *TypeWorld*, and his personal recollections constitute an extraordinary archive of historical materials about the evolution of cognitive typesetting devices. Among these materials is what appears to be a transcript of a seminar Louis Moyroud gave to MIT engineers in the 1970s. From Moyroud's first-person narrative (prefaced by Romano's comment "This is Louis speaking"), we can see with detailed precision how the transition from electromechanical operation to computational cognition evolved.

Moyroud, an electrical engineer working at an ITT branch in Lyon, France, noted that his office had been asked to publish a French patent gazette and that his supervisor, René Higonnet, who knew nothing about printing, accordingly went to visit a printing shop. There he saw that for offset printing "it was necessary to cast lines of type, lock them in chases, set them up on the press and then produce only one good repro proof." Higonnet, an amateur photographer, immediately saw the possibilities for a phototypesetting machine that could be simpler and far more efficient than this "extravagant" procedure. Moyroud agreed, commenting that "the idea seemed simple to me," so they jointly set about creating a photographic-type composing machine, which they thought they could do in their spare time working in a basement. As it turned out, it took them almost five years of virtually full-time work and became "a task that would change our lives."[14]

At this point, it may be helpful to give a general idea of how their invention, the Lumitype phototypesetter, worked. A typist input text using an electric typewriter; this input was fed to the phototypesetting machine, which translated the alphanumeric bits into an image by positioning a spinning glass disc inscribed with the negative images of alphabetic characters to

2.7 Section of type disc from a Lumitype phototypesetter showing alphabetic characters, 1954.

Source: Image by jeronzinho, flickr.com/photos/jeronzinho/3375353476. Creative Commons license, https://creativecommons.org/licenses/by-ne-nd/2.0.

be transmitted to photographic paper (see figure 2.7). When the relevant letter was in the proper position, a xenon strobe flash was used to "freeze" the image and, with mirrors and prisms transporting it, provided escapement (that is, reflected the beam horizontally across the paper). Each disc was initially inscribed with only one font style in uppercase and lowercase letters as well as with numbers from 0 to 9. A series of lenses controlled by stepper motors and positioned between the disk and paper allowed the image to be enlarged or reduced as desired.

As with much in the material world, the machine that seemed simple in conception proved diabolically difficult to fabricate so that it actually worked. Moyroud and Higonnet decided on arithmetical calculations to accomplish justification (rather than spatial means such as quadrats), noting that "we were directing our efforts toward digital and electromechanical solutions."[15] A related problem was line storage. Although some later machines used punched-paper tape,[16] Moyroud was concerned about error correction, noting that he "could hardly type 10 lines without making numerous errors." Therefore, "we wanted to give the keyboard operator the capability of automatically erasing characters by back spacing." Reasoning that erasure would be easier with digital storage than with a punched-paper tape, "we decided to develop a mechanical memory directly controlled by the carriage of the typewriter." By 1947, after the first prototype was created, the two men "decided to use the binary system in practically all the functions of our machine . . . but we had to produce binary accumulators from scratch for nothing was commercially available at the time, digital computers having hardly been born and being totally unknown to us."[17]

The binary system paved the way for the next improvement, a mechanism capable of variable spacing on the film to accommodate proportional spacing typefaces. Summarizing, Moyroud explained that by 1948 they had created a machine with "an electromechanical programmer . . . a binary width accumulator using home-made flip-flop switches, an 18-value variable escapement, a disc with slits to time flashes of very high precision, and an electromechanical timing unit." In retrospect, although they did not realize it at the time, "we had in this machine the basic ingredients of a digital computer: a memory, a computing unit and a program all operating on the binary system."[18]

Despite their accomplishment, the inventors did not find much interest in the machine in France. Romano reports that in 1946 Moyroud carried an early prototype in his suitcase to New York to show it to W. E. Garth, president of the Lithomat Corporation. As an indication of the slim budget on which the inventors operated, Higonnet split Moyroud's travel expenses with Garth, each paying half. Garth then had the machine examined by Samuel Caldwell, an electrical engineer at MIT, who verified that it had potential as a commercial photo-composing machine. The inventors estimated that they would need $10,000 to get the machine to a commercial stage, and Lithomat signed an agreement by which it would provide this amount in return for the option to manufacture and distribute the machine in the Western Hemisphere.[19] Introducing the machine commercially in 1951, Lithomat branded it "the Photon" in line with the company's new name, "Photon, Inc."

To prepare for the machine's commercial introduction, Photon, Inc., exhibited it in April 1949 at the American Newspaper Publishers Association convention at the Waldorf Astoria in New York. Romano reports that at this early point "competitors were strictly excluded from the Photon demonstration and identification had to be shown to gain entrance to the exhibit."[20] In part because of the enthusiasm for the machine among publishers, in July 1949 the printing industry established the Graphic Arts Research Foundation, contributing $100,000 annually for three years to support the development of a photo-composing machine.

Moyroud, in a section entitled "The Search for an Ideal Universal Machine" (a retrospective nod to Alan Turing's Universal Computer), commented in his seminar that "to satisfy those who wanted a universal machine [specifically the Graphic Arts Research Foundation and more generally the printing industry] and partly because of our own enthusiasm for a new application of telephone relays and logic circuits we went back to the drawing board in 1949."[21] The result in 1951 was a machine that was "universal" in the sense that it featured sixteen typefaces (not only one, as had the prototype of 1949), eight different sizes achieved through lenses; a "width accumulator circuit" that allowed mixing of sizes on the same line; as well as a number of other automatic features that moved the machine closer to a fully automated computational device.

This preproduction model, nicknamed "Petunia," was again exhibited at the American Newspaper Publishers Association convention in April 1951, and the enthusiasm it generated

Print Into Postprint

2.8 Commercial version of Lumitype/Photon, 1954.

Source: Photograph by Michael Pilat, https://www.flickr.com/photos/mikepilat/
3836200658/in/photolist-bETN03-0Gw8vS-4yjGQ2-7sHWtD-7sMS
Au-7sMScU-6QZwW3-6QZwNE-3bSdZy-F.

encouraged Photon, Inc., to produce an initial lot of ten commercial machines (see figure 2.8). Meanwhile, research continued on more improvements, now bolstered by the muscle (and deep pockets) of the Photon corporation. In 1952, the Graphic Arts Research Foundation wrote in its *Report to the Subscribers* about the prospects for further development, noting that "the transistor was hardly known in 1949. Now it offers the opportunity to perform complex computation and control operations with compact, light, and rugged circuits. . . . [Further] improvements in magnetic recording techniques and materials make this a likely substitute for the present mechanical memory unit."[22] With these changes, implemented in 1955 with the second-generation Photon, the interpenetration of computation into typesetting was firmly established.[23]

A Digression: The Digitization of Light, or Sending Photons Through a Tube

Computerization was taken further in the late 1970s with the introduction of third-generation machines that employed a cathode ray tube and extensive computer software. We can trace this transition through the Computer Assisted Typesetter (C/A/T) developed by Graphic Systems International (GSI) in 1972. One advantage of this machine was its introduction of a flexible coherent fiber-optic bundle to convey the image from the font film negatives (which replaced the glass-disc negatives used by the Lumitype) to the photographic paper. To understand this advantage, we can briefly review how a coherent fiber-optic bundle works. In previous machines, the image was conveyed by a complex arrangement of mirrors and prisms, which could easily become misaligned, covered with dust specks, and so on. By contrast, the fiber-optic bundle encloses the light carriers in a conduit (see figure 2.9). The bundle is composed of roughly a million individual optic fibers, each about ten microns in diameter and capable of carrying a single pixel of light along its length.[24] At the output end, each fiber maintains its precise position relative to all the other fibers that it had at the input end (this is the meaning of "coherent" in this context). This coherence yields a resolution equivalent in pixels to the number of fibers in the bundle (in this case a million).[25] Because the bundle is flexible, it can be moved to achieve horizontal placements across a line without the use of mirrors. In computer terms, its location is programmable—that is, the bundle's location is highly addressable to very fine resolutions. This precise control of optics and image position made the interface to computer programs reasonably simple; in effect, image digitization was already accomplished through the fibers in the bundle.

Here is the glass-manufacturing company Schott North America's description of how fiber-optic bundles are manufactured:

The "mono-fiber" is assembled with a core of high refractive index glass and a cladding of low refractive index glass, heated and drawn down to 2mm. It is then precisely assembled into a 45mm "multi-fiber" grid and again drawn down to 2mm. Again it is assembled into a 45mm "multi-multi fiber" grid and drawn down yet again to 2mm. The "multi-multi-fibers" are then assembled into a "block" and fused without further drawing down. The "block" may then be used as a solid inflexible image conduit, heated to a taper for magnification or minification, or twisted to invert the image.

In the case of a *flexible* fiber-optic bundle, however, the technique of inflexible fusing will not work because then the desired flexibility of the cable would be lost. A clever technique instead assures precise point-to-point matching between the input and output ends, without causing worry about what is happening to the relative placement of the fibers in between as the cable bends into different positions. This is how Schott explains it:

> A flexible coherent fiber optic bundle does not, in theory, require the same precise assembly. In the "hoop winding and assembly process" all that is necessary is for the fiber to pass through a shaping fixture at a single point along the hoop or loop. As long as the fibers are packed tightly into that fixture, regardless of their order, they can be fused within that fixture, and the loop cut within that fused region. The result is that each of the two resulting windows will register a precise mirror image of the other.[26]

The cut means that there can be spaghetti in the middle, and it will not matter to the precision matching of the two ends.

The Gessler "Things That Think" Collection includes a fiber-optic bundle taken from a C/A/T machine, as shown in figure 2.9. Page layout for the C/A/T phototypesetter was determined by the software used to generate the paper tape it used for input; later versions dispensed with the paper tape, connecting the phototypesetter directly to the input computer. When Bell Labs purchased a C/A/T phototypesetter in 1973, its engineers created an interface to the UNIX operating system, and thereafter the C/A/T became standard for UNIX typesetting systems. This important step liberated the system from expensive proprietary input software that worked only for a specific machine, as had been the case, for example, with the Lumitype and subsequently the Photon. At Bell Labs, Joe F. Ossanna and Brian Kernighen developed the troff (pronounced "t-roff") software. Troff was derived from an earlier software, roff, a condensation of the term *run-off*; "t-roff" stood for "typesetter-roff."[27] Troff expanded typesetting capabilities beyond alphanumeric symbols to mathematical tables, graphs, and formulae.

In *Plain Text: The Poetics of Computation*, Dennis Tenen has an elegant explanation of how this software worked, explaining that the program "embodied the idea of text independent of its medium and free of form. The digital writer edited text in a 'virtual' location, without knowing its output in another physical one."[28] In this way, formatting instructions were mixed with content in the input stream, but in the output the commands controlling "representational structure," as Tenen puts it, were only implicitly present in how the text was formatted. It was precisely this division that bestowed the flexibility to combine alphabetic text, tables, graph, and equations on the same page.

GSI was a small outfit, and in 1975 it signed an agreement with Singer Corporation to market and distribute the C/A/T machines. Someone at Singer apparently noticed belatedly that the typesetting business was far removed from the corporation's core interests, and within a few years Singer notified GSI it was terminating the agreement, although it continued to support the machines through 1979. Left without marketing and distribution capabilities, GSI was bought by Wang Laboratories in 1978, which continued to market the C/A/T as Wang Graphic Systems through the 1980s.

2.9.a (top), 9.b (middle), and 9.c (bottom) The top image shows the complete fiber-optic bundle (with coffee cup for scale), one of the most expensive components of the C/A/T phototypesetter; note its flexibility in being able to bend (within limits). The middle picture shows an image being captured. And the bottom picture shows the image after transmission through the fiber bundle; note that the image is inverted, as in a camera, which indicates the bundle has a 180-degree twist in it.

Source: Courtesy of the Nicholas Gessler "Things That Think" Collection. Images courtesy of Nicholas Gessler.

The End of the Phototypesetter Era

As phototypesetters were more and more tightly integrated with computer software, the increased speed of production ironically changed the media ecology in ways that doomed phototypesetters to obsolescence. When the era of phototypesetters began, their main competition was mechanical typesetters such as the Linotype, a contest in which phototypesetters had the advantages of lower cost, cleaner operation, easier methods to change typefaces, and less storage and operating space. The incorporation of computational components changed the nature of the game, however, so that the competition then shifted to handling more and more data faster and faster. With the push to produce fully assembled pages mixing text, graphics, and color, laser devices became the technology of choice, and by the 1980s laser imagesetters began to replace the phototypesetting machines.

Romano reckons that the peak period for phototypesetters was 1980–1984, during which the market was largely saturated with this technology, with 282,000 first-, second-, and third-generation machines in use worldwide.[29] As is so often the case with computational media, the full flowering of the phototypesetter was inevitably followed by its decline and eventual demise. Romano accordingly ends his account of the phototypesetting era in 1985, less than four decades after its beginnings in Moyroud and Higonnet's "part-time" basement project.

Let us now return briefly to the heady days of the phototypesetting era's beginnings for a final glimpse of its accomplishments. The first book to be produced entirely by phototypesetting was Albro Gaul's *The Wonderful World of Insects* in 1953 (figure 2.10), composed, as a special page inserted at the end of the book proclaims, by "the revolutionary Higonnet-Moyroud photographic type-composing machine. Absolutely no type, in the conventional sense, was used in the preparation of this book." The note continues:

Print Into Postprint

2.10a and 2.10b Page and image from Albro Gaul, *The Wonderful World of Insects* (New York: Rinehart, 1953) (left side and right side of page spread), the first book to be produced entirely by phototypesetting. The elegant design features wide margins as well as horizontal and vertical separator lines. The book has copious photographs of various insects, with the images bleeding to the page's outer edge.

Source: Courtesy of the Nicholas Gessler "Things That Think" Collection. Images courtesy of Nicholas Gessler.

In 1949, the Graphic Arts Foundation, Inc. of Cambridge, Massachusetts was formed to provide high-level research in the printing industry. It has as its objective the creation of new, better and less costly printing methods. In the Higonnet-Moyroud, or Photon, photographic type-composing machine—its first project—the Foundation has perfected an entirely new, faster and far more versatile means of composition that does not employ metal type. If, as we believe, time proves the Photon to be the replacement for past typesetting methods, then the printing and publishing industry is at the threshold of a new era. Rinehart & Company is proud that its book was chosen to be the first work composed with this revolutionary machine.³⁰

I purchased this work from a rare-book dealer so that I could examine it closely firsthand. Scrutinizing the pages for small errors in placement, I was not able to find any. On the contrary, I was struck by the elegance of the design, with its generous margins, innovative play of vertical and horizontal line dividers, and aesthetically pleasing spatialization. As my eye traveled over the letters, I imagined the Photon alphabetic disc spinning around while a strobe light flashed, freezing each letter in its proper place with a precision that would become routine and indeed taken for granted once computers fully transformed typesetting. In the production of this book, however, the accomplishment was nothing less than revolutionary, even astonishing. The history of cognitive redistribution instantiated in this book is implicitly revealed to the casual reader only on the final page. Lacking a number, the page is neither fully inside the text nor outside it. Its paratextual position hints that the media ecology within which the print book was conceived as a passive conduit between a human author and human reader had already begun to change. From this point on, cognitive capacities would increasingly inhere not only in humans but in the cognitive assemblages of postprint productions.

Obsolescence as Corporate Strategy: Device Independence, a Printer on Every Desktop, and Xerox's DocuTech

While phototypesetters were becoming standard in commercial print shops, a parallel line of innovation and development focused on desktop devices such as the dot matrix, daisy-wheel, and electric typeball devices such as the Selectric—a trajectory that

Print Into Postprint

entered a distinctively new phase with nonimpact printers. Edward Webster notes in his admirably detailed and richly illustrated history of these developments that during the 1950s and 1960s computation speeds increased by a factor of three thousand, whereas impact printing speeds merely doubled.[31] Clearly, the physics of impact printers was acting as a bottleneck to the new speeds possible with computers, and so the search was on for desktop nonimpact technologies, similar to the revolution that phototypesetters created in the commercial world. Whereas the use of phototypesetters began in the 1950s, as we have seen, it was not until the 1980s that desktop devices using nonimpact technologies, in particular ink jet and laser printers, were sufficiently developed to initiate a comparable revolution in desktop publishing. During the same decade, desktop computers were revolutionizing how and where publishing took place. IBM introduced its personal computer in 1980, and the Apple Macintosh appeared in 1984. The 1980s, then, were the breakout years for all these developments: printing software, desktop publishing, and laser and ink jet technologies.

One important event was the creation of the Adobe software for full-page description. Adobe was founded by John Warnock and Charles Geschke in 1982, and their development of page description language (PDL) and specifically page description format (PDF) achieved device independence for the transmission and printing of digital documents. This development accelerated the shift, already gaining momentum, from thinking of proprietary solutions that worked for only one device to a systems view in which interfaces were developed that allowed for flexibility and adaptability—the principle that made the web possible. It is somewhat ironic, therefore, that in the mid-1980s Steve Jobs recruited Warnock and Geschke for Apple—a company built on keeping the computer's operating system proprietary—where they developed the software for the first LaserWriter printer. In 1985, Apple launched the Macintosh,

LaserWriter, and Pagemaker as a package. With this launch, Warnock recounts, "the 'desktop publishing' concept was born."[32]

How that concept in turn transformed the desktop-printer industry is recounted in an interview with Hewlett-Packard's (HP) Dick Hackborn (reprinted in Webster's book from the HP Company Archives but not dated). Hackborn and others at HP knew that desktop publishing was destined to spread, so "time-to-market was critical to success." Time pressure meant that the standard practice in HP of developing its own technology would lose the competitive edge, so HP partnered with Canon, which already had the technical and manufacturing expertise for the printer engine, and focused on "developing the controller electronics that told the marking engine what do to." The first LaserJet printer hit the market in 1984 (scooping the Apple LaserWriter by two years). Hackborn emphasized that in addition to high print quality and speed, the LaserJet also had "an *upgradeable* printer command architecture ensuring broad support from personal computer software applications," an enhancement possible only because it also had increased cognitive capacities.[33]

Time pressure had another aspect, too: the relentless cycle of innovation had its dark side in increasing the pace of obsolescence. HP not only was aware of this aspect but also embraced it. Hackborn commented that "we believed a continuous stream of innovative products, achieved through the rapid introduction of new models, was necessary to maintain market leadership, even when this meant obsoleting our own products before our competitors did." As an example of HP "obsoleting" its own products, we may consider the LaserJet IIP of 1989, successor to the LaserJet II introduced two years earlier, "half as big, half as fast," but with a price cut of more than $1,000, bringing the cost to less than $2,500.[34] This price point enabled the shift from thinking of printers as something only business offices would buy to seeing them as a commodity that ordinary consumers would purchase, leading to still further innovations in hardware and software design.

From Photons to Electrons: The Invention of the DocuTech

In 1990, Xerox launched the multiple-prize-winning DocuTech, the machine that single-handedly created the market for print-on-demand (figure 2.11).[35] The DocuTech was arguably the first printing device not only to change how printing was done but also radically to transform the functions that counted as "printing." Its increased cognitive capacities rippled through the cognitive assemblages formed around printing, changing how humans within the assemblages functioned as well as how book production itself was envisioned.

As printing technologies grew more complex, the emphasis shifted from individual inventors such as Moyroud and Higonnet to large corporate teams and consequently to the managers who led them. As mentioned in chapter 1, the person recognized as the manager most responsible for the DocuTech's successful

2.11 Xerox DocuTech 128HLC.

Source: Photograph by Dave Wolnick, https://www.flickr.com/photos/mossbeep/2345124782/in/photolist-hR2viD-697YN-qbAjr7-pwp9xK-6QST36-4zenTU-btLKq2-btLKMv-btLK5g-btLJJV-btLJo4-5A2xPU-hR3WfJ-hR3XoH-hR3MiT-hR3F4i. Creative Commons license, https://creativecommons.org/licenses/by-sa/2.0/.

creation was Chip Holt, corporate vice president of Xerox's Wilson Center for Research and Technology. Interviewed by Webster in 1999, Holt articulated with remarkable clarity and insight what that creation required and the changes it initiated. As a manager, Holt was alert to the corporate politics involved as well as to the paradigm shift that the DocuTech instantiated.

Holt had been involved in developing software for carrier-based aircraft in the 1960s, recounting that he had moved to Scientific Data Systems in 1970 in part because it had been acquired by Xerox. He had heard the expression "the architecture of information" and was eager to think about how an informational view might change the printing industry. After joining a task force to think about how electronics could change Xerox, he was assigned to the new Electronics Division to supervise a team in Rochester, New York (Xerox's home base), and moved there in 1979. At the time, the Rochester-based engineers were creating copiers using hard-wired logic circuits. Holt's vision was to replace these hard-wired circuits with microcontroller-based computerized circuits that ran on software, which would have vastly more flexibility as well as more cognitive capacity. In 1983, his team initially thought that the machine they envisioned might require 200,000 lines of software; by 1991, after the DocuTech's launch, 1.3 million lines of code had been written, with code development still ongoing.

A clear theme in Holt's interview by Webster in 1999 is his retrospective realization that changing from photons to electrons, as he put it, required successive layers of insight, thinking, and innovation. Each layer was achieved at considerable personal and corporate cost; like peeling an onion, each revealed yet more layers underneath that needed to be rethought. The team began by assuming that they "were going to build a reprographics machine electronically" but did not yet fully understand that this task required more than "a one to one replacement of the conventional reprographics machine." We may note the echo here of the Paige Compositor, whose inventor also began (and ended) with the notion of a one-to-one replacement of human thinking with machine cognition. Holt and his team gradually realized that this strategy would not work; "we needed to think about the features of the product in an integrated systems way." At that point, according to him, the team "virtually locked themselves in a room for a year" to think through the desired features and come to grips with the reconceptualizations these required.[36]

When Holt subsequently described the machine they had envisioned to Xerox CEO David Kerns, Kerns realized that "DocuTech could hurt" both of Xerox's two core businesses, printing and reprographics. With admirable courage, rather than scuttling the project, Kerns decided to locate the DocuTech team outside both of these divisions, ensuring that internal resistances would not be able to throw up too many obstacles (a move reminiscent of Hackborn's claim that to maintain market leadership HP had to be willing to obsolete its own products). Even so, Holt commented that the DocuTech "was a product the existing businesses of Xerox did not want," and internal debates continued to rage around certain of its features. This debate led Holt to conclude that "market-making events can occur [only] on the basis of competent true believers railing against the infrastructure of a corporation."[37]

Listing the DocuTech's features shows how deep the revolution went. First was the issue of productivity. Electromechanical devices could handle only one original at a time, but the enhanced cognition of computational circuitry enabled the DocuTech to scan and store in memory several originals, printing out each in turn. "While jobs were running out the back end," Holt commented, the operator could perform make-ready tasks on other originals; thus, "concurrency [was built] into the system."[38] The scan-to-memory feature also meant that each original needed to be sent through the machine only once, reducing the possibility of damage that might be incurred in multiple runthroughs. The documents could also be modified through their scans: merged, reduced, enlarged, cropped, and cut and paste.

These possibilities led to debates within the company about whether operator skills were up to the task because with traditional machines operators needed only to input pages and collect output. Holt told Webster, "The concepts of concurrency and ease of use were lost on traditional planners and developers of the old reprographics machine. Here with the push of a button the technology . . . made the operations very easy. It turned out that operators became empowered and in fact became more enthusiastic about his [sic] job. The new system became a real motivator."³⁹ In a positive-feedback loop, enhanced machine cognition in this instance led to enhanced use of human cognition, illustrating that a redistribution of cognition within a cognitive assemblage may not necessarily be a zero-sum game but may rather lead to higher cognitive functions for both human and machine partners.

Another function performed by the DocuTech was duplexing, or imaging pages on both sides. The old reprographics machines required room for output trays that would hold the sheets until all were imaged; then the sheets were turned over, inverted, and fed back into the machine for imaging on the other side, a task usually performed by an experienced operator because it was easy to make a mistake. But the DocuTech had a "dynamic duplex process" in which the computer rather than a human figured out whether the first or second side needed to be imaged, saving space and thus allowing room for 11-by-17-inch sheets, something previously prohibited by lack of storage space. An especially neat feature was the DocuTech's ability to move the margins outward as the number of pages in a book increased to compensate for the larger turning radius (in a conventionally printed paperback, I sometimes find it necessary to push the pages so far apart that I risk cracking the spine, a problem I would not have with a book produced by the DocuTech).

The net result of these innovations was the creation of the print-on-demand market, a development with profound implications for how university presses in particular think about their backlists and intellectual property, as we will see in chapter 3. Throughout the 1990s, the DocuTech dominated the print-on-demand market, bringing in for Xerox a $30–35 million revenue stream, with yearly margins of almost $1 million. With a market this attractive, it was inevitable that competitors would follow the path that the DocuTech had blazed, and by the end of the 1990s several other machines had entered the print-on-demand market. With these developments, printing was "unchained" (as in the title of Webster's book) from the necessity of large runs. Intellectual property as instantiated in books was suddenly plunged into an entirely different temporal regime, and book production was changed forever.

Ethics and Information Technology Innovation

The Lumitype and DocuTech are exemplary of successful innovations; rarely do we remember those innovators who gave up or who were overwhelmed by institutional politics, bad timing, lack of financial support, or other adversities. These kinds of contingencies—the distinctions between those who succeeded and those who did not—also have important effects on the trajectories of technological development. The stories about who won in the development of computational media within the printing industry can be used to test the procedures that Sarah Spiekermann advocates in *Ethical IT Innovation: A Value-Based System Design Approach*.

Rather than try to articulate new values or critique old ones, Spiekermann starts with broadly consensual values: "The success of a value-based approach therefore depends on a broad social, historical, and philosophical consensus on what constitutes a value or what ideals form an epoch," she writes.[40] So she defines widely accepted values such as dignity, honesty, integrity, and privacy and then breaks them down into incremental steps in the design process to show how they can be implemented from management and engineering points of view. She is, of course, correct in her insight that values cannot be added on at the end, like sprinkling powdered sugar on a pound cake; they have to be baked in at the beginning. She also wisely acknowledges that such reflections require time to achieve and think through. Hers is an attractive vision for how ethical innovation might work, and one wishes that every engineer and manager designing information technology (IT) systems would make this book compulsory reading for themselves and their employees.

However, if we measure this vision against the actualities of innovations in the print industry that brought about its computerization, we notice several aspects in which the reality contradicts the vision. For example, Spiekermann cites the "hype cycle," illustrating it with a curve that sharply zooms upward as an innovation is touted as completely transformative, then just as sharply plunges downward after the innovation fails to live up to the hype, and thereafter slowly crawls upward again as its more limited usefulness is discovered.[41] She locates many technologies along this curve, specifically mentioning radio-frequency identification (RFID) as an example. RFID was initially hyped, as she says, as a transformative technology that would revolutionize warehousing along with much else, but then it was discovered that warehouse metal shelving interfered with the signals, making RFID much less useful than initially imagined. The implication is that innovative practices might save a lot of time and money by avoiding the hype and investing the savings into thinking more carefully about the values that the technology would embody or foster, in effect cutting off the first part of the curve and leaping directly to the slowly rising adoption portion. The point, Spiekermann argues, should not be adding new features simply for the sake of novelty, which will lead to "feature fatigue," but instead thinking through the values, explicit or implicit, that the design conveys and exploring alternatives that may foster better ones. "People are so used to constant new functionality that its magic quickly wears off," she writes. "My advice to deal with IT hype is: Treat them [sic] with suspicion and think first. Envision the sustainable *value* that you want to create with the new technology. Don't invest unless you see that value. Only go to market with a fully tested, trustworthy and mature technical product."[42]

The reality, however, is that the hype is what attracts venture-capital funding, either from inside corporations or from the outside, without which the product might not be developed at all. Moreover, this chapter reveals the intense market pressures that innovators are often under, when a delay of a few months or a year could mean the difference between a product's success or its failure. If a competitor wins a majority market share and "locks out" devices that use other formats, that might be a death knell for anyone seeking to compete with another kind of machine (the VHS versus Betamax situation). A final objection can be made to Spiekermann's admonishment to think about the "sustainable *value* you want to create." When a new technology is being developed, it is difficult or impossible to envision all the uses to which it might be put as it matures. As a consequence, new kinds of values—positive or negative—might emerge that are very different from what was envisioned at the beginning. Because these values are unknown (and perhaps are unknown unknowns), it is impossible for them to be evaluated correctly or sensibly at the beginning of product development. Does this mean that the value system that Spiekermann advocates will not work? I would not go that far, but it does indicate that her approach may be of more limited usefulness than she tends to suggest.

Another way to interpret the gap between her vision and the reality of technical innovation is to say that her approach does not go far enough, that a more radical revolution is necessary to free innovation from the notorious short-sightedness of corporate investment and profit seeking.[43] It is obvious from myriad indications (as well as from this chapter) that *ethical* IT innovation is made more difficult by the pressures associated with capitalism; to cite just one example, witness HP's strategy of obsoleting its own products, a situation that on an industry-wide scale has led to myriad electronic artworks becoming unplayable when the software used to create them becomes obsolete, as we will see in chapter 5. The ethical issues raised by cognitive technologies in printing come front and center with e-books and e-readers, particularly with regard to surveillance, licensing, and consumer-specific product placements.

E-readers and Their Cognitive Capacities: Transforming the Landscape of Book Consumption

The decisions bounded by Higonnet and Moyroud's midcentury practice of using binary inputs up to the end-of-the-century decision to use software instead of hardwired logic circuits for the DocuTech had two enormous consequences that unfurled in the gale-force winds of change that blew in the new millennium. The first was to open the door to the rapid development and expansion of the cognitive capabilities not only in the devices that produced books but also in those that served as electronic reading platforms for them, the e-readers. The second was to accelerate already-existing trends to separate content from its material manifestation by introducing a clear delineation between electronic data and the devices that interpreted them, a development that made e-books conceptually and practically distinct from e-readers. The first consequence led to radically changed relationships between electronic reading devices and human readers; the second to a seismic shift from books that were owned by those who bought them to content that was merely leased and subject to significant restrictions on how it could be used.

Let us consider first the changed relations between devices and human users. With e-books and e-readers,[44] the cognitive developments that had been in the background of readerly practices vaulted into visibility (although the extent of this visibility

Print Into Postprint

depends in part on a given reader's habits). This is where a media-archeology perspective becomes invaluable because whereas each (human) reader may vary in the extent to which she accesses the cognitive functions available in an e-reader/e-book, making generalizations difficult, a media-archeological perspective focuses on the viewpoint of the device itself, enabling a clearer view of the ways in which its cognitive functions make it very different from a print book. So dramatic is this break, in fact, that it is no exaggeration to say that it constitutes an ontological rupture from the print era. Moreover, e-readers and e-books have changed the media ecology of reading itself—for example, reviving possibilities for communal readings that had faded into the background after print books displaced medieval practices of reading aloud and transferred the scene of reading to an individual's private rooms.

What are the capabilities of cognitive reading devices? Here I focus on the Amazon Kindle and the multiuse Mac iPad because the Kindle, more than any other of the dedicated e-readers (Kobo, Nook, Boox, etc.), has been the most successful in expanding the market for e-books, and the iPad, for its part, has been largely responsible for expanding the sensory inputs associated with reading e-books, in particular touch and gesture. The iPad and some versions of the Kindle (in particular the Kindle Fire) have accelerometers that know the spatial orientation of the device and can shift the screen accordingly, along ninety-degree increments. Some have an internal GPS that knows the device's geographical coordinates and can report on them if asked. The iPad and some e-readers have touch screens that utilize capacitance technology to sense when they are touched by a human finger and can respond to gestures according to algorithms that interpret this input.[45] Most e-readers have clocks and can report on the time as well as use the clock to keep track of readerly activities.

In addition to these sensory system, e-readers of all kinds instantaneously transform ASCII strings into binary digital and vice versa, allowing for vastly more storage space than a print book (indeed, consumers often cite this capability as the single most important advantage of e-readers). The Kindle Oasis and Fire as well as the iPad have text-to-speech functions that enable a user to convert words to sound (possible because once a text is stored as a binary file, it can be outputted as either alphanumeric symbols or as speech sounds). The Kindle, iPad, and most e-readers can change and resize the font, highlight passages, as well as record, store, and retrieve notes a reader makes on specific passages. Most have the functionality to call up definitions of words. Moreover, the iPad and some versions of the Kindle come with wireless transceivers, allowing remote databases to draw content from them and vice versa. In addition, this capability enables the device to report back to a centralized database on the reader's activities, including such fine-grained analytics as how long a reader has perused various sections of the e-book, which sections were skipped or read quickly, how many notes were taken or highlights activated on what passages. Because the relevant database has this information not only for a given reader but for *all* readers who purchased that same e-book, the Kindle and iPad also have functions that enable a reader to see how many other readers highlighted or took notes on a given passage. In this sense, e-readers reinstitute communal reading (for some software packages, the networking possibilities go much further).[46]

Many readers may not realize or think much about an e-reader's cognitive capabilities, in part because the extent to which a reader utilizes that potential varies from person to person and in part because e-readers are designed, as a deliberate marketing strategy, to screen from readers the full extent of the e-readers' capabilities, especially with regard to their surveillance potential. **For someone who regards an e-book as a convenient way to access print content, reading text on an e-reader may not seem very different from engaging with a print object. Nevertheless, an adequate understanding of the interactions**

```
466    <p class="X">Many readers may not realize
       or think much about an e-reader's cognitive
       capabilities, in part because the extent to
       which a reader utilizes that potential varies
       from person to person and in part because
       e-readers are designed, as a deliberate
       marketing strategy, to screen from readers the
       full extent of the e-readers' capabilities,
       especially with regard to their surveillance
       potential. <span class="B _idGenCharOverride-
       4">For someone who regards an e-book as a
       convenient way to access print content, reading
       text on an e-reader may not seem very different
       from engaging with a print object. Nevertheless,
       an adequate understanding of the interactions
       between a user and an e-reader requires a model
       of distributed cognition and, as a necessary
       corollary, an understanding of the interactions
       between user and e-book as instances of
       distributed agency. As a result of its cognitive
       capabilities, the e-reader immerses the user in
       a very different media ecology than a print book
       does. Once the device is not only a cognitive
       support, like the print book, but also a
       cognizer in its own right, it becomes in effect
       a collaborator with the human reader, able
       to sense and respond to the reader's desires
       and execute commands of a quite sophisticated
       nature.</span> In the larger context of the
       cognitive assemblages within which e-readers and
       e-books operate in postprint technologies, their
       significance is that they bring the experiences
       of distributed cognition and distributed agency
       up close and personal so that they are no longer
       abstractions or implications of historical
       accounts but everyday realities, perched right
       under our noses.</p>
467    <p class="H1">Ownership, Access, and
       Surveillance <br />in the Postprint Era</p>
```

Here is the code to transform the print page into an ebook format for the passage describing the cognitive capabilities of ereaders.

between a user and an e-reader requires a model of distributed cognition and, as a necessary corollary, an understanding of the interactions between user and e-book as instances of distributed agency. As a result of its cognitive capabilities, the e-reader immerses the user in a very different media ecology than a print book does. Once the device is not only a cognitive support, like the print book, but also a cognizer in its own right, it becomes in effect a collaborator with the human reader, able to sense and respond to the reader's desires and execute commands of a quite sophisticated nature. In the larger context of the cognitive assemblages within which e-readers and e-books operate in postprint technologies, their significance is that they bring the experiences of distributed cognition and distributed agency up close and personal so that they are no longer abstractions or implications of historical accounts but everyday realities, perched right under our noses.

Ownership, Access, and Surveillance in the Postprint Era

In the next chapter, we will encounter the belief held by some (many?) that the print codex is a superior format for scholarly research compared to an e-book. However that may be, it is clear that the print codex has greater cachet and cultural capital than does the utilitarian e-book. We often tend to treat this ranking as obvious, but Ted Striphas reminds us that the early twentieth century saw a concerted campaign concocted by the "father of spin" Edward L. Bernays, who was hired by book publishers to inculcate the belief that print books were necessary accoutrements to the well-furnished middle-class home. Bernays's ingenious approach was to work with architects and others to incorporate built-in bookshelves into new homes. For people who accordingly found themselves with more bookshelf space than books to put on them (a situation I can scarcely imagine), "mimic books," wooden or cardboard forms that looked like books but were not, could be purchased by the yard to fill out the space. Striphas comments that these developments initiated a transition that "redefined the private home from a space of moral and spiritual uplift to one increasingly focused on domestic leisure."[47]

As the campaign succeeded and more people bought print books, publishers began to wake up to the fact that the lending of books among friends or even from libraries was cutting into their potential sales.[48] Responding to this concern, Bernays had the further inspiration to sponsor a contest in 1931 to "look for a pejorative word for the book borrower, the wretch who raised hell with book sales and deprived authors of earned royalties."[49] Implicit here was the notion that the ownership of a book did not entitle the consumer to convey its content to someone else—an implication somewhat masked by the fusion of content and vehicle in the print book. Although this idea never acquired much traction in its day, the situation was exacerbated by the commercially viable photocopiers that began appearing in the 1970s and 1980s. When the lawsuits brought by publishers against the Gnomon Corporation in 1980 for unauthorized copying and then against Kinko's in 1989 were successful, the implication became clearer because now the content was actually transferred from its original location in a print book to a photocopy, making the case for violation of copyright much stronger. As Striphas observes, implicit in these suits but unacknowledged as such was "the question of what it means to own books . . . in the late age of print."[50]

This story may be regarded as the prehistory of the legal and informational constraints that became fully explicit with e-books. When one buys a print book, one owns it, but buying a text formatted for an e-book does not confer possession of its content. Rather, what one buys when purchasing an e-book text is a *license* to access its content.[51] This is very clear when the text itself resides "in the cloud" rather than on the individual device. Even in the latter case, however, the content may be recalled if the relevant corporation judges that the terms of the license have been violated.

One ironic instance of such recall involved Amazon deleting George Orwell's novels *1984* and *Animal Farm* from its customers' Kindles, apparently because the texts had been added to the Kindle store by a company that did not have the rights to them. Other reported instances involved Harry Potter books and the novels of Ayn Rand, apparently also because of copyright issues. As a result of the furor, Amazon agreed not to delete texts directly from people's Kindles, but it continues to erase them from Kindle archives—which means that if someone wants to redownload onto her Kindle an archived text she purchased earlier, she will not be able to access it. This situation poses special problems for libraries because it is not clear that they have the right to make an interlibrary loan of an e-book text to another library. With print books, they could load the objects onto a truck and physically transport them elsewhere, but the licenses for e-books do not allow someone to give the contents to someone else—including another lending library.

Striphas interprets these developments in a way consistent with his Marxist perspective as a historically situated and culturally specific movement to focus on controlling consumption rather than on increasing production (although obviously the two are related). From my perspective, this interpretation misses the larger point that as knowledge work became more important and the amount of data exploded exponentially with the advent of the web near the twentieth century's end, there was an overall shift of emphasis from ownership to access. For example, you can look up at your bookshelf and see the book you bought last week; if you feel like it, you can pull it down and see your marginal notes, marks that make it a unique object, uniquely located in space and time. With respect to information, however, knowing that it resides in one location does not prohibit it from residing in another (or a thousand other) places as well. In the web world, information can be duplicated and sent almost anywhere

Print Into Postprint

at almost no cost, so what becomes important is not so much who owns the information as who can access it.[52] Moreover, access is not only a legal but also a technical matter. Questions arise with e-books that simply never occurred with print books. You can access your e-book in the cloud (or on your own machine), but can you also access the code that underlies the surface inscription?

Many of these issues are highlighted in Dennis Tenen's book *Plain Text: The Poetics of Computation*. Noting that "an electronic book governed by digital rights may subsequently prevent readers from copying or sharing stored content, even for the purpose of academic study," Tenen points out that the U.S. Digital Millennium Copyright Act of 1998 "prohibits physical circumvention of copyright protections. An electronic book encrypted to prevent copyright infringement could also prevent readers from examining codes and codices embedded in the device, rules governing accessibility, preservation, or freedom of speech." Moreover, the inaccessibility of these enforced rules "exposes a glaring problem at the heart of smart contracts."[53] Mireille Hildebrandt points out in *Smart Technologies and the End(s) of Law* that traditional English contract law requires that valid contracts must be explicit and available to both parties; as Tenen puts it, they must exist in "an objectively verifiable manner that is mutually accessible for analysis."[54] If readers cannot even access the code for smart contracts, much less study it, they are illegitimately forced to abide by a contract whose terms they do not even know.

This situation is bad enough, but for a literary community dedicated to practices of close reading, the implications of how the code is constructed do not remain at the subterranean level and instead, Tenen argues, "affect all higher-level interpretive activity." Tenen no doubt speaks for many when he acknowledges that "some of my deepest intuitions about literature relied on assumptions firmly attached to print media."[55] For those of us trained in literary study, one assumption born of print is that the

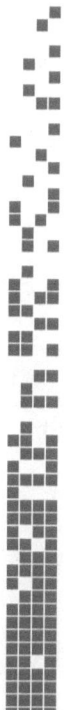

text will remain relatively stable. Of course, there are exceptions, such as texts with complicated histories of different editions and authorial revisions. Even here, however, literary readers expect that such a history is likely to have been adjudicated through editorial practices that have evolved over decades and centuries. Moreover, if one is motivated to recover this history, one can be reasonably sure (at least for important works) that a deep archive of textual scholarship will be available through variorum editions and other resources.

Nothing in this experience prepares literary readers for the reality of e-books that may be tailored in content to appeal to different audiences—much as the algorithms on Amazon, for example, choose for us books that our shopping data suggest we are most likely to buy. Tenen describes the situation like this: "Traditional strategies of close reading, which limit interpretation to the parsing of visible content, risk missing the concealed machinations of naked circuit control. It looks as though we are reading books [when engaging with e-books], but this book may change depending on the reader's race, gender, ethnicity, geography, or political affiliation."[56] Such fine-tuning of content, an everyday reality when one surfs the web, is a startling development for the books we read. Nevertheless, it clearly is well within the power of contemporary coding practices.

Readers who feel that e-books are not significantly different from print books are not simply being willfully ignorant. Rather, the technology is designed precisely to foster this illusion, from screenic displays of "turning pages" to highlighting functions and scrolling procedures that mimic the eye traveling down the page. Tenen is particularly astute in calling out this kind of simulation as a deliberate strategy of "dissembling to conceal [the technology's] material foundations." Moreover, he exhorts readers not to accept the comfortable illusions that such dissembling offers: "Metaphor sustains our lives in digital worlds artificially by analogy to habituated media [that is, print]. Replicators dull the discomfort of contact between human and machine. But we should not forget that computational ecologies are always constructed environments." Warning that "our grasp on the medium weakens the more convincing its simulation," he concludes that if we are "alienated from the base particulates of the word, we lose some of our basic interpretive capacities to interrogate embedded power structures."[57]

For Tenen, the answer to these problems is a practice that he calls "computational poetics" by analogy with the poetics of close reading. He explains that "the methodology of computational poetics insists on recovering the full shape of the inscription, across surfaces and domains. It makes the extent of the dissimulating figures available for interpretation."[58] But this is not quite a full explanation of his methodology, which includes, as observed earlier, close attention to contexts, historical documents such as patent applications, and situated analyses of when, how, and by whom technological innovations were made.

From my perspective, Tenen demonstrates in exemplary fashion that contexts and embodiments are crucial to understanding how cognitive assemblages are created from hybrid human–technology interactions, how they function, and how they work incrementally to transform human cognition as well. In exploring the printing technologies that moved us from print to postprint, this chapter and book aspire to contribute to the collective project of understanding more fully the implications of this massive change. From the shifts, ruptures, and transformations described in this chapter, the effects of postprint rippled throughout the publishing industry, including academic publishing and scholarship.

3

The Mixed Ecologies of University Presses

No one who has closely studied the history of invention is likely to agree with technological determinism. The historical record of invention is littered with accidental discoveries, diverging paths, quirks of financing and timing, and other contingencies that mock the idea of an inevitable trajectory. For example, in the history of printing technologies, Ichiro Endo and his team at Canon were trying to use the piezoelectric effect to move ink out of a nozzle, but then he happened to place his fountain pen next to a heated soldering iron, and he noticed that it spurted out ink: so thermal ink jet was born. Another example: the large connection plugs first used by Centronics matrix printers, which subsequently became standard throughout the industry, came about because Robert Howard, CEO of Centronics, was friends with Dr. An Wang of Wang Labs; Wang happened to have an inventory of twenty thousand unused plugs and gifted them to Howard.[1] These instances can be multiplied endlessly. Consider the possible contingencies of the history recounted in chapter 2 as examples: if Higonnet's office had not been asked to print brochures and he consequently never visited a print shop, if the Graphic Arts Research Foundation had never given funding, if Moyroud's suitcase had been lost during his flight to New York, if David Kerns at Xerox had ordered Chip Holt's team to be subservient to the existing reprographics and printing divisions, and so on, events might have played out very differently.

Let us grant, then, that an actual historical path evolves through an interplay of many forces, contingency prominent among them. I make this case explicitly at this chapter's beginning lest I be misunderstood as arguing for technological determinism. This chapter instead documents pervasive technological *influence*. Once a trajectory (or set of trajectories) comes into existence through a series of contingent and contextually situated events, it can have enormous influence on how people read, write, and think. Such is now the case with digital inscriptions and the resulting fracturing of the sign into surface display and underlying software and hardware. Dennis Tenen argues that instead of following the path of least resistance with regard to our digital-inscription practices, we should think about the implications of our actions and make conscious (and conscientious) choices. He points out, for example, that using Adobe PDF software forces us to agree to the company's licensing terms, which include unacceptable (to him) limitations on how PDF documents can be created, stored, and disseminated. He writes, "From the many available visions of human–computer interactions, I argue for choosing ones that align with a humanist ethos, whatever the reader's politics."[2] Leaving aside the minor inconsistency created by that last phrase (because such choices are always inherently political, a reader's politics cannot be beside the point), Tenen's focus on a "humanist ethos" as the acid test for such choices highlights the importance of knowing precisely what is at stake when we create, disseminate, store, and share digital inscriptions.

In this chapter, we follow these implications to ground zero of postprint book scholarship: university presses. In my view, university presses have been slow to follow the path that Tenen urges—that is, fully taking into account the deeper implications of their engagements with computational media. The likely reason, I suspect, is their deep allegiance to the ethos of print and the

The Mixed Ecologies of University Presses

humanistic values associated with it. A contributing factor is their partial insulation from the capitalist demand for profitability. Unlike commercial publishing, university presses have a margin of financial freedom in their operations because they are typically not expected to generate profits from monograph sales. At the same time, though, their universities are increasingly asking them to become self-financing. Some losses in book publications may be tolerated if they are offset by surpluses elsewhere—for example, in journal sales. On the whole, however, university presses aim to break even with their monograph costs, which, as we will see, is increasingly a herculean task (see John B. Thompson's figures substantiating this claim[3]). Dedicated to the mission of making the best and most important scholarship available in book form (among other formats), university presses tend to have a conservative bias that tilts them toward the print book as the privileged vehicle of communication. Nevertheless, digital technologies are now accepted as pervasive components of the press's everyday work flow, so almost all university presses operate in a mixed ecology of print, postprint, and digital practices.

These mixed ecologies make university presses a good site through which to explore urgent questions confronting humanities scholars and others in the digital age. What is a book, and how does it signify in different media ecologies? How does (or should) the life of a scholar proceed? What counts as scholarly production? Is scholarship a matter of articulating complex issues so that they achieve polished final form, or is it rather a flow that continues to modulate and change without an end in sight? Is scholarly production typically achieved by someone sequestering herself so she can think deeply on the issues that concern her, or is it a boisterous, many-sided, and raucous conversation in which no single voice predominates? If many of our deepest intuitions about literature and literary analysis are bound up with print, as Dennis Tenen suggests, no doubt the same is true of how scholarship is regarded by university presses. Their deepest intuitions about what constitutes excellent scholarship are bound

The Mixed Ecologies of University Presses

up with print practices, and these presuppositions linger as these presses advance into the digital age.[4]

Protocols and Limitations

In preparation for writing this chapter, I interviewed personnel from five university presses: California, Chicago, Columbia, Duke, and Minnesota. I chose these presses because I have some kind of working relationship with them and because they represent a typical sample of Research 1 institutions.[5] This focus leaves much out of account, notably the large, semicommercial university publishers Oxford and Cambridge, whose monograph publishing volume each year puts them in a class by themselves, numbering 3,000–4,000 books annually compared to the typical output of 90–250 books per year for each of the five presses I investigate. It also ignores European publishers, who typically charge higher prices for their monographs but are willing to publish books that may only sell 100–200 copies. It neglects regional university presses, some of whom have specialty areas in which they are highly competitive with Tier 1 presses; for example, Bucknell University Press is internationally known for its monographs in Luso-Spanish, Irish, and eighteenth-century studies; the University of Mississippi Press for its books on southern culture; and so forth. Perhaps the most serious limitation is my focus on scholarly monographs in the humanities and interpretive social sciences, which leaves out textbook publishing, journal publishing, the lucrative field of business publishing, and scientific areas in which the journal article rather than the scholarly monograph is the accepted form of scholarly production. Nevertheless, monographs arguably occupy a crucial position in scholarly publishing for several reasons. They often make a press's reputation as well as the reputations of individual scholars; they continue to be regarded by humanities tenure and promotion committees as the most important form of publication;

and they are the pinch points where financial considerations bite most fiercely into a press's bottom line and thus pose the most risk to its long-range financial stability.

Limitations notwithstanding, my interviews identify important trends in scholarly publishing, including how different presses are dealing with financial precarity, how they envision the future of scholarship and scholarly publishing, and how their attitudes and practices are affected by the incorporation of cognitive technologies into the printing and publishing business. Perhaps most importantly, they reveal the powerful transformative effects of moving from a mode of thinking, writing, and publishing where the focus is on the individual to a networked model of scholarship. This transition affects every assumption we have about scholarly productivity, including how presses position themselves, how scholarly careers are envisioned and practiced, and how scholarship is evaluated and disseminated. Happening in diverse ways and with various intensities at different sites, the shift from individual cognizer to cognitive assemblage enables us to glimpse a landscape of postprint scholarship profoundly changed after the hundreds of years in which print reigned supreme.

Without necessarily putting the transition in these terms, scholars and publishers know as well as anyone that the cognitive capacities of computational media are crucial for making the networked model of scholarship possible. The capabilities of computational media include creating collaborative platforms, facilitating communications between participants, enabling dissemination through the web, and employing many other functionalities. The transition to a networked model literally would not be possible without the collaboration of cognitive technologies with human scholars at every step of the way. Humans naturally like to think of ourselves as in control of this process, but anyone who has seriously worked in this way has experienced the collective force that technological configurations exert on the process, from new apps that make something possible that was previously impossible to the technical obsolescence that brings to a premature close many promising avenues of scholarly development simply because a tech company did not find it profitable to continue producing a certain product.[6] Humanities scholars, writers in electronic media, and university presses rely extensively on computational technologies, but they are not the ones who control the media's development.

Although the framework of cognitive assemblages is not how these scholars and presses typically conceive of their relation to computational media, they would have no trouble in recognizing the problem I have sketched here. Nor would they find it difficult to agree that computational technologies' increased capabilities have taken over many everyday and routine tasks, such as template design, formerly done exclusively by humans. The novel element that might take them by surprise is the realization that computational media are no longer simply better tools but also cognizers in their own right and that the media's cognitive capabilities move them closer to being collaborators rather than, say, to being hammers that can do more things.

The next step for scholars and presses, of course, would be a reevaluation of their own positions as participants in cognitive assemblages in which agency is distributed between human and nonhuman entities. Many might strenuously disagree with this conclusion put this way. But if we were to ask the question differently—for example, inquiring whether computational technologies have influenced the way everyday tasks are done—they would no doubt agree. And if we asked again if they (the humans) can completely dictate how that influence is wielded, we would again find substantial agreement that certain developments in the technical realm are beyond their control. The sticking points would likely be the related realizations that computational technologies have cognitive capacities and that agency is distributed, no longer residing solely in the human participants. The interviews in this chapter demonstrate both the

The Mixed Ecologies of University Presses

reluctance to embrace conceptually the assumptions underlying a cognitive-assemblage framework and the implicit recognition that computational technologies have an increasingly large role in scholars' and university presses' everyday tasks. The cognitive-assemblage framework enables us to put these positions together in a coherent way that makes sense of the mixed ecologies now typical of the contexts in which contemporary humanities scholarship is practiced.

The Precarious Future of Monograph Publishing

I had met Jennifer Crewe, director of Columbia University Press, many years ago at an English Institute conference; I was impressed then by her good sense and astute insights, and my background research into her career made me more impressed. When she took over as director, she was the first woman to serve in that capacity at an Ivy League university press. Moreover, she had worked her way up through the ranks, serving as an editorial assistant while still engaged in her MFA work in poetry at Columbia University, advancing to assistant editor after graduation. After a stint at Scribner's (later taken over by Macmillan), she returned to Columbia University Press as acquisitions editor. Finally, after working at the press for nearly thirty years, she was named interim director for nine months and then was appointed president and director in 2014.

Asked about the influence of digital technologies, Crewe identified a sea change about twelve years ago when digital-book readers appeared, along with the rise of Amazon as the press's primary customer for sales of print and e-books to individuals.[7] At the time, the staff at Columbia thought e-books might eventually supersede print, but she said that in a trend confirmed by other university presses Columbia's e-book sales plateaued at 20–25 percent, averaging just 5 percent for literary criticism.

On one point, Crewe was crystal clear: monograph sales are in trouble. The press has seen a decline in library sales from around 400 copies of each new book ten to fifteen years ago to as low as 100–200 copies even for a book heralded as important in its field. Moreover, scholars are buying fewer monographs, too, a somewhat counterintuitive result of having more books available in their fields. She mentioned a scholar in Islamic history who twenty years ago considered it necessary to buy every new book published in his area, but as the volume of books in the field grew, he abandoned this idea and settled for purchasing only those he considered truly essential, thus purchasing fewer monographs overall. With budgets squeezed by the rising costs of journals, libraries were making similar decisions. Instead of each library feeling that it must own every important new scholarly book, libraries began forming consortiums in which members specialize in different areas, with the understanding that others can obtain monographs through interlibrary loan from the specializing library. The combined effects of these changes have drastic implications for monograph sales. Thompson cites 2,500 copies as a typical run for which a press could reasonably expect to sell a monograph in the 1970s. By the early 2000s, that number had shrunk to 400–500 hardback copies of a monograph for many university presses.[8]

To put some flesh on these bones, we may consider concrete numbers. Although it is difficult to estimate the "average" break-even price point for a print book because costs and revenue vary by length, number of images, list price, and other factors, Crewe mentioned that in a typical case it costs $25,000 to publish a single monograph. It would be necessary to sell around 600 copies of a book with a list price of $60 and a net return of $42 to earn back costs. Even for a book well reviewed and considered important in its field, the sales might not rise above 400 copies, leaving a deficit of approximately $8,000. Such a loss-heavy business practice is clearly not sustainable, and, as we will see, different presses are adopting a range of strategies to make up the shortfall.

The Mixed Ecologies of University Presses

Many are counting on journal sales or profitable areas such as business or regional books, which sell in much larger quantities to general readers. In addition, most university presses occasionally publish books that sell far more than the average, and these books help to subsidize those that do not achieve break-even sales. In Crewe's terms, this dependency puts a premium on finding the "right mix" of books—a tricky strategy because publishers can't really know how well a book will sell, and a breakout book is not infrequently difficult to predict. In addition, Columbia, like many university presses, is turning to endowments and grants to help it balance its bottom line. This strategy, too, is not without problems because endowments take years to raise, sooner or later even a successful grant will run out, and then the budget problems return.

One bright spot is the emergence of short-run digital printing and print-on-demand (POD), technologies that enable Columbia, one of the country's oldest university presses, to make available its archives dating back to the press's founding in 1893. By partnering with a European e-book distributor and sending material to Romania to be digitized, the press is now able to offer its deep backlist in digital form to libraries and other interested parties. An additional option is to offer these materials in print form as well because the digital file can be repurposed for print with only a minimal amount of additional coding.

Despite the challenge of finding a sustainable business model, Crewe is optimistic about the future of print and although more cautious about the future of scholarly monograph publishing is upbeat about it also. As mentioned earlier, a key factor is tenure and promotion committees' preference for scholars to be the authors of university press imprints. At the same time, like Lindsay Waters, executive editor for the humanities at Harvard University Press, Crewe is reluctant for the press's publishing decisions to be seen as an arbiter of academic careers. In an interview in the *Chronicle of Higher Education*, she wrote, "University-press editors are quite uncomfortable when they think that a tenure decision has been 'outsourced' to them. A book is just one factor in the tenure or promotion decision, and we would prefer that it remain just one factor."[9]

Despite the financial precarity of monograph publishing, Crewe (like most university press directors) believes passionately in the press's mission to bring the best, most important, and most transformative scholarship into book form, thus making it available to scholarly audiences—as she put it, the "kind of book we were put on the planet to publish." The press's strategic plan going forward is to align its mission more with Columbia University's intellectual strengths and to continue the effort to find the "right mix" while still maintaining its traditional emphasis on quality.

For information about the impact of digital technologies on the press's workflow, I spoke with Michael Haskell, production editor and publishing systems manager, who, like most of my interlocutors at Columbia and elsewhere, has been with the press for more than a decade.[10] Previously holding the title of manuscript editor, **Haskell explained that the manuscript editing and production departments had been combined. He noted that book designs are increasingly done by templates, in which decisions about font, headings, and other structural elements are predetermined, thus reducing the amount of effort designers need to spend with a given book—a prime example of how everyday tasks are increasingly performed by computers rather than by humans.** This change might provide an opportunity for designers to introduce more exotic or imaginative features because they no longer have to concern themselves with mundane matters. Haskell noted that, given the current state of monograph publishing, this opportunity might be more dream than reality. He ruefully acknowledged that university presses are squeezed by the mandate to break even, including those situated in well-financed universities that are nevertheless less willing than in the past to subsidize operating losses.

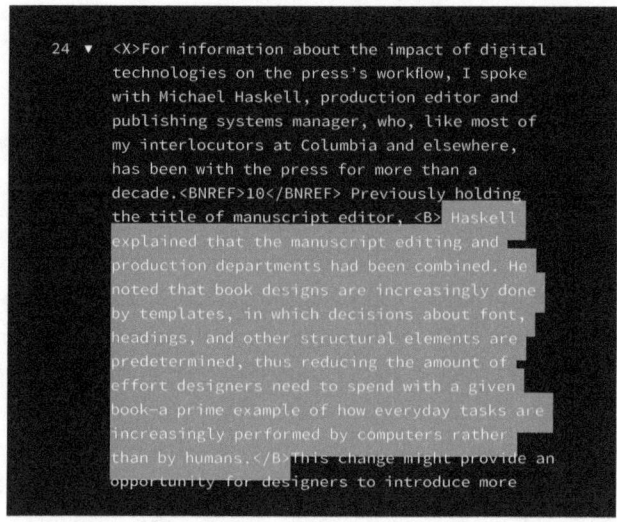

(*Above*) HTML code for typesetting the text; (*below*) the template sample page showing measurements and markup for the compositor.

Like Crewe, Haskell thought that book sales are deeply entwined with attitudes toward the monograph held not only by tenure and promotion committees but also by universities. "It's a weird niche that exists at the pleasure of the university." "If the gold standard moves away from the book," he continued, then "the publishing industry won't need scholarly monographs." As it is, the printed book, along with its e-book version, is perceived to bring prestige not only to the individual scholar but also to the publishing press as well as to the university sponsoring the press.

Although Haskell thinks that the current climate of precarity suppresses innovation because "the margins are so thin," Philip Leventhal, the editor for literary studies, is more sanguine about possibilities for exciting developments.[11] One direction he particularly likes is the emergence of scholarship directed to a variety of readers across disciplines and outside of academia rather than toward specialists. Specialist discourse has been a particular problem for literary criticism; since the advent of deconstruction in the U.S. academy in the 1970s, the public has come to believe that literary criticism is inscrutable if not altogether nonsensical. But now Leventhal sees publishing opportunities opening up for different modes of scholarly address through such venues as the online review *Public Books* and the *Los Angeles Review of Books*. "Authors are trying to find their voice and write in a different way," he commented, "and this is a good thing." For younger scholars still trying to land a tenure-track job, he notices another trend, which he calls the "two-tiered approach": a book project that will establish their scholarly credentials but also a "more public persona" in which they write for a broader audience, a mode of address typically reliant on networked computers. Here we see the mixed ecology in action, wherein codex books coexist with blogs, online reviews, and opinion pieces disseminated through social media. Leventhal is cautiously optimistic that the trend might lead to the resurgence of scholars writing for readers beyond their own subfields and addressing issues of public concern. If he is correct about younger scholars pursuing a two-tiered approach, implicit in this development is a dilemma that touches on the fundamental values assumed to govern the standards of academic scholarship. Although the print book still has the larger cultural capital within academia, online discourses arguably have more reach and influence with much larger audiences, so a situation emerges in which evaluators such as tenure committees must weigh having wider public influence against reaching much smaller numbers of experts through print publication. Which is more important, and how should each be weighted in the recommendations that tenure and promotion committees must make?

My overall impression is that the full scope of this dilemma has not been fully realized or debated, either within academic contexts or in university presses. Similarly, from this visit at Columbia I concluded that digital technologies have changed the way books are designed, edited, processed, and manufactured, but they have not caused significant changes in what I call the worldview of university presses, notwithstanding the difficult economics of publishing scholarly monographs. Columbia University Press is representative of many university presses that remain committed to long-form arguments and therefore continue to invest in monograph publishing, hoping to offset deficits with profits elsewhere in their production. How long this model can be sustained is not clear. As Leventhal commented, "University presses will need to think of other models to fund what we do. Book sales alone won't be a viable option." Nevertheless, the staff at Columbia and at many other university presses carry on because they deeply believe in their mission to make the best scholarship available as print and e-books, which, in their view, the scholarly community continues to value and to demand as credentials, even while diminishing sales make it more difficult to carry out this mission. These presses are the unsung heroes of an uncertain era when print is modulating into postprint but when print values continue to dominate the scholarly imaginary, both within the press and within the larger humanities community that it intends to serve.

The Chicago Model

My next visit was to the University of Chicago Press. My first impression: massive and overwhelming competence, Columbia on steroids. The largest university press in the United States, Chicago also benefits from its connection with the Chicago Distribution Center, which has as clients more than one hundred other presses. Even so, the director, Garrett Kiely, says, "costs keep going up," and "margins are getting smaller."[12] Among those aggressively competing with the Chicago Distribution Center is Ingram, a for-profit distribution center. Other challenges include growing demands from Amazon, Chicago's largest customer, which imposes an array of requirements on its suppliers and levies fines on publishers for missing them. Missing a shipment window on an Amazon order or failing to heed packing guidelines results in onerous "chargebacks." When turnaround times are tight, Chicago uses Amazon's CreateSpace, an inventory-management service that prints on-demand books from digital files. CreateSpace takes Chicago's digital files, prints the book, and ships it, all in a transaction invisible to the customer. Publishers benefit from CreateSpace and similar services but must also contend with pressure arising from Amazon's strategy of serving as both printer and retailer.

Because the use of POD is growing, I asked about its quality. Although saying that the digital-printing technology keeps improving and the cost of services is declining, Kiely also acknowledged that POD does not produce the same-quality graphics as offset lithography. Another issue is the different way in which the economics of POD works. Whereas with offset the price per book drops as the quantity increases, with POD there is no savings for quantity; if 500 books are ordered individually, each one costs as much as if only one book in total were ordered (although there are some cost savings if POD books are ordered 200–300 at a time). Nevertheless, POD is the technology of choice when current events push a book into the spotlight and there is a short-term spike in demand, as when David Ferry won the National Book Award in 2012 for his book of poems *Bewilderment*. POD also carries the significant benefit of eliminating the risk of overprinting, a situation necessitating that the publisher must write down the value of unsold inventory. With books not expected to sell many copies, university presses are increasingly using POD even for the first run, forsaking the "pristine" quality of offset, but this practice is still relatively rare at Chicago, which uses POD primarily for reprints.

Even as Chicago expands its use of POD, the press is mindful of POD's limitations. Kiely remarked that if a book has color images that require high-quality reproduction, Chicago will not use POD (although some illustrated books that are primarily documentary or technical in nature are produced with POD). The POD vendors "tout their color," he said, "but if you look closely at the dot patterns, it is nowhere near" offset quality. Curious, I asked if most readers notice the difference in quality between offset and POD (mainly because I have been the unfortunate purchaser of a book with noticeably deficient margins and type clarity, clearly a POD product, although not specified as such by Amazon). In addition to this problem, sometimes egregious mistakes occur with POD, such as printing sections in the wrong order or repeating sections (as happened with Italo Calvino's *If on a Winter's Night a Traveler*). In these cases, Chicago immediately examines the digital file and corrects any mistakes. "My job," Kiely commented at the beginning of the interview, "is to ensure we have the best books and the best journals."

One unintended consequence of POD is the emergence of a trust economy between book publishers and booksellers. "Technology has moved beyond our ability to understand it entirely,"

Kiely remarked. "We sell books [as digital files] through Amazon, Barnes & Noble, etc., but we have to trust that they are selling what they say since we have no physical objects to check" against the reported sales—no stacks of books in a warehouse that diminish as the orders go out. Such a "trust economy" never existed before, he continued, and "publishers worry" that they may be getting ripped off, whether by design or simply because of mistakes in the large volumes of files moving through cyberspace. Here is another example of how a press has no choice but to participate in a computationally managed situation that its staff may not completely understand, much less control. The obvious, although unarticulated, implication is that the press operates within a cognitive assemblage in which agency as well as cognitive capabilities are distributed.

Notwithstanding his uneasiness with this lack of control, Kiely readily acknowledged that digital formats have introduced cost savings. For example, when professors request examination copies, these copies are now sent out as digital files. If someone specifically requests a print examination copy, it is accompanied by an invoice, and the professor is expected either to adopt the book for classroom use or pay for it. Warehousing costs have also decreased because fewer books are stored in physical form. In addition, with a few exceptions, Chicago rarely puts books out of print anymore because POD has made it possible to keep most books in print indefinitely and at little additional cost. But POD income is not all gravy because files need to be updated for new formats and operating systems, and paper and ink still need to be paid for.

One of the innovations that Kiely has introduced at Chicago is a more balanced way to account for income from print books versus from e-book sales. Whereas many publishers attribute all fixed costs to the print format and consider e-book sales as "free" income, Kiely has worked out a more realistic accounting system that apportions costs such as typesetting and overhead across both print and electronic editions. Like university presses

The Mixed Ecologies of University Presses

everywhere, Chicago is feeling the economic pressure of declining library sales and libraries' increasing tendency to opt for access rather than for possession, renting books instead of buying them. In the short term at least, this rental system decreases the profits that publishers will make because the rentals are handled through micropayments that scarcely make a dent in the large up-front costs of acquiring, editing, and publishing a book, even though the payments will presumably continue for a longer period.

Another problem accompanying the transition to digital files is piracy. Kiely noted that many websites hosting pirated copies are located in Kazakhstan or elsewhere beyond the reach of U.S. laws and copyright protections. Like many publishers, Chicago employs a "cease and desist" service to protect its intellectual property, but piracy sites tend to pop up like mushrooms after a rain, so such services are of limited usefulness. Moreover, sometimes the metadata is there on a piracy site, but the digital files are not; the game is to lure readers to the site and then insert malware onto their computer. Another unsavory practice is the "fake" journal that requests several more copies of a book than any journal can actually use for a review; the practice is frequent enough that Chicago and other publishers maintain a blacklist to help identify such fake journals.

Asked what advice he would give a young scholar, Kiely emphasized the importance of knowing the ecology of his or her respective field. Young scholars, he noted, frequently do not realize how many books are published each year and lack a realistic sense of where their books fit. He also recommended strategies of repurposing material, writing in a way that lends itself to recombination. He notes a trend toward open access not only within the publishing industry but also among grant funders. Many funders—for example, the Wellcome Trust—now require that publications resulting from their grants be available through open access. To some extent, open access is orthogonal to a press's desire to protect its intellectual property as a revenue source. At

Chicago and many other university presses, these issues largely remain to be worked out, although, as we will see, Duke University Press, the University of California Press, and others are already experimenting with business models that reconcile these two imperatives.

I have worked with Alan Thomas, now editorial director at Chicago, for more than twenty years as an author, but my interview with him presented an opportunity to explore his views on a much broader range of topics. I found him delightfully opinionated and forthcoming; he is an eloquent spokesperson for what I came to think of as the "Chicago Model." Asked why he thought e-book sales have leveled off to something like 20 percent of the market, he had a ready answer: "The codex is a better technology."[13] E-books short-circuit some of the most useful elements of printed books, he said, pointing as an example to the difference between a search function and an index. The index is superior, he argued, because "it has intelligence behind it"; it is compiled by someone who understands the book's argument and has thought about what readers will want to know, whereas a search function is merely an all-purpose algorithm looking for certain strings. Even if an e-book includes an index, he commented, it is not as useable as an index in a print codex because the user cannot easily flip back and forth between pages. Moreover, print books have a spatial dimension that e-books lack, including volumetric clues to where in the book one is and two-dimensional spatial clues about where specific passages are located. He also pointed out something that others have noticed as well: it is much easier to remember the title and author of a print book than of an e-book, presumably because one often turns to the title page when opening a codex, whereas in an e-book it is cumbersome to keep traveling back to the title page.

Like other presses, Chicago faces challenges with monograph sales, although in the past fifteen years occasional surpluses in the Books Division and consistent performance by the distribution center and Journals Division have allowed the press to build a modest endowment, making financial precarity less a concern. Nevertheless, Thomas is keenly aware that "long term trends present a more challenging picture." Part of the Chicago Model (widely shared by American university presses) is to rely less on sales to libraries than to individuals and consequently to invest much more in copyediting, peer review, design, and marketing than in for-profit ventures that emphasize quantity over quality. The Chicago Model may be sustainable in the future, Thomas believes, but "it will take real creativity" and depends on publishing a diversity of genres because "monograph sales alone have never been self-sustaining."

Of open-access publishing, Thomas fears there will be a "race to the bottom," in which the emphasis shifts from quality, or publishing the best scholarship available, to quantity, or making a higher number of different books available to readers. The Chicago Model, he pointed out, cannot compete on that basis because it presumes that quality control, with its attendant costs, is all important and that books benefit from an investment in sales and marketing. Of self-publishing he is openly scornful, saying that "it is not publishing" but rather "making available." At the same time, he thinks that tenure and promotion committees' emphasis on top-tier university press books is far too narrow a criterion, pointing out that many regional and state universities have presses that excel in certain areas and specific lists. (In this opinion, he echoes concerns voiced by Crewe and other press directors.)

Along with a certain view of what constitutes publishing are Thomas's opinions about the relation between an author and editor. The role of an editor, he believes, is not just to shepherd a manuscript through the publishing process but also to work with the author to make the book a better one, somewhat on the model followed by famed Scribner's editor Maxwell Perkins (my analogy, not Thomas's). Authors tend to approach presses too soon with their first book, he said, and too late with their second book. Although many authors have a strong support network for their first book—dissertation committees, networks of mentors, and advisers at their institutions—this network often fades away by the second book, which is where a good press editor can pick up the slack, offering advice and suggestions that will help the author turn a mediocre manuscript into a much stronger book. Obviously, this role also has implications for upfront costs in terms of an editor's time, experience, and expertise showered on the would-be author to help her succeed. But this aspect of his job seems to offer Thomas the most satisfaction. It is what keeps him from seeing book manuscripts as so many commodities moving along an assembly line but rather as unique intellectual endeavors, each with its own achievements and challenges.

Like Leventhal, Thomas thinks that young scholars should experiment with writing in different genres and in styles suited to diverse audiences, including the educated public. Not only is this diversity good for its own sake, but it also "makes them better book writers" and "more effective collaborators" with the press because they have a more capacious sense of the intellectual ecologies in which their writings are located.

Although the acquisition process Thomas described seems only marginally affected by digital technologies, a very different picture emerges from the marketing and design departments, where digital technologies are now central to the ways in which they do business. Dean Blobaum, whose work includes the Chicago website, online marketing, and direct-to-consumer selling, recounted how in 1991 he discovered the internet (remarkably early) and has since made it the central focus of his marketing strategies, calling it a "profound change."[14] His efforts include trying for a more favorable standing in Google's search results, offering discounts at Chicago's website to lure buyers there and away from Amazon, and using Facebook, Twitter, Instagram, and other social media: "each has its marketing uses."

Asked about the future prospects of scholarly monograph publishing, he, like many others, pointed to the importance of how tenure and promotion committees favor university press books. "If the humanities have a future," he said, "then so does university publishing" (although, to be fair, Chicago also has substantial lists in the social and life sciences). "We are just collateral damage on the crisis in higher education generally," he remarked. At the same time, he acknowledged that Chicago, as the country's largest university press, is in a particularly favorable position. "We bring something to the reputation of the university, and we even bring something to the bottom line."

When I asked Blobaum what advice he would give to young scholars, his comments echoed Thomas's and Leventhal's. "Find out about scholarly publishing," he advised, adding, "it always amazes us how little first-time authors know." He emphasized the importance of knowing how books are put together, how they are marketed, what the book marketing ecology is like, and how reviewing spaces are configured. Asked how a young scholar can acquire this knowledge, he suggested turning to mentors and colleagues who are experienced in scholarly publishing as well as to books and online resources dedicated to these topics.

On the future of scholarly publishing, he emphasized that people *are* reading; to him, it is a minor matter whether they read a print book or an e-book. In a fascinating comment, he said, "You market a book; you distribute formats." Perhaps nowhere in my interviews does the mixed ecology of university presses come through so clearly. The print book *is* obviously a format, but his memorable aphorism identifies the work as a whole as a "book," using the term *book* as a synonym for the text independent of the output form. In this small gesture, one sees the enduring hold of print on how many, perhaps most, university presses think about their relationship with the works they publish.

Not surprisingly, Krista Coulson, digital-publishing manager for Chicago, had the keenest sense of how digital technologies are affecting work flow, design, and production. Her position at Chicago, created in 2011 when she was hired, consolidated functions that previously were split among several staff members. She remarked that in designing e-books, she aims for the "most common denominator" because different e-book readers use different platforms; even when a platform is shared, different brands support it differently, so that a function supported by one vendor may not be supported by another.[15] Moreover, certain design features found in print books are not used at all because e-books have a functionality that allows the reader to resize the font, so images with a caption, for example, would be partially obscured if the font were enlarged. Starting with monograph files coded for print, she described the e-book version as a "gentle mirroring" that does not necessarily push every design element all the way through. To make this generalization specific, I asked her about a design feature Chicago used in the print edition of my book *Unthought* that struck me as ingenious: in headings where a large font is used, certain capital letters thin as they progress down the page, as if they were on the verge of disappearing, an effect created by Chicago's designer Matt Avery that is exquisitely appropriate to the book's content. Coulson confirmed that this detail would likely not be carried over to the e-book version, which instead would revert to default fonts.

She pointed to an important difference between e-book coding and PDFs. Although PDFs preserve precisely the look of the print page, e-books use "reflow" design, wherein if the font is resized, the lines automatically fill in, a technique that results in lines breaking at different points for different font sizes. As a result, texts where line breaks carry significance, especially poetry, cannot easily be carried over to e-books because the reflow feature could destroy the author's intended line breaks and thus annihilate important clues to meaning.

Partly for this reason, Coulson agrees with Alan Thomas's view that e-books are not as suitable for scholarly writing as print books. She pointed out that scholarly apparatuses for print have evolved through centuries of experiment and codification, whereas e-books have a history as short as a couple of decades. She contrasted e-books delivered on an e-reader with websites, which have much more flexibility. "You can do anything with a

The Mixed Ecologies of University Presses

website," she remarked. At the same time, however, she does not recommend individual websites as modes of scholarly production because they can easily get lost in the vast landscape of cyberspace, whereas e-books have established ecologies and marketing practices that make them visible. When one searches for a given work on Amazon, for example, the e-book format will be listed as one of the available options. Coulson wistfully imagined a future for e-books in which the scholarly apparatus would be fully mature, so one might, for example, make annotations on one e-book text that would automatically be carried over to a copy on a different device simply by syncing the two texts together.

In summary, digital technologies have not yet been as transformative for university presses or as challenging to their business models as anticipated by either utopians or doomsayers. For university presses operating on the Chicago Model, most of the experimentation has been in mastering digital work flow, converting to e-book formats, creating metadata, and fulfilling orders for POD rather than experimenting with open access.[16] Even the staff at Chicago, however, recognizes that the model's long-term future may be in doubt, a prospect they find disturbing. Their commitment to quality so far continues to be a primary value, but market pressures are challenging that commitment. It may be that the Chicago Model will in future years be regarded as representing a golden era that has by then faded from view. If so, then the impetus to think constructively about more radical changes may be the best path forward.

Monograph as Mistake

I served a term on the Editorial Board at Duke University Press, and my contacts made the press's staff a natural for interviews. Steve Cohn, the press director 1993 to 2020, has a good sense of the press's history and context. He explained that when he arrived, the press was running a deficit and in danger of closing. To justify its continued existence, he wrote a comprehensive strategic plan that outlined the press's relation to the university, how it could achieve a more distinctive focus, and what its goals should be; it was, he said, a matter of "plan or die."[17] Because Duke styles itself an international university, Cohn argued that this should also be the press's identifying feature. Its focus should be on scholarly publishing (as distinct, for example, from a regional university press that might include cookbooks on its list). Moreover, its distinctive strength should be in "pushing fields forward and in particular helping fields develop that cut across the traditional disciplines." "We see ourselves as innovative," he said, "always looking for the next development," an ambition related to the press's five-year plans. "We take planning more seriously than any other press I know," he said, a legacy from the crisis in the 1990s.

As an example of planning's payoff, Cohn mentioned that the press is in the process of combining its journal and book divisions. He explained that the two had historically been separate because they had different access pathways: books were sold through bookstores, journals through subscriptions. But in the digital world these differences are going away; both books and journals are marketed in a variety of ways, including the press's own website, social media, Amazon, and so on. Moreover, books are now available as rental subscriptions, making them more like journals. When I remarked that such a change seemed overdue, Cohn replied, "That may be so, but almost no one else has come to that conclusion," indirectly confirming the inertial pull of tradition that characterizes most U.S. university presses.

Perhaps the interview's most startling moment came when Cohn remarked, "We don't publish monographs, and when we do, it's a failure." When I asked what he meant by "monograph," his answer was precise: "a book that only libraries and a few specialists would buy." He said that Duke looks for books that are "methodologically or theoretically interesting" and that "will

The Mixed Ecologies of University Presses

appeal across disciplines and regions," with potential for course adoption. This distinctive focus, he commented, makes it easier for scholars who write such books to think of Duke as a potential publisher. He contrasted this approach with presses that "publish a little of this, a little of that," which is the kind of press Duke used to be, he ruefully acknowledged, before it forged a recognizable identity in the 1990s.

When I asked what percentage of Duke's revenue comes from e-books, he estimated about 30 percent, which is "about as high as it gets in the university press world." He mentioned that Duke sells its e-books as collection for libraries. "We promise them at least one hundred e-books that are not available in any other collections," he said, explaining that "those who subscribe for the current year have access to all the back content, well over two thousand books." Duke has also taken the lead in opening up books no longer in demand on their backlist through the Hathi Trust at the University of Michigan. On its new website, the press lists these titles, telling users that all these books are available free. To pay expenses, it asks authors to help it find subventions. "When a little college comes up with $500, we celebrate," he said, "and if its Princeton, and it's an art book, we [might] get $25,000," and (of course!) the press celebrates that also. In addition, Duke recently asked its authors to consider donating royalties to a First Book Fund, a Translation Fund, or a fund for the World Reader series (for example, books that document how Peruvians think about Peru through songs, newspaper clippings, and other material).

Kenneth Wissoker, editorial director for books, has like Cohn been at Duke since the 1990s. Like others, he agrees that open peer review, although sometimes useful for an author, does not accomplish the same objectives as press-commissioned reviews, which he noted are more likely to catch large structural problems.[18] He also noted that open-forum contributions are less likely to be candidly critical because in general they are not anonymous. Speaking with more than two decades of university press experience, he has an interesting perspective on where scholarly books are moving in the future. He suggested that as writers experiment with different forms of writing, the market will turn toward books that are relevant not only to one's scholarship but also to the way one lives, instancing Aimee Meredith Cox's book *Shapeshifters: Black Girls and the Choreography of Citizenship*.[19] He sees the turn toward more public rhetoric and experimental forms such as creative nonfiction as cause for optimism, one of the major reasons why university press book publication will remain resilient despite the financial challenges that Duke, like virtually all university presses, faces.

Innovating Costs

The idea behind the Luminos initiative at the University of California Press is simple, although the details are complicated: shift part of the financial burden for publishing a scholarly monograph from the publisher to the author or her institution or both and make the text open access, giving it away free on the web. In a sense, this initiative kills two birds with one stone: increasing the potential audience for university press texts, especially in the global South, and reducing the financial risks to the publisher in doing so. The first objection to this practice that springs to mind is the burden it puts on scholars who are not associated with wealthy universities. To get a better sense of the initiative and the reasons inspiring it, I interviewed three academics on the Luminos board: Kathleen Fitzpatrick, currently director of digital humanities and professor of English at Michigan State University (when I interviewed her, she was also associate executive director and director of scholarly communication of the Modern Language Association); Christopher Kelty, a professor in the Graduate School of Education and Information Studies, with joint appointments in the Anthropology Department and the Institute for Society and Genetics at the University of

The Mixed Ecologies of University Presses

California, Los Angeles (UCLA); and Todd Presner, a professor in UCLA's German Department, with appointments in comparative literature and Jewish studies, and chair of the Center for Digital Humanities Program.[20]

As Kelty explained, the primary focus for Luminos is changing the economic model while maintaining intact the rigorous peer-review practices of university presses and their focus on scholarly excellence. Scholars who publish in Luminos are asked to contribute at least $7,500 to the cost of publishing, a contribution to be shared between the author and his or her institution, with additional amounts required if the work uses many images, exceeds the specified word length, has multimedia components, and so on. All the works available through Luminos's open-access platform may also be ordered as print books through POD, but profits from these sales go back to Luminos to offset the costs of future publications rather than to the author. Importantly, works accepted to Luminos go through the same peer review as a print book and must also be approved by the University of California Press's Editorial Board. Once a book has been accepted for publication, the author may choose to have it appear as a conventional print book rather than in Luminos. The main advantage of Luminos, from the author's point of view, is having the work available free to a global public, including scholars in South America, Southeast Asia, the Middle East, and other areas where people may not have money to buy the book. According to Fitzpatrick, preliminary statistics show considerable uptake in developing countries, especially India, Brazil, and Vietnam.

To this basic idea, many wrinkles have been added to offset the principal objection that the Luminos model shifts the problem of access from the consumer (how to pay for the book?) to the author (how to pay for the subvention?). The press hopes to build up a fund, the Author Waiver Fund, that will offset costs for those scholars or institutions that cannot afford them. Other ideas include partnering with libraries, who by paying a subscription fee will enable authors at that institution to pay a smaller amount for the subvention; the University of California Press website specifies that the library fee will provide $2,000 toward the subvention cost. As Fitzpatrick explained, this idea is aimed particularly at institutions that do not have a university press associated with it. Whereas universities with presses often provide financial support to the press, the authors who publish with that press but have appointments elsewhere can be seen as "free riders" benefitting from the university's support but not contributing to it as faculty.

Another idea, mentioned by Presner, is to broaden the basis for the subvention beyond the institution to specific centers within it. The Center for Jewish Studies at UCLA, for example, sets money aside to support two books per year in the broad area of Jewish history and culture and written by any faculty member anywhere in the world. Still other ideas echo strategies that other university presses are also employing, such as getting outside grants and building up endowments for the Luminos project.

It is too early to tell if the Luminos open-access texts will bring money back to the project through POD sales. (It should be noted that Luminos has so far accepted only works that can be printed out, although Kelty, Presner, and Fitzpatrick are pushing the Editorial Board to think about what will happen if works are submitted that cannot be printed because of their extensive use of digital affordances.) If we assume conservatively that POD books will not result in significantly increased income, then the economic issue may be stated in simpler form: Is $7,500 plus enough income for a university press to be able to publish a work for free? Let us assume, for the sake of comparison, that a conventionally printed university press book is priced at $45, and production costs are $20, leaving a profit margin of $25 per book. Then to generate $7,500 in income, the press would need to sell 300 copies or, if selling through bookstores or online retailers such as Amazon, about 600 copies (because Amazon typically takes about half of a book's price for its services). If we suppose that the book sells partly through Amazon and partly through the press's own site, then on average, as a rough estimate, 450 copies of a book would need to be sold for the press to break even. These figures are consistent with what I was hearing as a break-even point for scholarly monographs, so from this point of view the Luminos project looks like a win–win for the press and the author, especially if the author's institution picks up the cost and the author has the benefit of open access.

But there are many ways this scenario could go wrong. For example, the Mellon Foundation in April 2014 provided a grant to Ithaka S+R to estimate the actual cost of publishing a scholarly monograph. The panel of experts identified all expense components for a single monograph, including direct costs such as staff time and indirect costs such as overhead, and then asked twenty university presses to estimate what each of those components cost. The estimates ranged from a low of $15,140 to a high of $129,909 per monograph.[21] If we take a middle point of $35,000, then the Luminos project is not sustainable over the long run, for the press would need to absorb about $27,500 of the remaining cost after the subvention. These figures are for a print monograph, of course, but perhaps no more than 20 percent of this amount would be saved by digital production (that is, printing and distribution costs), still leaving a total around $22,000 to be absorbed per monograph published.[22] Moreover, by shifting to digital distribution and open access, the press is inviting competition on its subvention costs from publishers who will do it less expensively, initiating what Alan Thomas called "the race to the bottom." Finally, because of the open-access policy, the press would generate no income from sales other than what POD might yield. The hope expressed by Kelty and others that the Luminos model would enable the press to publish more scholarship does not solve this problem but exacerbates it, for the more open-access works the press publishes, the more losses it sustains. This is not to say that the Luminos initiative is doomed to failure, for much remains to be determined. There is a fair chance it can succeed, especially if the POD sales take off. Selling as few as

200 such books could change the picture from a deficit to a break-even or profit scenario.

Perhaps the most audacious part of the initiative is not its cost-sharing feature but its vision of how open access might expand the global marketplace of ideas, making the best of U.S. scholarship available throughout the world while preserving the commitment to excellence at the core of the university press mission. Fitzpatrick has already argued for this aspect of digital publication in her book *Planned Obsolescence: Publishing, Technology, and the Future of the Academy*, which advocates for, among other things, an open-composition process that invites peer review throughout the process, not only at the end.[23] She put this idea into action during her stint at the Modern Language Association, where she initiated and oversaw the MLA Commons, which facilitated just this kind of communal peer review. (I should note that Crewe at Columbia, Thomas at Chicago, and Wissoker at Duke were skeptical of communal peer review and felt it was not as objective or useful as assigned evaluations commissioned by the press.) Nevertheless, rethinking how peer review works might function as a point of intervention for tenure and promotion committees because it would spread the range of evaluations beyond a press's commissioned readers and editorial board to a broader scholarly community (as we have seen, such committees' preference for university press monographs is a major reason for their continued existence).

Moreover, one can argue that peer-reviewed open access not only fulfills a university press's core mission better than books for sale but also contributes powerfully to the research university's mission of creating, disseminating, and preserving knowledge. All three of my interviewees at the University of California Press—Fitzpatrick, Kelty, and Presner—have strongly supported open access in their research and service commitments. Kelty, for example, authored *Two Bits: The Cultural Significance of Free Software*, exploring how open access in the form of sharing source code has transformed humanities scholarship, science, music, and film, among other fields. He makes the case that freely sharing code results in what he calls a "recursive public," committed to maintaining, improving, and innovating the very knowledge that constituted it in the first place.[24] Fitzpatrick similarly argued in my interview with her that although achieving open access in humanities scholarship would not be easy, the "increased impact that openly distributed scholarship" would have makes it a highly desirable goal. Presner shares this view, as is evident in the open platforms he has developed for mapping projects, inviting collaborators from all over the world to contribute their local knowledge to the growing database of geolocative knowledge, as discussed in his coauthored book *HyperCities: Thick Mapping in the Digital Humanities*.[25]

All of the Luminos interviewees have thought about how digital technologies might affect university presses and scholarship in general; Presner's vision is especially compelling, perhaps because of his hands-on experience in developing large-scale digital projects. In addition to the HyperCities project, he is also the director of Mapping Jewish Los Angeles, another digital venture bringing together archives, neighborhood geographies, historical and contemporary narratives, local knowledge, and augmented-reality applications to collect and exhibit Jewish citizens' contributions to the Los Angeles area, thus making them available for further research.[26]

To illustrate the transformative effect of digital projects on scholarship, Presner instanced the work of UCLA classicist Christopher Johanson, who with colleagues developed models in the Unity game engine of the digital Roman Forum modeling project for time-based events such as speeches and funerals.[27] The Unity platform is well suited to combine spatial exploration with time-sequence events and in this sense provides a valuable addition to the virtual-reality model of the Roman Forum developed at the University of Virginia. In one version, the work combined funeral music with ritual chanting to enhance the effects. Presner commented to me that such installations allow the scholar to test "assumptions about spatiality, embodiment, and events. For example, it allows a scholar to test sightlines, sound cones, crowd sizes and crowd movement, and other features of embodied, built spaces, using a GIS [geographic information system] filled with modern and other data" from material and archaeological histories.

As Presner noted, the digital Roman Forum project functions not only as a product of scholarly effort but also as a tool to enable further discoveries. Immersed in the game environment and surrounded by relevant stimuli such as sound, motion, and sight, even a scholar knowledgeable about the forum might gain fresh insights. For students struggling to comprehend the past in all its complexity and dynamism, the experience could be altogether transformative. Because of the project's research aspect, Presner said that it is difficult for work like this to stand on its own as a fully explicit demonstration of scholarship; an article or book is often necessary to explain the various interpretive possibilities as well as the assumptions built into the model. Even though in these cases print and digital work together, it is important to note that the print addition explicates the digital project, which remains the central exploratory artifact.

This example as well as Presner's own work with Hyper-Cities and other digital projects illustrate how the ground shifts when digital technologies come to the fore as the primary vehicles for scholarly exploration. New criteria emerge as a result of the networked and programmable nature of these projects, including how much uptake they have with communities of scholars who build on them, how much their affordances are recombined, remixed, and modified by other scholars, how much utility they have in classrooms as teaching models, how much their databases are extended as others add to them, what kind of research results from exploring their complexities, and what kind of

The Mixed Ecologies of University Presses

modifications, extensions, and additions are made to the initial archives, to list only a few of the possibilities. Some of these criteria have analogues with print literature—for example, providing a foundation on which other scholars build—but this is literally true of digital projects as platforms are extended and modified, upgraded, and disseminated. I am reminded of John Unsworth's distinction between a cooperative community of scholars engaged in now-and-then exchanges often separated by intervals of weeks or months and a collaborative digital project where the interactions are direct, extensive, and continuous.[28] His argument also applies to the networked model compared to the print one: the difference is not simply quantitative but also qualitative.

Along with this transformational change go related changes in the metaphors used to describe the work. I remember when scholars were praised for their "crystalline prose" and books were seen as especially strong when they could remain relevant for a decade or longer. The underlying values expressed by such rhetoric were endurance without change, language so precise it could not be improved upon, replication through time. For digital projects, in contrast, another set of metaphors have emerged: contagion, extension, mutation; remixing, recombining, upgrading, disseminating; extensible, exportable, importable.

Accompanying these new metaphors is a changed vision of a scholarly career. Whereas book projects are seen as essentially complete when a publisher accepts the manuscript, one is never really done with a digital project, which continues to grow, mutate, and develop as new collaborators appear, operating systems become obsolete, applications change, new platforms and applications emerge. We might describe the former as a nodal model, in which scholarly effort and thought move from one book to another, with each book marking a point of completion and closure before moving to the next, and the latter as a flow model, in which the project rarely achieves closure and continues to modulate and change as the years go by. The two models are not necessarily mutually exclusive. Many scholars, including Presner, write books as well as create digital projects. Presner told me in an e-mail that in his view the two platforms "remediate" each other. "I've developed books from digital platforms and vice-versa, and physical exhibitions from digital ones and vice-versa. Each enhances and transforms the other."²⁹ Nevertheless, the two platforms also provide distinctly different kinds of rewards. Perhaps most importantly, they represent different models of scholarly achievement and hence require different criteria for evaluation.

Presner, Fitzpatrick, and Kelty agree that scholarly monographs should not be seen as the only valid or valuable mode of scholarly production. Fitzpatrick emphasized that there should be a "whole lot of ways" to convey the promise of a scholarly career other than a university press monograph, including "a series of articles published in good journals" or a "digital project like a scholarly edition" that has the richness and depth of a monograph. Presner noted that "obviously" the monograph "is not the only form that knowledge production can take," further arguing that when tenure and promotion committees consider digital projects, they should modify their criteria along the lines suggested by the metaphors given earlier. For example, committees might consider asking whether a scholar's work has been extended and modified by others, whether it has attracted collaborators to contribute to its database, and how extensively it has been used in classrooms. If a digital project is published outside of an academic press, additional modes of evaluation might be provided by successful grant applications, peer reviews by scholars knowledgeable about digital projects, awards from professional organizations for "best practices," and so forth. The effect, clearly, would be to challenge the privileging of a university press's imprimatur as a guarantor of scholarly excellence. In one sense, press directors such as Crewe and Kiely have already indicated they would welcome this change, but in another sense

The Mixed Ecologies of University Presses

the long-range effects might also be to undercut the university press's reason for existence.

A New Model: The Networked Book

My interview with Douglas Armato, director of the University of Minnesota Press, revealed another way forward for university presses. Minnesota received a grant from the Mellon Foundation to develop Manifold, a networked publishing platform that, as Armato put it, is "multimedia friendly."[30] Manifold has two sides: on the one side, as a project is developing, it provides a way to post drafts and invite comments, much as in Fitzpatrick's vision of open peer review; on the other side, it enables the importation of variety of materials in different formats into a scholarly work, including making the work interoperable with digital humanities projects. The first side is illustrated by John Hartigan's manuscript in progress *Social Theory for Nonhumans*. Two completed works serve as examples of how the Manifold platform can transform monograph scholarship: Grant Wythoff's edition and analysis of Hugo Gernsback's writings, editorial work, ideas, and inventions, *The Perversity of Things: Hugo Gernsback on Media, Tinkering, and Scientification*, and Stephanie Boluk and Patrick LeMieux's *Metagaming: Playing, Competing, Spectating, Cheating, Trading, Making and Breaking Videogames*.[31] The Gernsback Manifold project includes covers of magazines where Gernsback's original essays appeared, PDF excerpts from books he authored, as well as PDFs of many of the pulp science-fiction magazines that he edited. These resources enable readers to see Gernsback's work in context, a value-added feature too voluminous to include in the print book but valuable for any scholar seeking better to understand and evaluate Gernsback's contributions. The *Metagaming* Manifold resources include custom games designed by the authors, video games described in the book that readers may want to play, video advertisements for new video games, and videos of lectures by others relevant to the project—all multimedia and interactive material indigenous to the networked platform and so unable to be printed out.

Armato pointed out that Manifold is a "both/and" rather than an "either/or" proposition. Asked about the nodal versus flow model, he indicated that Manifold makes it possible to have both. For the Gernsback project and *Metagaming*, print books already are available,[32] and in these cases Manifold provides additional resources that in theory can grow without limit. For projects that are networked and ongoing, such as *Social Theory for Nonhumans*, authors still have the option of designating a "final-release" version that will provide closure. Moreover, the platform's flexibility makes it open for entirely new applications not originally envisioned. Armato mentioned an anthropologist who wants to use Manifold to provide annotations for open-access scientific articles. Another example is a digital scholar working with disability issues who plans to embed sound files in the work, which he says are necessary for his argument to make sense. Yet another instance is a project whose author wants to provide annotations for government documents. In cases like these, the marked-up digital text has two kinds of functionalities. A cube in the text indicates a media object, which when clicked displays on the left side of the Manifold screen display, and a caret when clicked opens comments or annotations, displayed on the right side.

Armato acknowledged that working in Manifold means more labor for both the author and the press. He estimates that having a project in Manifold adds perhaps 20 percent more labor for the press than for a conventional print book. As a consequence, the University of Minnesota Press is still in the process of discovering how many Manifold projects it can take on, estimating perhaps six to eight per year (out of ninety books published annually). A visit to the Stanford digital-publishing website, Publishing Digital Scholarship, indicates what is required from the author for a digital project: providing metadata, obtaining permission for all media objects, citing all tools used as well as sources, identifying tools or application programming interfaces embedded in the project, and acknowledging all the contributing parties to a project.[33] Manifold also offers the opportunity for readers to contribute comments, links, and annotations. "We are trying to get people to network the book for us," Armato explained, but this feature also adds work for the author because she needs to curate and organize the annotations as well as to provide interpretive and explanatory commentary for any video or other digital object readers may add.

The payoff for the extra work is to "make scholarship interoperable with other places where scholarship is happening," Armato commented, such as digital humanities projects. Comparing Manifold with e-readers such as Kindle that allow a reader to contribute annotations and see those of other readers, Armato pointed out that these annotations "remain in the Kindle universe." Manifold, by contrast, enables maximum distribution and dissemination by offering networking functionality across the web. Thus, a critical issue is the ability of any digital project to become a node in the Manifold network. For this reason, Armato said it is "really goofy to have a website along with the book. Let's put these together; that is what Manifold does." Manifold admittedly imposes some restrictions on authors regarding formats and work flow, so in this sense it is not as open-ended as one's own website, but such restrictions are the price, Armato pointed out, for interoperability.

Obviously, the more Manifold is used, the more useful it becomes. Minnesota is thus offering it for free to other publishers, and Armato said he has gotten "some pretty serious" inquiries from other university presses. A common platform capable of ingesting digital objects as well as texts, offering capabilities for readers to contribute to the project, and extending the book into an entire networked infrastructure while also allowing for the convenience and closure of a print book is indeed appealing. It is what Krista Coulson was dreaming of when she imagined a digital platform that would have the flexibility and interoperability of a website instead of being confined to the universe of an e-reader. It is easy to see why Armato is excited about the possibility. "It's more fun than I've had in a long time," he said. He also sees it as an appropriate project for Minnesota to take on. He pointed out that in the landscape of university presses Minnesota is known for breaking ground. It was the first press to publish simultaneously in paperback in the 1970s, and "we are always thinking we need to be in front." He is proud of the report on Mellon grants to university presses that identifies Minnesota's Manifold project as one of the two most adventuresome developments (the other is a project at Stanford University Press).

The Future Ecology for University Presses and Humanities Scholarship

If we compare the print book of the 1950s with a print book as it exists within Manifold, the full scope of the changes brought about by computational media becomes apparent. Among the important differences are accessibility, speed, interoperability, remixing, criteria for scholarly evaluation, and the role of cognitive media in scholarly production. Taken together, these factors are initiating profound transformations in how scholarly communities form and communicate, how scholarly contributions are evaluated, and how young scholars should proceed if they wish to establish themselves as important voices in ongoing scholarly discussions. University presses, operating with serious financial constraints and in historical traditions informed primarily by print, reflect both the inherent conservatism of the humanities as well as the possibilities for transformative projects that envision and create new kinds of ecologies for scholarly production. By exploring these factors, we can appreciate both how scholarship is changing and how inertial forces moderate the pace and scope of change.

ACCESSIBILITY

In 1950, print books circulated through warehouses, bookstores, lending libraries, and direct communication with publishers through mail and phone calls. Two or three weeks were required for a print book to make it through these channels, so owning one's individual copy paid dividends for scholars with limited time to create their own articles and books. Moreover, once a print run had sold out, the scholar either had to wait for a new print run or get the book through a library or interlibrary loan, adding more weeks to the waiting time. Citations came at a price, paid in time to receive the materials and/or labor to access its content through indexes, reviews, or the book or article itself.

In the new millennium, almost all new books are available instantly as e-books, and most older print books can be accessed through Google and other online venues. If a print copy is desired, the book can be purchased as POD and, with accelerated shipping, arrive within two days. Locating relevant references is as easy as typing the title and author's name into a search engine, and specific passages can easily be found as well. Research shows that the number of citations a work receives is influenced by its standing in Google search results, particularly if it makes the first screen. These factors influence how citations are accessed and deployed, how wide a net scholars cast when researching a specific topic, and what kinds of resources they locate. In addition to accelerating the speed of scholarly production, easy digital access has less salutary effects, such as favoring superficial skimming rather than careful close readings of entire books or articles. As the cost of obtaining information decreases, breadth tends to predominate over depth, horizontal lists of many citations over vertical analyses of specific instances, and contemporaneity over historical traditions. As scholarship moves more rapidly, fashions, instead of being measured in years or decades, now emerge and disappear in weeks or months.

SPEED

Speed is intimately tied up with accessibility. Whereas it would often take a year or more after publication for reviews of print books to appear, in the current ecology blog entries may show up as soon as the text is available online, and if the book is networked to allow peer review and commentary, reviews may be available to the author and online community while the text is still being written. Instead of taking weeks to communicate with an author by U.S. mail, readers can now send e-mails the day the book is available, contribute comments, ratings, and brief reviews to such online sites as Goodreads and Amazon, and immediately incorporate published results into their own research. Citations and quotations, rather than being typed out by hand, can be incorporated as digital files, along with links to YouTube, Vimeo, or other video sites. What it means to be part of a scholarly community has changed, broadening beyond academics to the interested public and changing the diction from scholarly decorum (including complex ironies and subtle insults) to hip language, inflammatory rhetoric, emoticons, acronyms, and other digital rhetorical forms.

INTERCONNECTIONS AND INTEROPERABILITY

Platforms such as Manifold can ingest text and graphic files in seconds, video and sound clips in minutes. Before Google Earth discontinued some of its mapping functionalities, digital projects such as HyperCities could incorporate data, including geographical, narrative, and historical material, from local projects around the globe into their databases and display the results in a series of coordinated displays. Projects developed in the Unity game engine, such as the Roman Forum project by Johanson, are compatible with other projects in the same software. Data-visualization projects in environments such as the data-analysis environment R are interoperable with others developed in the same software. All this contrasts strongly with print books as individual objects, which are limited to cross-referencing through scholarly apparatus. The networked book not only will be capable of connecting to media objects across a wide spectrum of materials but will also interconnect with other networked books in the platform, leading to new possibilities for scholarly inquiry and exploration—a prospect already on the horizon in the projects under development in Manifold.

CURATION AND REMIXING

As the amount of material grows exponentially and search functions increase our ability to find it, curation, remixing, and recombination become more potent as scholarly activities. As Mark Amerika argues in *remixthebook*, the mashup, the remix, and the recombinant may be the defining cultural forms of our era.[34] His print book comes with an associated website, which includes the work of musicians, artists, graphic designers, and others that exemplifies the theories and possibilities of remixing as a dominant cultural form. Suggestions made by Kathleen Fitzpatrick, Garrett Kiely, and Todd Presner extend this idea to scholarship, pointing out to young scholars the potency of these strategies for their own work.

CRITERIA FOR SCHOLARLY EVALUATION

A thread running through my interviews is the assumption by tenure and promotion committees that a book published by a well-regarded university press guarantees scholarly excellence, which seems to leave the tenure decision in their hands. As noted, university press directors are uneasy with this assumption and emphasize that tenure decisions must include other factors. Presner, Fitzpatrick, and Kelty agree that scholarly production cannot be limited only to the book or article but must be extended to include a variety of scholarly productions, such as websites, virtual-reality installations, data-visualization projects, and other digital or hybrid productions.

The shrinking market for scholarly monographs is the flip side of another issue: audience size and uptake. Although publications such as the *Citation Index* are increasingly taken into account in tenure deliberations, they refer only to printed materials, leaving out of their accounts the influence of websites and digital projects. As Presner suggested, for the latter types of projects other criteria should be considered, including whether the data have been used by others, how many other projects link to a given project, how much material on a site has been remixed and recombined with material on other sites, and how many other sites are connected with a given site so as to be interoperable with it. The humanities in general have been protective of publications that reach only a few hundred or even a few dozen readers, and there are good reasons not to equate quality simply with numbers of readers (otherwise, President Donald Trump's tweets would be rated as literary masterpieces). But influence should rightly be included in estimating the importance of scholarly projects as one factor among many, including hits on a website.

As younger scholars begin experimenting with more public venues and modes of address, the conservative bias toward print materials will increasingly come under pressure to take into account the importance to the humanities of reaching a broader audience through well-researched blogs, podcasts, YouTube videos, and other digital platforms. We know that the humanities suffered in general esteem because of the specialized jargon of movements such as deconstruction. Attempts to reach out to the general educated audience have the potential to reverse this trend, with long-reaching effects not only for the individual scholar and her institution but also for the humanities as a whole. I agree with those at the university presses—Thomas, Leventhal, and others—who believe this trend is a positive development and who want to see it become more pervasive. To do so, it must receive recognition within the academy as worthwhile and important in the contexts that matter most—tenure and promotion.

COGNITIVE TECHNOLOGIES AS COAUTHORS AND COLLABORATORS

As software becomes more intelligent and aware, its cognitive capacities advance from functionalities such as making spelling corrections and autocompletions to detecting trends in large corpora, organizing ideas into an outline, and drawing linguistic inferences from text "in the wild" through natural-language learning and language-processing programs (for example, Tom Mitchell's Never Ending Language Learning, or NELL). In addition, neural networks have mastered not only chess but the "intuitive" game of Go (through DeepMind's neural-networking programs AlphaGo and AlphaGoZero).[35] Text-generation programs are already used for artistic purposes (especially poetry) and for formulaic writing such as stock and sports reporting. Software is thus increasingly not just formatting human-produced text (a functionality, as Dennis Tenen argues, that has unrecognized importance[36]) but also creating, reading, and analyzing text. In short, it is moving from the position of scribe to the position of collaborator and coauthor.[37] The Stanford University Press website's explication of the information that digital projects must include comes close to recognizing this movement when it indicates that information on platforms be made explicit; in another section, the site emphasizes that *all* collaborators must be acknowledged. It is a small step to combining these two imperatives and requiring that projects recognize the software as collaborator.

NETWORKED BOOK AS COGNITIVE ASSEMBLAGE

In contrast to the print book of the 1950s, the networked book of the new millennium is not just a cognitive support but a cognizer in its own right. As argued in chapter 1, most of the world's work is now done through cognitive assemblages, networks of human and technical systems through which information, interpretations, and meanings circulate. The software platforms of networked books are examples of cognitive assemblages, correlating information, performing search functions, interpreting data from texts both inside and outside the book, formatting and controlling work flow, and linking to texts and digital objects in the database. Because cognition is distributed between authors, readers, texts, and software programs, agency is also distributed, a constraint that Armato alluded to when he acknowledges that Manifold requires authors to follow certain work-flow procedures. All of the issues articulated earlier—speed, accessibility, interoperability, remixing, software as collaborator, and criteria for scholarship—crucially depend on envisioning postprint book productions as cognitive assemblages, so it may be regarded as the umbrella term under which everything else fits.

Lessons from and for University Presses

The generally conservative bias of university presses is in a sense appropriate, reflecting the reservations that many humanists feel toward the shift from print to postprint. Assertions in this chapter that now seem controversial or even outright wrong may in another generation come to appear as mere common sense. (Of course, some of them may be wrong as well. As Yogi Berra says,

The Mixed Ecologies of University Presses

"It's tough to make predictions, especially about the future.") Nevertheless, given what we know about the exponential development of digital technologies and their ever-deepening penetration into the infrastructure of global communication, it seems clear that the mixed ecologies in which university presses operate at the moment are more a matter of the inertia of tradition than they are harbingers of the future. In my view, scholarly monographs sold as individual copies will constitute a smaller share of overall scholarly production, and presses will come to see their reputations not as tied primarily to this form but as expanding outward into the other kinds of services and facilitations, including but not limited to platforms, websites, blogs, videos, and other networked possibilities. Of one thing I am certain: their mission to bring the best scholarship to as wide an audience as possible may take new forms, but it cannot and should not be abandoned, for it is crucial to the future of universities and, indeed, to our culture as a whole.

4

Postprint and Cognitive Contagion

In chapters 2 and 3, we saw that computational media have interpenetrated every aspect of book production, transforming typesetting, editing, printing, warehousing, distribution, and sales. We explored how university presses are coping with the transition to digital production and touched on the hold that the printed book as a transcendental object still has on a press's work. We ventured into the near future—the kinds of differences digital media might make in how scholars think about their research and careers as well as new possibilities for open-access and open-publishing platforms. In this chapter, we turn to the effects of postprint on a larger cultural imaginary, expressed as pervasive anxieties about the relation of digitally produced and mediated language to human thought and being. If symbolic expression is entwined with the essence of what it means to be human, as Terence Deacon and others have argued, then fundamental changes in how language is transmitted, learned, and used may have wider implications for the meaning of being human.[1]

Two postprint novels provide the focus, *The Silent History* by Eli Horowitz, Matthew Derby, and Kevin Moffit and *The Word Exchange* by Alena Graedon. In both novels, language rendered digitally catalyzes transformations that radically alter the relation of humans to spoken and written discourses. They imagine traffic across biological and technical boundaries so that the operation of digital devices becomes inextricably entwined with the processing capability of human brains. In *The Silent History*, the (in)ability to use verbal language is the lever prying apart two different factions: those who regard the loss of language as a terrible tragedy and those who welcome it as an opening onto new abilities and new ways for humans to live in the world. By contrast, in *The Word Exchange* the combined digital and biological threats to language are presented as unmitigated evils. One of this novel's contributions is its exploration of the role that semiocapitalism plays in the corruption and potential loss of human language, a topic about which *The Silent History* is, well, silent. In details as well as in larger narrative arcs, the two novels reveal the anxieties of a print culture—indeed, a print world—that seems both enabled and threatened by the digital.

The New Illiteracy

Contemporary research into the effects of digital reading and writing on brain function indicate that even a moderate amount of web reading causes significant changes in synaptic networks as brain plasticity responds to environmental conditions.[2] The younger the cohort, the more extensive the changes, so many experts now recommend that very young children either be limited in their screen time or prevented from using screens altogether. My own observations indicate that college teachers across the nation are experiencing a cognitive shift from deep to hyper attention.[3] Several critics, notably Nicholas Carr and Bernard Stiegler, have raised the alarm about the inability of young people—and of older folks too—to engage in sustained attention to complex written texts; others have written about the new "attention economy" emerging as corporations struggle to attract eyeballs to their sites.[4] These texts, along with similar ones, are powerful stimuli generating anxiety about how our contemporary relations with digital media may be affecting us neurologically in addition to culturally, socially, and economically.

One aspect of these entangled influences is highlighted by Dennis Tenen, who points out that digital texts instantiate coding protocols that create what he calls "a new kind of illiteracy, which divided those who could read and write at the site of storage from those who could only observe its aftereffects passively, at the shimmering surface of archival projection."[5] All screenic inscriptions are underwritten by multiple layers of code, creating what Tenen calls "laminate text," an allusion to laminated products such as plywood consisting of multiple layers fused together. Like laminate plywood, laminate text can fuse the layers when printed out in hard copy, but the code can also expand again into multidimensional networks of international reach when instantiated in connected and programmable machines. As Tenen notes, few people have the expertise to understand these deeper code levels. Moreover, for propriety software such as Adobe, there are legal prohibitions on even accessing the code, much less intervening in it. **As a result, Tenen writes, "we find ourselves in a position of selective asemiosis"—that is, a lack of semiosis or a deficiency in our ability to read signs.** We are unable to parse the executable scripts that generate the inscriptions we see on the screen. One might argue that because we can still read the surface, these coding levels do not matter in our understanding of texts, but Tenen argues persuasively that "these technical details affect all higher-level interpretive activity."[6] They determine, for example, how font is sized and placed on the screen, how users can (or cannot) interact with the text, and in some instances even how the content is determined. As indicated in chapter 2, some e-books use their GPS capability to locate the user geographically and to interject place-names, product placements, and other texts based on this knowledge. Tenen's response to these cultural conditions is to urge us to adopt "plain text," observe its aftereffects passively, at the shimmering surface of archival projection." All screenic inscriptions are underwritten by multiple layers of code, creating what Tenen calls "laminate text," an allusion to laminated products such as plywood consisting of multiple layers fused together. Like plywood, laminate text can fuse the layers when printed out in hard copy, but the code can also expand again into multidimensional networks of international reach when instantiated in connected and programmable machines. As Tenen notes, few have the expertise to understand these deeper code levels. Moreover, in propriety software such as Adobe, there are legal prohibitions on even accessing the code, much less intervening in it. **As a result, Tenen writes, "We find ourselves in a position of selective asemiosis," that is, a lack of semiosis or a deficiency in our ability to read signs.** We are unable to parse the executable scripts that generate the inscriptions we see on the screen. One might argue that since we can still read the surface, these coding levels do not matter in our understanding of texts, but Tenen argues persuasively that "these technical details affect all higher-level interpretive activity." They determine how font is sized and placed on the screen, for example, how users can (or cannot) interact with the text, and in some instances, even how the content is determined. As indicated in Chapter 2, some ebooks use their GPS capability to locate the user geographically and interject place names, product placements, and other texts based on this knowledge. Tenen's response to these cultural conditions is to urge us to adopt "plain

observe its aftereffects passively, at the shimmering surface of archival projection."[v] All screenic inscriptions are underwritten by multiple layers of code, creating what Tenen calls "laminate text,"[vi] an allusion to laminated products such as plywood consisting of multiple layers fused together. Like plywood, laminate text can fuse the layers when printed out in hard copy, but the code can also expand again into multidimensional networks of international reach when instantiated in connected and programmable machines. As Tenen notes, few have the expertise to understand these deeper code levels. Moreover, in propriety software such as Adobe, there are legal prohibitions on even accessing the code, much less intervening in it. **As a result, Tenen writes, "We find ourselves in a position of selective asemiosis,"[vii] that is, a lack of semiosis or a deficiency in our ability to read signs.** We are unable to parse the executable scripts that generate the inscriptions we see on the screen. One might argue that since we can still read the surface, these coding levels do not matter in our understanding of texts, but Tenen argues persuasively that "these technical details affect all higher-level interpretive activity."[viii] They determine how font is sized and placed on the screen, for example, how users can (or cannot) interact with the text, and in some instances, even how the content is determined. As indicated in Chapter 2, some ebooks use their GPS capability to locate the user geographically and interject place names, product placements, and other texts based on this knowledge. Tenen's

Here is the bolded sentence in plain text (top) and pdf (bottom). The file size for plain text is 163 bytes, and for pdf, 18,816 bytes, more than 100 times the size. In addition, the code for the pdf version is proprietary and cannot be accessed by the author without special software editors.

Postprint and Cognitive Contagion

text created with programs such as TextEdit that use a minimum of coding to display and process the text, all levels of which are open access and easily examined by the user.

Admirable as this stance is, it forecloses the opportunity to explore more deeply the implications of selective asemiosis. It suggests that the solution to progressive industrialization (or asemiosis in our case) is to adopt a simpler way of life, reminiscent of Henry David Thoreau's retreat to Walden, which is positioned as the *antidote* to corrupt practices, including corrupt language. Note, however, that this seclusion presumes one retains full linguistic and semiotic capacities, an assumption Thoreau enacted through his journals by presenting his writing as inspired and enhanced by his natural surroundings. But what if language capabilities are damaged and cannot be cured by communing with nature? Moreover, what if the human capacity for language, far from aligning synergistically with nature, is precisely what *estranges* us from the natural world, filtering our perceptions through linguistic categories that always already determine what we can perceive and experience?[7]

This is the uneasy and intensely ambivalent terrain opened up by *The Silent History*, a work that articulates the anxiety associated with our selective asemiosis by literalizing it into a biological condition. The title inscribes the text's central oxymoron: a generation of children is born without the ability to understand or use language, a condition that causes them to be labeled "the silents." By definition, they cannot write their own histories, so the novel's episodic texts are presented as digitalized transcriptions of oral testimonies given by those who have relationships with the silent generation. From the beginning, then, readers are aware of the text's digitally mediated status, a realization deepened by the novel's first instantiation as an iPhone app, with 120 episodes, each downloadable every weekday from October 1, 2012, to April 19, 2013. Only after the installments were complete did the text appear as a print book. The print version flattens the laminate text of the digital original into the traditional form of the codex, but as we will see, the mark of the digital is everywhere apparent, proclaiming the book as a postprint production in multiple senses.

Mark of the Digital

In its digital instantiation, *The Silent History* consisted of Testimonials, the episodes that became the print stories, and Field Reports, short crowd-sourced narratives tied to specific locations. The Field Reports could be accessed only when a reader was at the relevant site, as indicated by her iPhone's GPS. As this division between authorial and crowd-sourced narratives suggests, the major parameters along which the digital work progressed were temporal and geographic, signaled within the authorial narratives by the date and location indicators that precede each Testimonial and within the locative Field Reports by constraints of access.

The temporal aspect was further developed by the psychological and social evolution of the characters and their world. The narrative's thirty-year span, from 2011 to 2041 (with the epilogue extending to 2043 and the prologue to 2044), is presented in six volumes that chart the beginning of the silent epidemic through its eventual conclusion, visually represented in the app as six segmented circles that functioned as portals through which the narratives of individual speakers could be accessed. Moreover, once a narrative by a given speaker came on screen, a button allowed the reader to see all the narratives by that character, a display mode emphasizing the diachronic progression of a character's development while simultaneously making it more difficult to grasp the synchronic rhythms of the different characters' interactions with each other.

The app's geographic dimension, for its part, was reinforced by the meshlike quality of the narrative progressions—the paratactic juxtapositions of different speakers that created openings into which the Field Report contributions could be inserted to give a local habitation and name to the narrative action. Amy Hungerford, who interviewed Eli Horowitz, recounts that he prepared elaborate instructions for users who wanted to contribute Field Reports, his suggestions running to six pages.[8] This indicates how strongly he considered the Field Reports an important part of the work, highlighting the central role he wanted them to play in establishing the work's geographical rootedness. His idea was that the Field Reports would help to offset the parataxis of the Testimonials; they could be disconnected because the connective tissue necessary for coherence was supplied by rooting the action in terrains that users would navigate by themselves, experiencing the landscape firsthand and seeing landmarks connected to the narrative action by the Field Reports. However, there was a price for the resulting abrupt juxtapositions, paid in the coin of character interactions. The effect, particularly at the beginning, was narrative cacophony: each small narrative, comprehensible in itself, was preceded and followed by jump cuts to different speakers that made it difficult to understand the interrelations between them and challenging to reconstruct anything like coherent narrative progressions. The app's design and function were thus crucial not only to how the digital work presented its material but also to the meanings it enabled and those it suppressed.

Moreover, the app's digitality was further emphasized by recursive mirroring. As coauthor Matthew Derby explained in an interview in 2016, the app itself is incorporated into the diegesis of the authorial narratives.[9] The prologue (called "The Condition" in the digital version) is narrated by a government archivist commissioned to create a historical record in the fashion of the report on September 11, 2001. He mentions the "Meme," an "ambient dictation application that allows key subjects to record their testimonials anywhere in the world."[10] The narrative texts are presented as the digitized results of these oral dictations, a fiction that mimetically reflects the delivery of digitized text to users' iPhones, devices designed (like the fictionalized Meme) to transform analog speech into bitstreams. That the narratives originated as speech, not writing, becomes important later as the characters' language abilities erode, and even talking coherently becomes a challenge for them, never mind matching speech sounds to written marks.

The episodes, usually only a few screens long, were deliberately kept short so they could be read while waiting for the subway or bus. Derby commented, "Everything we did had to support the behavior patterns of a reader who was mobile, connected, and expectant of a fluid, intuitive experience."[11] Given that the silent epidemic expresses cultural anxieties about the spread of digitally mediated asemiosis, the very form this expression takes—brief narratives displayed on a digitally generated screen—participates in catalyzing the synaptic reconfigurations that are moving the population into hyperattention and away from the deep attention necessary, for example, to read long print novels. The digital work thus furthers the "Condition" causing the anxiety in the first place, an ironic circularity rendered visually in the six segmented circles of the narrative portals.

If one were to imagine how a population might be forcefully severed from its participation in contemporary cognitive assemblages, the ability to use symbolic language would be a logical capacity to target. The silents communicate with each other, it is discovered, by using microfacial gestures; they can communicate with their parents through body language, touching, and other embodied actions. But without the capacity to use symbolic language, their communications with digital media are severed at the root. Unlike today's generation of young people, they would be incapable of being mesmerized by cell phones.

Cleaved from cognitive assemblages by their condition, the silents are later readmitted to the realm of verbal communication through the mediation of computational media. A brain implant is developed that partially restores their verbal capabilities, reconfiguring their neural networks so they can speak and understand words, but at the price of having their thoughts irreversibly joined with the streaming bits that have literally penetrated their brains. Their participation in cognitive assemblages is depicted as being as coercive as it is involuntary (most silents are implanted as infants and have no say in the matter). As a consequence, the implanted can have no illusions about being autonomous subjects independent from the implants that have become their indispensable symbionts.

The implant functions within the work to create a paradoxical similarity between the silents and the novel app users. As Hungerford astutely observes in a passage quoted briefly in chapter 1, "Walking silently around the site of a field report, looking where your device bids you, noticing what it tells you to notice, you find yourself manipulated by a central processor that pipes language into your brain . . . attaching the novel to the devices that render us silent even as we communicate furiously through them makes us into the very figure of the wandering silent."[12] In this sense, the cultural anxiety revealed in *The Silent History* about the selective asemiosis to which digital media have subjected us is conveyed in part through our embodied participation in the digital work. It is because we actively join the cognitive assemblages created by *The Silent History* that we feel the anxieties undergirding the work not only through our ears, eyes, and brains but also throughout our bodies as we trace the geography of the digitally augmented terrain of the Field Reports and associated narratives.

The Silent History as Postprint Production

Hungerford documents that Eli Horowitz was the mastermind behind the work, recruiting colleagues Matthew Derby and Kevin Moffit to do much of the actual writing and persuading tech guru Russell Quinn to create the app (significantly, Quinn's name is omitted from the list of the print book's authors). As noted in chapter 1, the collaborative nature of the project recalls J. J. Abrams and Doug Dorst's *Ship of Theseus*, where a celebrity media person enlists what Hungerford calls "subsistence" writers (writers who cannot earn a living through writing alone) to implement their ideas. These projects suggest that one of the effects of postprint's digitization is to facilitate cross-media projects that involve teams of people with significantly different skill sets, perhaps resembling in this respect small independent films more than they do a print book written by a single author and printed by a book-only publisher.

Nevertheless, the team had to coordinate closely to bring the project to fruition. According to Derby, when they were conceptualizing the project, they focused entirely on its digital instantiation, with no thought that it would become a print book.[13] Only when the app version exploded in popularity did the idea of a codex version surface. Hungerford recounts that Horowitz had some reservations about the print version because he did not want it to eclipse the app instantiation.[14] Nevertheless, the print project not only moved forward but also entailed significant revisions; it was far from being simply a matter of porting the material from one format to another. The essential structure was already determined by the episodic narration, so it could scarcely be changed without rewriting the entire work. But much fine-tuning could be and was done.

As Derby explained, "The pacing of the thing just didn't work when it was printed out on paper. So we did a lot of editing, merging, and excising to make the print version flow. It was a really interesting process, actually."[15] By my count, these changes reduced the number of episodes from 120 in the app version to 97 in the codex (including the prologue and epilogue), with a resulting damping down of the cacophonic effect. In addition, synchronic connections between episodes were strengthened, an effect particularly noticeable as the narratives arc toward the denouement, where there is a point-by-point convergence between narrators as they relate the same events from their respective viewpoints. The relation between the two versions should not be mischaracterized as print versus digital, however. Rather, both manifest deep connections to computational media, although they do so in different ways; both are postprint productions whose material existences are completely entwined with digital media.

As indicated earlier, the narratives in the codex were revised to make them less disjunctive and more novel-like. Referring to the codex version, I have traced this change through the distribution of characters throughout the episodes. The peripheral characters who appear only once are most numerous in the early Testimonials, whereas the major characters predominate at the end, a distribution that means the narrative cacophony is greatest at the beginning, with the interconnections between characters swelling toward the end. The major characters are depicted as a core group clustered around the silent center: Flora, a beautiful and charismatic silent who marries the silent Spencer, neglected as a child by his mother and semiotically marked by the terrible scars running down his arms, the result of smashing his arm through a window when his mother left him alone, and Slash, their son, a "double silent" born of silent parents who has never been subjected to the attempts to make him speak that haunted Flora's childhood. We understand these silent characters, of course, only through the major characters' narratives. Unable to enter the narrative directly and speak their own stories, the silents nevertheless function as the ineffable absence around which the verbal articulations swirl.

The central tension emerges between, on the one hand, this silent family and associated core group and, on the other, August Burnham, a scientist determined to overcome the silents' dysfunctionality (as he sees it), and his student Calvin Andersen, a silent whose parents take him as a child to Burnham and who thereafter becomes the doctor's primary object of experimentation or, as he later calls himself with retrospective bitterness, "Lead Guinea Pig." The tension has ideological as well as practical implications. Burnham is convinced that the "urge to speak is deeply human. It's woven into our DNA, into the structures of our brains. In very real sense, thought requires language," a position that quickly leads to the conclusion that the silents are less than human or in any case severely disabled. "It was just so clear that they were chronically unprepared to take on the challenges of the world," Burnham remarks.[16]

On the other side are the many comments from the core group and others speculating that the absence of language may be a blessing rather than a curse. Patti Kern, a New Age seeker more than a little kooky, tells a fellow traveler, "We have so much to learn from these people. You have to understand, words are just conduits. We invented them because we needed something to hook at the truth—but words have become an obstacle, a smoke screen." Her advice about the silent children: "Listen to all they're not saying." The theme is introduced in the prologue, when the administrator witnesses a mass escape of the silent children from SWAT-like pursuers who imagine they have the children trapped in an abandoned warehouse. When the pursuers close in, however, to the administrator's astonishment they find the place empty. "Somehow a group of fifty silents had managed to spontaneously coordinate an escape without being detected," a phenomenon that leads him to revise his opinion: "I had defined silents by what they lacked. I thought of them as hollow vessels, defective parasites feeding upon the speaking world. But in that lobby I saw them for what they might *possess* . . . Was the world somehow brighter, more tangible, without the nagging interference of language? Was the absence of words actually a form of freedom?"[17]

Throughout volume 1, the core group flirts with this idea, especially Francine Chang, the haphazard teacher so unenamored of her students that she arranges her classroom with the students facing forward and her desk in the rear. The exceptions are the silents, with whom she feels a growing sympathy. After she abruptly quits her normal teaching job in midterm, we are not surprised that she agrees to become a teacher at the first school for silents only, the Oaks. Here Francine makes the crucial discovery that the silents are in fact communicating with one another through microfacial gestures called "face-talking" in popular slang. Kourosh Aalis, a one-off who bizarrely hides in the ventilation shafts of the Oaks so he can photograph face-talking, calls it "a form of nonlinguistic communication with a depth and breadth that continues to surprise us."[18]

Theodore Greene, Flora's father, has a more ambivalent relation with face-talking.[19] After his beloved wife, Mel, died giving birth to Flora, he devoted years trying to teach her to talk. When face-talking is discovered, he and other parents of children at the Oaks go to sessions to try to learn to face-talk; he is coincidentally paired with Francine and finds himself attracted to her, an emotion that makes him profoundly uneasy. "She was kind of very attractive in an almost hostile way, like a wounded animal . . . but I didn't want the attraction I felt to transform into an obsession or anything, because I wasn't . . . I still felt the presence of Mel, even after eleven years." Conflicted about this (and so much else), Theodore writes that he "started avoiding the school altogether as much as I could, which was, I guess, just as well."[20]

Far less ambivalent is David Dietrich, the perpetual outsider and neglected child who, although he can speak, is attracted to the silents and wants to be as close to them as he can manage, if possible even to become one. "I trained myself to forget what word went with each thing. I wanted to unword it all." Unable to achieve this, he pretends to be a silent when transferred to a new school. Only after several months does his mother, in a parent-teacher conference, inadvertently reveal the truth. His teacher, chagrined that his ruse worked, makes him "stand in front of the class and confess." "There'd be no diagnosis for me," he mourns. "After I confessed, I went back to being nothing at all."[21]

The Soul Amp: Digitally Produced and Mediated Language

Burnham, equipped with a secondhand Hockman helmet capable of recording brainwaves and other equipment, begins probing the silents' brain patterns to determine the "dysfunctionality's" cause. He finds that the brain areas responsible for language acquisition and use have been selectively targeted by a virus contracted in the womb—hence, the silent children, unable to parse language from birth on. He begins cooperating with Prashant Nuregesan, a minor character driven to invent quirky devices to fill needs that he (and sometimes only he) perceives; together, the two concoct a digital implant device that supplies the functionality missing in the silents' brains. Burnham dubs it the "Soul Amp," with the obvious connotation that it enables the silents to become more human, more "soulful." Initially self-contained, the device was relatively bulky, but later it is miniaturized into an implant when its computational capabilities are transferred to PhonCom, a digital network that uses a server farm to connect with implants worldwide.

The language abilities bestowed by the implants are far from perfect. Many implantees find that they can speak but, like Joe Biden, not always as they intended. Indeed, all the expressions they can use are drawn from a database; Burnham proudly proclaims that "the pool is colossal—last time I checked we had over thirty-four billion unique phrases available." Despite his pride, even this number pales in comparison with the actual number of possible combinations in alphabetic languages. Moreover, some implantees have a difficult time adapting and find themselves saying phrases wildly off the mark. Persephone Goldia, a minor character, is used to illustrate the problem. Talking about her recent implant, she remarks that "some begin to talk instantaneously after the anesthesia wears off and some require an elongated unlocking period, and I must have been one of the primary threats to the osprey's nesting habits."²²

More disturbing than these limitations is the implants' surveillance potential. Because the verbal traffic is carried over a digital network, Burnham and his lackeys can listen in whenever they choose and intervene, forcing some phrases to be uttered and blocking others. Calvin is coerced into doing this when Burnham identifies in a female implantee what he perceives as a problem and instructs Calvin to force her to speak: "Looks like the issue here is an inability to verbally express sexual desire. So please do whatever you can to provoke that in her." Calvin's response is intense aversion: "I loathed this practice—I had to use the calibration helmet to massage a stranger's neural pathways in the hope of eliciting some kind of verbal response." Initially grateful for his own implant, Calvin experiences its coercion when out of frustration and anger he starts calling his mentor "Dr. Burned Ham." After saying this a few times, he discovers the next morning that he is unable to utter the phrase and surmises that Burnham has put a block on it. "Everything he did from that point on, every word he uttered, made me want to crush him to a pulp." His perspective and Burnham's now diverge completely, although Burnham remains oblivious to Calvin's true feelings. Calvin's reassessment extends to his implant. He realizes that "becoming his living experiment has in no way made me a happier person. My soul is not singing. So I can banter with chattering fools—so what? Before the implant . . . I was alone in my own head, and it was a sacred place I couldn't even begin to describe to you. There are no words for it, because it was a place outside of words. It was pure color."²³

In crafting these scenes, the authors set up an obvious allusion to the surveillance potential of the web and the many abuses, by institutions and companies ranging from the U.S. National Security Agency to Facebook, to which that potential has led. They also invite comparisons with more subtle ways in which digital mediation compromises our ability to use and understand language. The web is notorious for seeding memes that spread throughout its globally distributed sites—for example, in the thousands of Facebook accounts designed to spread Russian propaganda and Trump's repeated proclamation of "fake news" to describe the investigative journalism exposing his lies and corruption scandals. In this respect, the authors of *The Silent History* presciently understood that digitally mediated language, although often greeted as a powerful liberatory force in countries such as Iran, where it serves as a mouthpiece for oppressed groups, can also lead to the kind of scenarios George Orwell foresaw in *1984* when he invented "Newspeak." That this message was originally delivered over networked digital devices themselves subject to surveillance makes the warning all the more potent for readers—if they care to connect the dots or, in this case, to understand the connections between the episodic narratives and the iPhones used to access them. With the print codex, the connections become more subtle, but the fact remains that the text began as a digital file, both in its original app version and in the revised codex. As indicated earlier, the book participates in the postprint condition in multiple senses. Appearing belatedly after the iPhone downloads were completed, it necessarily incorporated many features of the digital version; moreover, as a contemporary book, it is interpenetrated by digital technologies in virtually every phase of its existence.

Crashing PhonCom

With the development of the implant, cultural attitudes begin to change toward the silents, becoming less sympathetic to their condition and regarding those who do not want to be implanted as akin to religious outliers who do not want their children vaccinated. Legislation is predictably soon passed to make the implants compulsory. This legal action ratchets up the pressure on the core group, which eventually retreats to an abandoned missile silo in the Midwest. Providing for the group is David Dietrich, who stalks stray dogs and kills them for the meat. David and everyone else know that this lifestyle is not sustainable; as Francine eloquently puts it, "We couldn't go, we couldn't stay. We were all perched on the crumbling tip of the present."[24]

David upends the game board by suddenly leaving without telling the group where he is going. He has decided to destroy the implant network at its source. Traveling across country, he makes his way to the bird sanctuary housing the PhonCom servers, cuts a hole in the roof, introduces a fatal worm into the network, and blows up the computers and himself in the process. Calvin, spending a late night at the facility, hears David and, going to investigate, catches him in the act. Once he understands David's intent, he turns and walks away, commenting, "There was nothing in that room that I cared to protect."[25] Still wearing the calibration helmet (a significant detail), he continues walking and through a series of unlikely coincidences joins the core group still hiding in the silo.

When the PhonCom system crashes, more than the digital network goes haywire. Children everywhere suddenly become uncontrollable; to say they behave like wild animals is to insult our furry brethren. Burnham grasps the problem most acutely. He realizes that the children, implanted at birth, have learned to perceive the world through the voice in their heads. When the network goes down, "the voice in their head was replaced with static. . . . The feeling must have been akin to a hand reaching down from the heavens and yanking their brains right out of their skulls."[26] The image vividly expresses how integrated their cognitions have become with the cognitive assemblages into which the children have involuntarily been incorporated.

Because there is no way to cope with the berserk children other than by putting them in holding pens and shooting them with tranquilizer guns, society falls into chaos. That is when Slash, back at the silo, comes to the rescue. This double silent, who received no verbal name from his parents and whose handle references a punctuation mark that divides and connects, sees a screen filled with images of the distraught children. Although he does not understand the reporters' talk, he is acutely sensitive to the children's distress and mesmerized by their acting out. He is given the calibration helmet, ostensibly to protect him when Theo brings him a skateboard, but in narrative terms a device that lets this small child solve an international problem of gigantic proportions precisely *because* he is a silent.

Leaving the silo and climbing a tree (conveniently an oak, recalling the name of the school that Flora attended), Slash begins a series of actions that we see from Francine's perspective. "I thought I could hear a low humming sound coming from the helmet . . . the boy's strained expression beneath the helmet softened. Sympathetic, almost. It went places. I watched him, and my mind went places too. I realize I sound like Patti now. But this is how it was." As usual, Burnham, a scientist, is used in the narrative to explain what happened. He is examining an out-of-control silent girl when the event occurs. "I saw something that passed over the surface of her features. It was as if I saw her go from animal back to human. I don't believe there is a word in our language, or perhaps any language, for what I saw on the girl's face. It was the primal spark of a mind recognizing itself." As he recounts, "The device [i.e., helmet] was designed to pass a predefined emotional impulse into the mind of a targeted subject. . . . We could pass these impulses to a single subject or a hundred of them. But by all indications the boy had simultaneously accessed all possible endpoints—in effect, all implantees worldwide."[27]

Although he remarks, "I couldn't imagine how [the helmet] was possibly still active" (neither can we!), he realizes that the "boy was able to act as a sort of neural beacon, broadcasting a signal of such strength and purity that it broke through the chaos of the implanted children's brains and established the kind of order and focus that afforded conscious thought." In effect, Slash

Postprint and Cognitive Contagion

shows the children that they are conscious beings even though they no longer have the (digital) voice in their heads; he opens for them the realization they are human. "You see," Burnham continues, "the children who had been affected most acutely by the destruction of PhonCom were all implanted within the first year of life, and of course none of them had ever developed an internal consciousness that wasn't brokered by the implant. They hadn't *learned* to be silent." One would think that Burnham, realizing this, would feel immense gratitude to Slash and proclaim him an international hero. The first thought in his mind instead is to acquire Slash as an experimental subject: "I wanted to study the boy. I had to."[28]

This explanation notwithstanding, issues such as the helmet's power source remain unexplained.[29] Since the helmet scene strains credulity, we may assume that the authors really, really wanted to keep this episode despite its implausibility. What is at stake in this scene that makes it so crucial? Its implications are indeed momentous, for it shows that consciousness does not require language to exist (a point now conceded by many neurologists but for a long time considered controversial). Moreover, it shows that empathy and deep understanding of what it means to suffer do not require language either. If we take these qualities to be essential to what it means to be human, the final implication is that the human essence can survive without language. Given this implication, perhaps we may forgive the implausibility.

Reimagining Humans

The issue of what humans would be without language, first introduced as a marginalized phenomenon affecting only the silents, starts to spread when the virus mutates and becomes airborne. Burnham cites figures indicating that 70 percent of the global human population is affected.[30] Even though the virus remains asymptomatic for some, everyone is aware that sooner or later they may be affected. How the authors position this eventuality very much depends on the final episodes. As the novel draws to a close, an increasingly tight correspondence between episodes gives a clear sense of denouement in the major characters' story lines. Significantly, no one-offs appear in volume 6, the only narrative section from which they are completely absent. Having served their special purposes, they are no longer needed. Moreover, the central silent family (Flora, Spencer, and Slash) around which the core group assembled, successfully catch a bus to Canada, thus exiting our narrative and defeating Burnham's obsession with capturing Slash. Thereafter, the novel is free to focus on the fates of the major characters.

Nancy Jernik, one of the first to be affected by the airborne virus, has retreated into silence, thus leaving the narrative as well. Patti Kern, ever the seeker, has drifted into a carnival and, in her usual happenstance way, taken up residence dealing a card game aimed not at profit but at interacting with whoever wants to. She remarks, "I spent my whole life like a hermit crab, sidewalking from notion to notion, trying them on like shells, finding them cracked or cramped or flimsy. Now I shuffle my cards for anyone, no one. I'm open for business for the brief spell until time makes me otherwise." Earlier she would have said the loss of language was a blessing, but from her present perspective, facing it as her own destiny, she judges that despite her earlier protestations against language, she was "rotten with the sound of things." Her attitude now is more measured, more nuanced. "We are endowed with many gifts. And often the only thing that makes you do a full inventory is to be robbed of one of them."[31] Carrying the weight of her new understanding, the term *robbed* concisely acknowledges that the loss of language cannot be so cavalierly dismissed as an unambiguous good.

A similar ending marks Theo and Francine's story. At last together, they are shown watching a foreign film, with Francine anxiously reading the subtitles and barely able to follow the narrative. Then Theo turns off the words, and she finds she can understand it much better simply by attending to expressions and gestures. Like Patti, she realizes that the loss of language can awaken awareness of other senses and ways to know the world. This cannot, of course, be the whole story about the loss of language worldwide. The authors wisely end with no attempt to fully imagine what global society would be like without language, eschewing apocalypse for gentle resignation.[32]

Calvin is saved for the epilogue. Always an ambiguous figure hovering between speech and silence, Calvin still has the calibration helmet. Recalling that the helmet can send impulses resulting in linguistic utterances and has its own database of phrases (though the power-supply issue is still unaccounted for), we can understand how he is able to produce words, but ironically he cannot understand his own utterances because he has retreated into the silent condition. "I can send signals to my own implant," he explains. "I can still speak. But I can only send signals outward. Without PhonCom there is no language processing. No comprehension. I can make words but I cannot understand them."[33] A clever ploy to account for Calvin's dictated narrative, this explanation leaves unexplained how his dictations are accessed by the archivist because he lives in the desert, in an abandoned miner's shack without electricity, alone except for a dog.

But we are far from the days when the authors of *Robinson Crusoe* and *The Scarlet Letter* felt obliged to account for how the written record was produced. So let us pass over this issue and focus on the reconfiguration between thoughts, words, and understanding that Calvin represents. Without verbal comprehension, he has become a creature much closer to the dog: conscious, able to have thoughts, even able to make sounds, but with very little comprehension of what those sounds mean in a linguistic sense. When Calvin tries to train the dog to fetch, he is remarkably unsuccessful, but he, too, strikes a final note of resignation. "Let the dog have its thoughts, whatever shape they may take. Let the unknown be unknown. The things we need will reveal themselves in time."[34] With this light touch, the authors suggest that one effect of losing language will be a reordering of humans' relations to the rest of the lifeworld, so that they are less domineering, less inclined ruthlessly to exploit other species for our benefit, less sure of their right to dominion over the earth. This is asemiosis in a very benign form.

Burnham speculates that the cause for the mutation may ironically be the spike delivered to the implants when the PhonCom network crashed. Thus, the very devices invented to produce digitally generated language end up destroying natural language ability in most of the human species. This outcome may be interpreted as a comment on our present condition of selective asemiosis. Like the implanted silents, we plunge ever deeper into digitally mediated language as social media increasingly replace face-to-face interactions.[35] Even our facial expressions are now transmitted digitally through an animoji app, a technology that uses facial-recognition software to project our facial gestures onto animated masks. Choose your mask—Donald Trump, Donald Duck—and he smiles when you do, frowns when your brow wrinkles. Like an evil twin to the silents' face-talking, animoji represent not a more embodied and authentic mode of communication but a digital transformation vulnerable, like all digitally mediated language, to commodification, surveillance, and capitalistic exploitation.

The deeper issue raised by *The Silent History* turns on the symbiotic relationship we have with our technologies, most acutely with cognitive technologies such as computational media. No one can deny the benefits of instant communication worldwide or the many other affordances that contemporary cognitive technologies bestow. But, as with any symbiosis, the continued welfare of the human species increasingly depends on maintaining functional relationships with our symbionts, especially our cognitive technologies. When digital technologies, with their always increasing linguistic and analytical capacities, interact with humans, they do not merely rearrange synaptic networks through external means (something books also do, although not as

The Silent History—What is This?

A generation of children forced to live without words.

It begins as a statistical oddity: a spike in children born with acute speech delays. Physically normal in every way, these children never speak and do not respond to speech; they don't learn to read, don't learn to write. As the number of cases grows to an epidemic level, theories spread. Maybe it's related to a popular antidepressant; maybe it's environmental. Or maybe these children have special skills all their own.

The Silent History unfolds in a series of brief testimonials from parents, teachers, friends, doctors, cult leaders, profiteers, and impostors (everyone except, of course, the children themselves), documenting the growth of the so-called silent community into an elusive, enigmatic force in itself—alluring to

```
<html xmlns="http://www.w3.org/1999/xhtml>

<head>
<title>The Silent History - What is This?</title>
<meta http-equiv="Content-Type" content="text/html;
      charset=UTF-8" />
<script type="text/javascript">window.
      NREUM||(NREUM={});NREUM.info={"beacon":"bam.
      nr-data.net","errorBeacon":"bam.nr-data.net","
      licenseKey":"d75ae37743","applicationID":"4702
      1","transactionName":"cwpaERNfXlpTRBlEVFcAR0oW
      WFNC","queueTime":8,"applicationTime":21,"age
      nt":""}</script>
<script type="text/javascript">(window.
      NREUM||(NREUM={})).loader_config={lic
      enseKey:"d75ae37743",applicationID:"4
      7021"};window.NREUM||(NREUM={}),__nr_
      require=function(e,n,t){function r(t){if(!n[t])
      {var i=n[t]={exports:{}};e[t][0].call(i.
      exports,function(n){var i=e[t][1][n];return
      r(i||n)},i,i.exports)}return n[t].exports}
      if("function"==typeof __nr_require)return
      __nr_require;for(var i=0;i<t.length;i++)
```

Here is the html code for the first part of an ad describing *The Silent History*. It dramatizes the differences between the print page, immediately accessible to readers, and the code layers underlying the text as it was delivered on iPhones and iPads.

powerfully). Rather, in these fictional scenarios, they are depicted as invading the physical boundaries of the brain, radically altering brain processes, including consciousness. However troubling the thought of digital media transforming us from the outside, far scarier is the idea that they can cross the blood–brain barrier and affect us from the inside. This is the territory homesteaded by *The Silent History* but then fully developed into globalized terrain by *The Word Exchange*.

Reading the Codex: Spatializing Narratives

Before leaving *The Silent History*, I want to reflect on the differences between reading the work as a codex and reading it as an iPhone app. In its digital instantiation, the novel was widely reviewed, but most reviews commented primarily on its novelty. In some, major plot points were misread or missed entirely, including that a virus is responsible for the silents' condition and that the virus then spreads to most of the population. One does not expect, of course, that everyone will read a print novel completely or even understand the major plot points, but I know of few who would dare to publicly *review* a novel without having done so.

Rather, I think that reading the work as an app inspires a different kind of reading than reading it as a codex, with different expectations for what "reading" implies. The app's design invites distracted (rather than immersive) reading—for example, reading with an eye toward when the bus arrives or the train rolls out. Distracted reading discourages attention to details and complex plot symmetries. Moreover, because digital reading is deeply influenced by web practices, there is also a tendency to skim and skip, without the compulsion to finish a text that the codex's linear progression often induces.[36] The same goes for reading every episode. If one is particularly busy and misses an installment or several, there is less incentive to find the missing parts and read them. Web reading, including e-mail, social media, and other forms of digitally mediated communication, is very much about the flow of words through time. Once one has floated past a particular marker on the river, it is easier to continue downstream than to buck the current and try to backtrack, especially when reading takes place as a leisure activity or as an activity done when someone is stuck on a bus or train.

Another difference is how the app and codex instantiate spatiality. As we have seen, the digital version was crafted with the expectation that users would contribute Field Reports and that these reports would fill out the episodes with locative-specific narratives anchoring the action to local landmarks, topographies, and architectures. The codex, lacking this kind of anchoring, relies instead on creating an *internal* topography, facilitated by the ease with which one can navigate between episodes, pages, speakers, and actions. Flipping back and forth, the reader is easily able to follow the progression of speakers and see how one plays off of another, either with syncopated repetitions or orchestrated differences.

With the app version, designed with more diffuse coherence, greater narrative cacophony, and more tenuous connections between episodes, the interpretive payoff for this kind of close analysis would not be as great. Indeed, to my knowledge, no one has attempted, for example, to map the distribution of major, minor, and one-off characters in the app version, although it is a fairly simple exercise in narrative analysis. Does this openness to close reading make the codex a better literary work than the app version? Although I am tempted to respond in the affirmative, I recall Tenen's comment that he realized his "deepest intuitions" about literature were formed with print.[37] So were mine, of course, so I hold open the possibility that the app version may offer satisfaction just as potent for a certain demographic of readers. Without doubt, however, the rewards are different in the two cases—as different as the diverse ways in which the two works mobilize spatiality for narrative purposes.

The Word Exchange: Capitalism as Culprit

Comparing *The Silent History* to Alena Graedon's debut novel *The Word Exchange* reveals an absence in the former that might otherwise slip by unnoticed: the role of capital in accelerating and expanding selective semiosis. *The Silent History* restricts capital's role to a bare minimum, the quirky inventor Prashant Nuregesan; Burnham, the narrative's antagonist, is driven far more by an obsessive need for control than by greed. Yet in the real world selective asemiosis is all about capitalism, in particular the proprietary code that corporations seal off from public access. In *The Word Exchange*, capitalist greed—aided by malicious hackers who may or may not be in the control of the aptly named Synchronic, Inc.—results in nothing less than a global assault on language capabilities and, just as catastrophically, the linguistic heritages of the human species.

The novel begins darkly enough with the disappearance of Douglas Samuel Johnson, editor in chief of the *North American Dictionary of the English Language* (*NADEL*), which is about to launch its third edition, the last to appear in print. His twenty-seven-year-old daughter, the palindromically named Anana (a.k.a. Ana), grows increasingly concerned when she discovers that not only is he absent, but his biographical entry in the digital *NADEL* has also been erased. This is very much a story of young adult daughters and their fathers. Virtually all of the characters fall into either her generation or his: no children, no teenagers, almost no middle-aged adults. The narration alternates between Ana's account and the journal kept by her father's protégé at *NADEL*, Bart, who is hopelessly in love with her. Despite Doug's gentle suggestions that Bart may be worthy of her affection, Ana remarks that she "wasn't quite sure why I wasn't attracted to Bart; he just wasn't my type."[38] Her "type," apparently, is represented by the charismatic Max (a.k.a. Hermes

Maxmillian King), who has recently broken up with Ana, leaving her devastated.

These relationships form the bones around which the conspiracy's flesh is molded. Our first introduction to its scope comes when Ana, deciding to search in the building's subbasement for clues to her father's disappearance, discovers the Creatorium, a clever neologism foreshadowing what she finds there. Under the watchful eye of a male foreman, Chinese and Russian female workers toil at screens showing *NADEL*'s digital corpus. As Ana peers over one worker's shoulder, the screen reveals a shocking sight: a "word—I think it was 'paradox,' but I couldn't quite see—disappeared. And in its place strange characters emerged: b-ay-n-o-k-c. Then the blocks of text below—its senses and textual examples—also vanished. Replaced by a single phrase 'that which is true.'" Ana knows that even "accidental deletions would . . . be devastating. Each term represented untold hours of painstaking labor," yet here alterations are deliberately being carried out by dozens of workers. Noticing that the room is smoky and hot, Ana also sees print copies of *NADEL* being thrown in an enormous furnace. "This was no ordinary book-burning," she realizes. "Our digital corpus was also being dismantled," so she understands the destruction as an effort to eradicate all traces of the texts that have been her father's lifework, or, more precisely, to contaminate those texts by substituting made-up "words" for real ones and simultaneously changing their definitions, in this case flattening the oxymoronic qualities of *paradox* to a much simpler Orwellian claim of "truth."[39]

The term *paradox* is a well-chosen example, for it recalls the paradoxical "creative destruction" that Karl Marx analyzed as characteristic of capitalism and Joseph Schumpeter argued was a harbinger of capitalism's ultimate demise. As Alan Lui has shown, however, neoliberal business literature heralds capitalism's "creative destruction" as a source of its perpetual renewal, thus converting what was a paradox into "that which is true."[40]

What Ana witnesses may more aptly be called "destructive creation," the erasure of communally understood words and their meanings (destruction) and the substitution of ersatz made-up terms with definitions flattened, distorted, or altogether rewritten (creation). "Destructive creation," like its inverse "creative destruction," carries the neoliberal agenda into the realm of language, sowing confusion about the proper forms of words and, even more devastatingly, their associated meanings in order to make a profit. It makes sense that *NADEL* is the site at which this "destructive creation" takes place, for dictionaries have traditionally been arbiters creating consensus about pronunciations and meanings; in addition, they document linguistic histories, enabling readers to have a deeply layered sense of how meanings have changed over time. This constructive work is highlighted when the defenders of reading, writing, and dictionaries call themselves the "Diachronic Society," named in part to contrast with the capitalist archvillain, Synchronic, Inc.

In *The Silent History*, the link between selective asemiosis and digital technologies arrives only retrospectively in the Soul Amp, but in *The Word Exchange* the connection is much more direct. Not only is the corpus of *NADEL* attacked, but also complicit are the media technologies Synchronic produces, futuristic cell phones named in successive generations the "Aleph," the "Meme,"[41] and the (about to be released) "Nautilus," each more deadly than the previous one. The relatively benign Aleph has no sensors and "could only roughly gauge mood states," but the more "aggressively" branded Meme has Sixth Sense software that anticipates a user's desires—for example, hailing a cab before the user can summon one. Further, an op-ed piece published by the Diachronic Society speculates that "Memes have commandeered user data not simply to predict but to *guide* behavior: . . . [for example] generating vindictive beams and tempting one to send them, order[ing] more drinks when you should go home."[42]

Deadlier still is the Nautilus, "the first commercially available device that integrates electronics with cellular biology" by utilizing "the already existing infrastructure of the brain."[43] Reminiscent of Neal Stephenson's novel *Snow Crash*, *The Word Exchange* imagines a technology that can communicate in either binary digits or DNA code; as in *Snow Crash*, the effect is to create a bridge between computer and biological viruses, each able to transmute into the other. Graedon tries to give a pseudoscientific account of how this might work. She writes that the Nautilus's "biojet" technology infiltrates cells by "integrating with the somas of the nearest sensory neurons to create new chimeric cells that can communicate with their cortical counterparts in the brain." By speaking the body's own language of proteins and cells as well as the binary code of electronics, the Nautilus creates a "seamless integration between the device . . . and the neuronal network it joins."[44]

Device sales, we learn, are only the tip of how Synchronic intends to make money. Much as printer sales are dwarfed by the continuing income stream produced by ink purchases, so the Meme generates income primarily from the Word Exchange, a handy little app that pops up whenever a user cannot quite remember a word's definition. At first, people consult the Word Exchange primarily for "obscure" terms, but their use later spreads to such common words as *clothed* and *bitten*.[45] What accounts for such expansion? Like the French philosopher Bernard Stiegler, Graedon's protagonists argue that the devices themselves are eroding cognitive faculties, seducing users into distracted states of mind in which concentrated, coherent thinking becomes more and more difficult. In a vicious cycle, the more one uses the devices, the more one needs to use them.

In a text that may have been one of the sources Graedon consulted for her book, *Taking Care of Youth and the Generations*, Stiegler argues that "psychotechnologies" typified by the programming industries, especially TV and video games, are undermining the very quality that defines humans at their best: critical consciousness. Eroding deep attention, these industries are creating instead short-term distractions, which Stiegler calls "attention without consciousness." In terminology that Graedon echoes, he argues that these industries are rewiring human brains, exploiting and also destroying its "cerebral plasticity" to produce instead an animalistic nervous system "forever enclosed within strict neurological limits." This future is almost upon us, he argues, with consciousness reduced to a "grammatized stream" for the "transformation of formalized machinic processes, as well as by devices recording and manipulating the information stream."[46]

Compare Stiegler's account with the looming future predicted by the Diachronic Society's op-ed piece: "As more and more of our interactions are mediated by machines—as all consciousness and communication are streamed through Crowns, Ear Beads, screens, and whatever Synchronic has planned next, for its newest Meme—there's no telling what will happen, not only to language but in some sense of civilization. The end of words would mean the end of memory and thought. In other words, our past and future."[47]

The Word Exchange accelerates this process by "rewiring" people's brains to the extent that they need to consult the Word Exchange simply to make it through a day's business of answering e-mails, reading news, corresponding with colleagues. Moreover, after Synchronic buys the digital copyrights for *NADEL*'s and most other dictionaries' word corpora, the Word Exchange becomes the *only* place where users can quickly and easily recover meanings. As the Diachronic Society predicts, once Synchronic has a monopoly, it jacks up the price of consulting the Word Exchange from two to twenty-five cents per word.[48]

The effects are not merely economic. In a long passage Ana quotes from Doug, the larger (Stieglerian) implications are made clear. "Moving all our words onto one consolidated exchange, changing the way we use and access language, through Memes— it wasn't just affecting our economy and culture, Doug had explained. The technology was actually rewiring people's brains. Changing neuronal pathways and reward systems. They were forgetting things, or not learning them in the first place. And if we didn't really have a shared, communal language—if we had nothing but a provisional relationship with words, a leaseholder's agreement, what would happen . . . if something went wrong?"[49]

Go wrong it does, big time. As if rewiring brains were not enough, the narrative also shows how word stores and words' meanings get corrupted through a video game, *Meaning Master*, invented by Ana's former lover, Max, CEO of the start-up Hermes. *Meaning Master* works by inviting a user to submit a made-up word, for which either she or someone else submits a definition. Underscoring its connection with capital, the game offers monetary prizes for words that get the most uptake. Pitching the game, Max argues, "We have to communicate not just better but differently. Invent a completely new kind of exchange." Echoing Humpty-Dumpty in *Alice in Wonderland*, a work that serves as *The Word Exchange*'s mirror-reflection text, Max boasts, "We can get words to mean whatever we want."[50]

When Synchronic buys Hermes, *Meaning Master*'s algorithms begin to merge with the Word Exchange, creating new versions of what Max and his friends call "money words." "Money words" originally denote the made-up words contributed by *Meaning Master* users, but they also covertly refer to the words most often looked up on the Word Exchange and thus the most profitable. In certain devices infected with a virus originating from a Synchronic project, these money words are increasingly supplanted by neologisms. Vernon, a former colleague of Max's who is sympathetic to Ana, explains that because people's internal memories have eroded, users "don't quite recognize the substitutions as fake. . . . But they *do* draw a blank, of course—a lot more often than with real words, even the ones they can't really remember. And just to communicate, they've started downloading meanings of some of the fabricated terms."[51] With both linguistic forms and meanings increasingly unstable, language's role in creating complex societies and indeed, the human species comes under attack.

The resulting crisis, in which computer virus and biological infection merge to create the "word flu," explodes during an aptly named gala, "Future Is Now." With hundreds of thousands flooding the *Meaning Master* site to compete for a $100,000 grand prize and more thousands infected through the Nautilus, whose roll-out occurs at the same event, the virus spreads like wildfire throughout New York, the United States, and from there most of the world as the virus leaps from English into many other languages. Word flu symptoms include "slips" in which nonsense words are peppered through speech and writing (although the infected person remains oblivious of such slips); blinding headaches; fever and chills; and in extreme cases death or the linguistic equivalent, Silencing, an inability to use language at all.

The global apocalypse can be combatted only by language therapy, Ana discovers when she finally finds her father at (where else?) the home of the *Oxford English Dictionary* in a building shaped like an open book. The therapy includes banishing all digital devices, a rigorous program of reading difficult print materials, and a daily discipline of writing, supplemented by learning additional languages and scholarly study. In an interview, Graedon remarked, "I'm part of the last generation to use print media"; her narrative in effect reverses this trend, sending those who survive back to print.[52]

Reading against the grain, I understand the climax as the answer to a hypothetical question: What would it take to reverse our present plunge into postprint and return us to a regime of print? The answer, apparently, is the end of civilization as we know it. Against its own intentions, *The Word Exchange* testifies to how pervasively and deeply print has been interpenetrated by computational media. Agreeing with Stiegler that nothing less than the human essence is at stake, *The Word Exchange* nevertheless shows the devastating price that would need to be paid to recover the supposed purity of a print regime uncontaminated by viruses or computational media. As a fictional narrative, it teases readers with an implicit question. Which would you choose: returning to a print era in which your participation in cognitive assemblages is limited to books that operate only as cognitive supports or continuing to participate in postprint, where your cognitive capacities are severely diminished and enslaved via digital media to global capitalism? In simpler terms, do you want your mind to remain your own, or are you willing to have your innermost thoughts captured by cognitive devices controlled by ominous forces?

For Graedon, only a looming global apocalypse is sufficient to express the gravity of our contemporary condition as participants in cognitive assemblages. Although I disagree with the black-and-white (and one-sided) nature of the dilemma the narrative constructs, my views align with Graedon's that cognitive assemblages differ qualitatively from the practices associated with the long reign of print and that the heart of the matter lies in the interaction between human cognitions and those of computational media.

Dictionary Through the Looking Glass: Reflection as Language Therapy

Through each chapter's epigraph, Graedon structures her narrative as a kind of dictionary or, better, a reflection of what dictionaries at their best can do: charge words with meanings that deepen their impact and encourage insight. Marching A through Z, each epigraph offers a word starting with the appropriate letter, a pronunciation guide, a designation indicating the part of speech, and a definition. These playful and clever aphorisms encourage the reader to reflect on their significance, both in general and in relation to the chapter that follows. One of my favorites: "I\i\n 1a. that which separates us from others b: that which separates us from ourselves <I am I>."[53] Like the Hegelian Thesis:Antithesis:Synthesis that serve as titles for the book's three sections, 1a seems to be in tension with 1b, the first pointing to the individual as distinguishable from all others, the second to an internal split in which the subject is divided within (against?) himself. In the chapter, narrated by Bart as part of his journal, this tension is resolved into a synthesis. Bart, the odd man out who is very definitely not part of the family group gathered at Ana's mother's apartment for Thanksgiving dinner (1a), at first is fractured by self-doubts and fears he may do something wrong (1b). As the ghastly dinner proceeds, however, he finally finds the courage to confront her family and scold them, especially her loathsome stepfather, Laird Sharpe, for not treating her better. This action not only endears him to Ana but also heals the split within himself, achieving a kind of synthesis that makes the episode a fitting finale for the work's first section. In addition, Bart's favorite philosopher is Hegel—"GWF," as he refers to him—so it is fitting that he is the character to undergo this transformation in I and Eye (both his and Ana's).

Another favorite epigraph: "com*mu*ni*ca*tion \ . . . \n 1: the successful bridging of subjectivities 2: the act of spreading disease 3: something foolhardy, to be avoided."[54] Definition 1 emphasizes a point made at several places in the text: that language is the primary way in which we, as individuals, come to know and understand each other. It follows, then, that an attack on language is nothing less than a blow to human community and solidarity. Definition 2, underscoring that implication, further plays on the pun with "communicable diseases." As people become infected with the word flu, they spread the disease by speaking with or writing to the uninfected. Definition 3 follows immediately from 2. As the people begin to realize what is happening, they institute prophylactic measures that include staying away from anyone who is infected.[55] The chapter headed by this epigraph recounts Ana's visit to the apartment of Phineas Thwaite, Doug's friend, who both shelters Ana and misleads her. He is wary in part because she has already been infected with the word flu from briefly trying on a Nautilus, and he fears that she may infect him as well, thus making good on all three of the meanings of *communication* given at the chapter's beginning.

As the epigraphs show, Graedon's writing is often nimble, clever, and effective. She sometimes has a tendency to overwrite, especially at moments of crisis when she tells (rather than shows) her characters' strong emotions. This flaw is minor, however, in this ambitious book that tries to imagine the worst possible outcomes of leaving the print era behind. Its core assumptions continue to be debated—that digital communication is less rigorous and more distracting than print, that our interactions with digital media are making us less capable of critical thinking, that the cultural and linguistic heritages of the human species are being put at risk by what Stiegler calls, in a double or triple pun, the "programming industries."[56] Although many argue that a more nuanced approach is needed than the broad brush with which Stiegler tars TV, video games, and other digitally mediated communications, *The Word Exchange* demonstrates with unmistakable clarity and considerable narrative force the deeper anxieties underlying selective asemiosis.

Postprint and/as Cognitive Contagion

This chapter's contribution to the book's narrative arc is to voice deep concerns about how not just print but also the whole of human language may be changing under the impact of computational media. A deeper implication is an idea explored by Bernard Stiegler, Mark Hansen, David Rambo, Andy Clark, and me, among others: that humans are engaged in a continuing feedback cycle with the technical devices we create.[57] From the stone axes of the Paleolithic period to the Memes and Nautiluses of an imagined future, our devices affect not only human culture but also humans ourselves, biologically, psychologically, and cognitively.

This tendency, evident from the earliest days of *Homo sapiens*, has accelerated exponentially with the invention of computational media. It has also changed direction. As Hansen's title *Feed-Forward* suggests, the thrust of what he calls twenty-first-century or "atmospheric" media has shifted from a *feedback* cycle, in which the device is first invented and then feeds back to affect culture and human neurology, into an anticipatory role in which human responses, including those involved in designing computational media, are affected by algorithmic governmentality and affective semiocapitalism even before fully conscious responses are formed.[58] Graedon picks up on this idea with her Meme, which not only anticipates the user's desires but also subtly shapes and directs them, operating in microtemporal regimes under the horizon of conscious awareness.

If intention is preempted before it can begin to operate on a conscious level, then postprint designates much more than the interpenetration of computational media into the printing business. It also signals a shift in which human being is so entangled with computational media that human intentions and desires literally cannot be thought without them. Although this entanglement has myriad benefits, from global communication circuits to more sophisticated detection of contagious diseases, to mention only a couple, these texts suggest that the feedforward/feedback cycles may also have less-desirable consequences. As with postprint, these texts' concerns center on how print, literacy, and human language are changing through the impact of computational media.

One can argue, of course, that the changes wrought by the invention of print were also immense. No one doubts that this was the case. Nevertheless, if the focus is specifically on the *cognitive* dimension of the relevant changes, the two novels discussed here (along with many other indicators explored in my book *Unthought*[59]) insist that the differences between print and postprint are not merely quantitative but qualitative and that postprint poses unprecedented challenges as well as benefits to humans in developed societies. The risks should be weighed in the balance, along with the thrill of invention and commercial success documented in chapter 2 and the new and exciting dimensions opened up by computational media in scholarly publishing and humanities scholarship explored in chapter 3.

How the balance is assessed and understood will, of course, vary from one person to the next, depending on his or her priorities, values, and judgments. This book does not so much seek to arrive at a conclusive answer to that conundrum as to clarify the stakes, analyze the contributing factors, and, most of all, argue that postprint and the related concept of cognitive assemblages should become part of the intellectual tool kit for people interested in these issues.

5

Bookishness at the Limits

RESITING THE HUMAN

This chapter is a fitting conclusion because it interrogates the status of the book as a print object in the computational era. Jessica Pressman leads the way by identifying what she names the "aesthetic of bookishness," calling it "a literary strategy that speaks to our cultural moment." She explains that this aesthetic refers to literary works that "draw attention to the book as a multimedia format, one informed by and connected to digital technologies."[1] Her specific focus is the novel, but I think her insight applies to other literary forms as well. Moreover, in keeping with the theme of cognitive assemblages that provides the throughline for this work, not only is the book's status bound up with computational media, but the status of the human is as well.

Two seemingly opposed literary projects illustrate how the status of the book becomes entwined with the resituating or, as this chapter's title puts it, the resiting of the human.[2] They are the print codex *Between Page and Screen* by Amaranth Borsuk and Brad Bouse (discussed briefly in chapter 1) and the books published by the Argentine writer Mirtha Dermisache. These books are "unspeakable" in the literal sense that they contain no words capable of being uttered, only marks that can be seen but not read in any conventional way. The two projects may be understood as pointing in diametrically opposite directions in their resiting of the human. Borsuk and Bouse embrace the cognitive-assemblage implication that the human practice of reading is now irreversibly entwined with the cognitive capacities of computers, whereas Dermisache resists algorithmically generated language by creating inscriptions that reference human gestures. Another way to say this is that the marks in Borsuk and Bouse's book can be read only by computers, whereas the marks in Dermisache's books can be interpreted only by humans. Together, the two point in opposite directions to the limits of bookishness in the contemporary era: complete immersion in cognitive assemblages on the one hand and complete avoidance of computer-legible inscriptions on the other. For Borsuk and Bouse, the directionality of writing reveals a posthuman future already here; for Dermisache's literary interpreter, it evokes a prehuman past to which we may perhaps return if apocalyptic intimations prove true.

Marks Legible Only to Computers

To find the words in *Between Page and Screen*, one must go to the website betweenpageandscreen.com and initialize one's computer by holding up the book's cover (figure 5.1), with its illegible mark, to the webcam. **After loading the Flash software reader, one can then access the words by holding each page's mark so the webcam can see and read it. With the proper placement, words flash onto the screen.**[3] The webcam, of course, images the user and book as well as the words, so every page's words appear on a screen already containing these images (see figure 5.2). This arrangement has several implications, chief among them the incorporation of the user's image into the reading process, a visual representation reinforcing the realization that the user is now incorporated into a cognitive assemblage. In addition, the words are projected in front of the user and book images. Although all the images appear on the computer's two-dimensional screen, the visual impression is that the words appear

5.1 Cover image of Amaranth Borsuk and Brad Bouse, *Between Page and Screen* (Denver: SpringGun, 2016).

Source: Image courtesy of Brad Bouse.

5.2a and 5.2b The projection of the text of one of the epistles between P and S in *Between Page and Screen* and the image of letters flashing away when the webcam cannot read them.

Source: Images courtesy of Brad Bouse.

```
<div style="width: 500px; margin: auto;">
<object type="application/x-shockwave-flash"
        style="width: 500px; height: 450px; margin: auto;"
        id="VideoPlayer" data="yourvideo.swf">
<param name="allowScriptAccess" value="sameDomain" >
<param name="movie" value="yourvideo.swf" >
<param name="quality" value="high" >
<param name="scale" value="noscale" >
<param name="bgcolor" value="#ababab" >
<p><a href="http://www.adobe.com/go/
        getflashplayer">Install Adobe Flash For
        Richer Experience</a></p>
</object>
</div>
```

Here is the code for the beginning of the Flash Player.

in the space intervening between the screen and the user, an augmented-reality effect accentuated by the three-dimensional appearance of certain projected animations.

In a reading/podcast at MIT, Borsuk made clear that she is committed to a materialist poetics, citing my book *Writing Machines* as one of her inspirations.[4] The idea of a materialist poetics is simple, although its ramifications are complex: to exist in the world, language must be embodied, and its embodiments matter. Reading screens is different than reading paper pages; reading on a Kindle is different than on a MacBook Pro; reading a folio is different than reading the pages of a quarto. In addition, a materialist poetics emphasizes the materiality of language, attentive to its history, pronunciations, etymologies, and other specificities that distinguish it as a medium of communication (a stance that Garrett Stewart exploits in considering language itself as a medium[5]). In addition, Borsuk also identifies as one of her important influences the constraint-based writing of the Oulipo workshop for potential literature.

These influences are readily apparent in the projected words that appear page by page of *Between Page and Screen* via the webcam. The book is situated as a dialogue between P and S (presumably "Page" and "Screen"); one mark appearing near the beginning generates flashing words that are all those anagrammatically contained in "betweenpageandscreen," a mode of algorithmic generation easy for a computer but more difficult for a human. Even at this early point, then, we encounter the two different ways of reading cojoined in this work. The projected images of the marks that follow are not about (human) psychology, as one might expect in a poetic form devoted to a lover's quarrel; rather, they foreground the materiality of language. This materiality includes elaborate plays on the etymologies and linguistic specificities of pages as opposed to screens and the differing technological capacities of the two.

The cover mark generating the opening salvo from P will give the flavor. "Dear S, I fast, I fasten to become compact, but listen, that's only part of your impact—I always wanted to fit a need, it's my character to pin, impinge, a twinge of jealousy."[6] To decode this passage, we can refer to the etymology of the term *page*; it comes via the French word *pagina*, which is from the Latin *pangere*, "to fasten." One idea about the derivation is that it comes from pages being "fastened" in a book, while another proposes that it alludes to vines being "fastened by stakes to a trellis, which led to columns of writing on a scroll" (etymonline.com/page). The latter explanation is referenced in one of P's last missives: "let's name this pagan pageant [two words that are among the anagrams flashed from the cover mark], these rows of lines or vines that link us together." More is at work here than etymology. There is internal rhyming and word play—for example, between "pin" (derived from the notion that the pages can be pinned as well as fastened in place) and "impinge," rhyming with "twinge." In addition, the two dimensionality of the page in contrast to the (relatively) thick computer screen provides the basis for "fast," as in becoming "compact," which in turn rhymes with "impact."

In several projections, images reference the shaped forms of concrete poetry, which Borsuk identifies as another formative influence. The passage from P's first missive continues, "Let's spread out the pent-up moment, pentimento memento. A pact: our story's spinto—no more esperanto." "Spinto," defined as a voice having both lyric and dramatic qualities, references both a poetic form (lyric) and a performance (drama). The next mark generates one of several animations, this one featuring a spinning circle of letters reading "spintospininintospinto" (see figure 5.3). The letters form a circle, so that where one begins and ends is arbitrary, leading to multiple anagrammatic possibilities. Other projections include a pig-shaped graphic filled with words and a rectangular column that revolves showing the words *pale, peel, pole, pawl*, and so on. This image references P's comment that "I didn't mean to impale you with my pin—my origin's to join, to stake a claim, but that root . . . leads both ways: to palisade and pole, but also to travel and travail."

5.3 Screen shot showing the "spinto" projection from *Between Page and Screen*, with book and user images in the background.

Source: Image courtesy of Brad Bouse.

The term *screen*, for its part, derives from *shield*, which in turn derives from the Old Norse Proto-Germanic word *skel*, "to divide, split, separate." "Perhaps the notion is of a flat piece of wood made by splitting a log" (etymonline.com/shield); *screen* is also related through *skirmish* to "Scaramouche," a comedic figure in a play who is a cowardly braggart. So S's mark flashes this initial passage: "I take your point—I don't mean to cut, but it is my stripe, my type, I'd rather shear than share. I wear a scarf to hide my scars, my scabs have scabs, my heart is a shard. I am that Scaramouch, I like a joust (my tattoo says keep out). I prefer arras to arias, you've guessed, a bard of scabbards, a chorus of cuirass." The point S takes relates to P's "pin," and the rest of the passage relates to the etymology of *screen–shield–skel*. Wearing a scarf relates to "scar," of course, but will later surface in the form of a veil, a veiled reference to S's inaccessible interiority. S later flashes, "My best subject was always division. I like partition. You only get a portion of the stuff that makes me up—or anyone. The rest hides," alluding to the code that underlies every screenic display.

This provides the opening that P will exploit to flash a riposte but also to suggest a possible opening: "Dear S, A screen is a shield, but also a veil—it's sheer and can be shorn. There's a neat gap between these covers, a gate agape, through which you've slipped your tang." If something can slip between the pages, which thus function as a "gate agape," then rapprochement is possible. The turn comes through referencing the trellis, which P uses as a metaphor that "props me up," asking S, "Be my support? What are boundaries anyway?" S responds, "We're running out of words, so I'll be curt curtal and curtail my tale. You're a core—a shore—a sight. I regret the fight. Don't forget to write," a cliché turned exquisitely appropriate sentiment when addressed to the paper bearer of words. There's a (joint) proclamation, a PS that isn't; the final projection flashes, "PS a co-script posthaste postface there is no postscript. Sleep tight," followed by an animation in which letter Ps and Ss fall down in the projected space.

The entire work can be seen as a "coscript," an orchestrated performance not only between P and S, Page and Screen, but also among author, reader, book, and computer. Given that it is not easy to hold the marks steady enough in exactly the right position for the webcam to read them and flash the projections, the hard-working (and not infrequently exasperated) reader finishes the work with a sense of satisfaction quite different from reading either a page or screen by itself. Every aspect of this work enacts an embodied performance that imprints onto muscles and brain what it means to be part of a cognitive assemblage as well as what it means to be materially immersed in language—and in code. Unlike the selective asemiosis discussed in chapter 4, this work positions code and language as synergistic symbionts. Code is necessary to display the words, while the words themselves playfully reference (human) language's complex historicity, verbal specificities, and rich interconnections. The aesthetic projected (in both senses) by this work is technically confident, saucy and sassy, brilliantly inventive.

The posthuman as it manifests here draws on the best of both worlds, human and computational. Not all about this project is roses (or pins and shields), however. The work is programmed in Flash, and as of the end of 2020 Adobe will no longer support the Flash reader. Like many artists working in computational media, Borsuk and Bouse are hostage to the large tech companies; they depend on these companies' software, but they are not in control of whether that software will continue to exist. If Adobe does not support Flash, as promised (threatened?), Borsuk and Bouse's full work may become inaccessible. The codex of course will continue to exist, but its marks will no longer be legible to human readers. This possibility is especially ironic because at the time of the MIT podcast in April 2011, Borsuk had only one instance of the book, which she had made as an artist's book. She mentioned that she would like to find a publisher for a print book and succeeded in achieving this goal when Siglio Press took on the project in 2012 (Spring Gun Press produced a new edition in 2016). But her desire to have the work be widely read and shared may ultimately be ambushed from the other side—the inaccessibility of the code.[7]

The Paradoxical Power of the Asemic

Asemic writing is sometimes defined as writing without semantics (*sem* as in *semiotics*, the science of signs, and *asem* as a negation of that). It is an artistic practice that uses wordlike symbols but remains illegible because the marks never resolve into recognizable characters. Michael Jacobson, an eminent practitioner, characterizes it as a "wordless, open, semantic form of writing that is international in its mission. . . . [A]semic writing is a shadow, impression, and abstraction of conventional writing. It uses the constraints of writerly gestures and the full development of abstract art to divulge its main purpose: total freedom beyond literary expression."[8] As Jacobson indicates, asemic writing is parasitic upon writing in the sense that it clearly alludes to writing and yet cannot be read. As I like to think of it, it is not writing, but it also is not not writing. The double negation of the second formulation distinguishes asemic writing, usually but not always inscribed on paper, from practices such as drawing, doodling, scribbling, and other nonstandard ways of making marks.

As we shall see, asemic writing takes our present condition of selective asemiosis, a cause for alarm in the texts discussed in chapter 4 and for literary critics such as Dennis Tenen, Bernard Stiegler, Nicholas Carr, and others, and it converts that condition into an occasion for exuberant artistic experimentation. In this respect, it shares with Borsuk and Bouse's *Between Page and Screen* a delight in the possibilities of "unspeakable" texts, books that cannot be read aloud. This celebration of the book indicates that digital textuality has not led to the demise of print, as some have predicted, but on the contrary has stimulated a renewed interest in book history, book culture, and "bookishness" in general, as Pressman points out. It has also led some literary critics to think more deeply about what constitutes a book, as do Johanna Drucker in *A Century of Artists' Books*, Garrett Stewart in *Bookwork*, and Kiene Brillingburg Wurth in her brilliant interpretation of the illegible "cross-written" texts of Louise Paillé.[9] A counterintuitive result of the postprint era, then, has been a renewed interest in print books and print culture, including books containing marks that evoke writing but are not writing as such.

Mirtha Dermisache, an Argentine artist whose works have been internationally exhibited and published, exemplifies the contemporary interest in asemic writing and print books (although, as we shall see, her relation to print is complex). Despite having reservations about acknowledging the role of publishers in producing her books, she prefers the book form. She published the first in 1969 with the unassuming title *Libro*

No. 1; each of the many others that followed used the same title, numbered in sequence. Although Dermisache died in 2012, there is robust continuing interest in her work, as indicated by the publication of her selected writings in 2017.[10]

Her career coincided with the transition from print to postprint. With her publications spanning from 1969 to 2017, it is virtually certain that at least some of them were produced by machines containing computational components, and multiple facsimiles exist on the web. Because her work is nontypographic, it represents the continuation of the gestural component of writing into the computational era. She seemed to want to position her work as if each volume were drawn by hand rather than mediated through the printing process. Writing about her legacy, Will Fenstermaker notes that in many of her books "she discards the identifiable characteristics of books themselves, empty colophons and covers left blank. The books were shipped with inserts denoting the publisher's information, but these were marked with notes requesting that they be discarded."[11] Nevertheless, Dermisache was adamant that her works should take the form of books meant to be read. In an interview, she commented that she wanted to see her work printed "because it was the only space adequate for the graphics to be read. . . . I was radically opposed to putting them on the walls like painting. There are people who saw the books and told me to take out the pages and put them in frames on the wall. I said no, this is not an engraving. It is not a painting. It has to be inside a book, to be read."[12]

For her, then, writing is an act of communication—but what does it communicate? Fenstermaker observes that "the unconscious impulse to write comes before the word, and it does not always take the form of language," a sentiment that Bernard Siegert, with his emphasis on cultural techniques preceding their formal expression, would very much agree with. Fenstermaker continues, "Everything that follows—in how we traditionally conceived of writing—is an attempt to capture that compulsion, to make approximate marks that convey our thoughts to others."

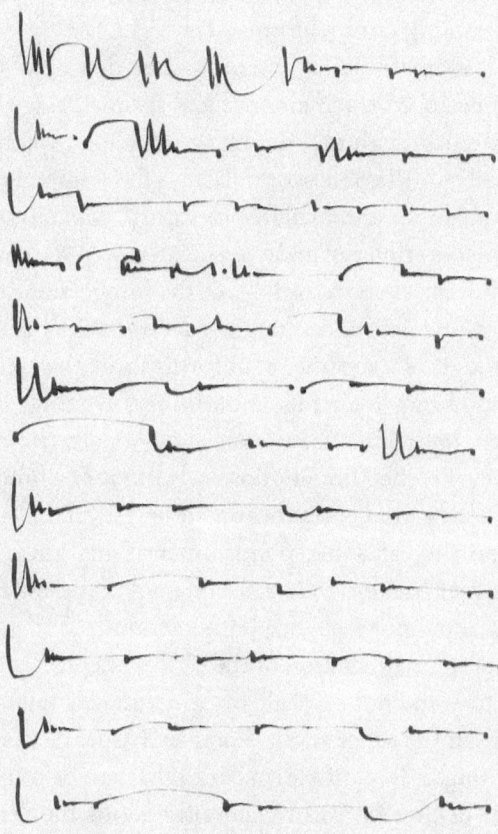

5.4 Mirtha Dermisache, plate 1 in *Selected Writings*, ed. Daniel Owen and Lisa Pearson (Catskill, NY: Siglio/Ugly Duckling Press, 2017).

Source: © Estate of Mirtha Dermisache, Buenos Aires, 2020.
Image courtesy Siglio/Ugly Duckling Press, New York.

Calling Dermisache's asemic writing "a sort of ur-language," he quotes Roland Barthes's letter to Dermisache saying that her work captured "the essence of writing." Concurring, Fenstermaker remarks that she "turned language back into something resembling pure, unformed clay."[13]

If asemic writing communicates first of all a desire to communicate, to reach another and form a bridge between subjectivities through making marks on paper, what does it mean to "read" an illegible work? Each of Dermisache's pages takes a graphic idea and explores its formal possibilities with the kind of elaboration normally associated with language. Whereas a novel, for example, spins out the implications of a character by narrating acts and thoughts, Dermisache's graphemes develop the logic of a specific set of forms through successive variations, amplifying, reducing, modifying, twisting, looping, circling back, inverting. Just as a novel has a narrative trajectory crafted to evoke specific emotions as different points, so her marks embody a kind of rhythm and progression that gives them a temporal arc, at some points intensifying the dramatic tension between background space and mark, at others quieting into subtler and more nuanced interactions. "For me," Dermisache stated, "the liberation of the sign takes place within culture and history and not on their margins. In this sense, my work is not behind the times at all. Graphically speaking, every time I start writing, I develop a formal idea that can be transformed into the idea of time."[14] This temporality marks the deep affinity of her work with writing in the conventional sense. Like ordinary writing, her asemic marks exploit the linear temporality of language but do so in visual rather than semantic registers. "What I did and continue to do," she remarked in an interview in 1972, "is to develop graphic ideas with respect to writing, which in the end, I think, have little to do with political events but with structures and forms of language."[15] Nevertheless, one could argue, as Fenstermaker hints, that the mere act of abandoning traditional writing in an oppressive era when speech and writing are censored constitutes in itself a political act (Dermisache wrote during the years of Argentina's junta rule).

Peter Schwenger, a prominent advocate for and interpreter of asemic writing, sheds light on a political subtext for the asemic in his essay tellingly entitled "Language Will Eat Your Brain." He references a scientific dispute over whether language can be appropriately described as a kind of "beneficial parasite . . . that confers selective advantage upon its human hosts without whom it would not survive."[16] Whereas *The Silent History* and *The Word Exchange* depict viruses that destroy language, there is a counterstory, as Schwenger points out, that positions language itself as a soul-destroying virus and runs from William Burrough's *The Ticket That Exploded* through Tony Burgess's *Pontypool Changes Everything* and Ben Marcus's *The Flame Alphabet*. "The word may once have been a healthy neural cell," Burroughs writes. "It is now a parasitic organism that invades and damages the central nervous system . . . the word is now a virus."[17] Even in as prolanguage a work as *The Word Exchange*, we glimpse the ways in which language replicates through its human hosts—for example, in the name Graedon chooses for her digital device, the Meme.[18] Although her protagonist Ana ultimately rejects the idea, Graedon signals her awareness of theories that argue we are trapped within language: language is the master, we its servants. In this context, the asemic may be positioned as a revolt against language's replicating power.

Rita Raley carries this thought into the computational era of postprint. She suggests that the history of asemic writing in the twentieth and twenty-first centuries can be characterized through three periods, proceeding from Henri Michaux's experiments in the 1920s recalling surrealist experiments in automatic writing to Timothy Ely's "meaningless scriptulations" in the second wave and through to the new millennium, where it joins with theorists such as Vilém Flusser in arguing that alphabetic writing has no future and will be replaced by binary code and other nonlinguistic modes of expression.[19] As Raley points

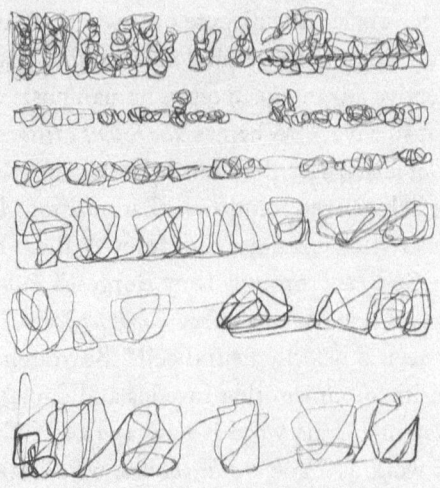

5.5 Mirtha Dermisache, plate 5 in *Selected Writings*.

Source: © Estate of Mirtha Dermisache, Buenos Aires, 2020.
Image courtesy Siglio/Ugly Duckling Press, New York.

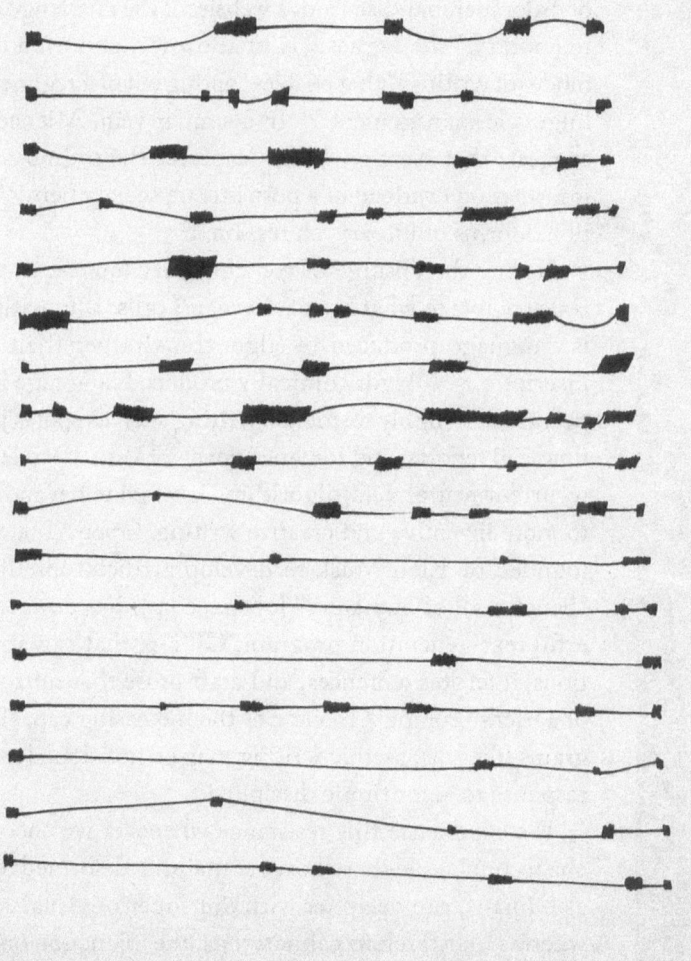

5.6 Mirtha Dermisache, plate 12 in *Selected Writings*.

Source: © Estate of Mirtha Dermisache, Buenos Aires, 2020.
Image courtesy Siglio/Ugly Duckling Press, New York.

out, computers regularly discipline human writing by determining the forms acceptable from an algorithmic point of view, as anyone can attest who has tried to book an airline ticket online or order merchandise from a website. "The challenge of the contemporary," she argues, "is to allow for, and even cultivate, a mode [of writing]" that enables "opting out of a regime of techno-linguistic management."[20] In a similar vein, Michael Jacobson suggests that asemic writing "captures the techno-anxiety and information overload of a post-literate society better than traditional forms of literary expression."[21]

Noting the upsurge of contemporary interest in the asemic, Raley points to what Franco Bernardi calls "automatisms"—that is, language produced by algorithms rather than by human inscriptions.[22] Algorithmically produced language is currently pervasive in highly formulaic writing such as sports journalism, financial reports, and romance novels.[23] With deep learning and recurrent neural nets, algorithms have gone beyond hack work to more inventive and creative writing. OpenAI (a corporation founded by Elon Musk to develop artificial intelligence that "benefits all of humanity" [openai.com]) has developed a powerful text-generation program, GPT-2, that can answer questions, interpret sentences, and craft prose that mirrors the style of a user's prompt.[24] In view of the increasing capacities of programs like this, asemic writing may be positioned as a resistant response to algorithmic discipline.

We experience this resistance whenever we encounter captcha technology—those boxes containing deformed text that we, as humans, can decipher with our superior visual capabilities, whereas (most) robots cannot: thus, the injunction on many such websites, "Prove you're not a robot." In this sense, the distorted alphanumeric characters can be seen as veering toward asemic writing. However, with captcha we are co-opted back into the service of algorithmic instrumentality; when we type the requisite letters into the box, they are regularized and made computer readable—and only then does the algorithm allows us to proceed to the next screen. Unlike captcha, asemic writing has not (yet) been routinized and so remains a form of writing that only humans can understand.

As we plunge deeper into our symbiosis with cognitive media, the asemic reminds us that the foundation on which the postprint era was built—from type pieces fashioned in metal to images flashed on photographic paper and binary signals interpreted as computer codes—originated with human mindbodies wanting to communicate, to express what is known, and to reach toward what may be known but cannot be said with words. If, as Vilém Flusser has argued, alphabetic writing has no future, the asemic will endure as long as there are humans to invest it with meaning and purpose.

Fenstermaker says it best. Ruminating on the end of civilization, "when we find ourselves again huddled in caves by firelight," he imagines that "we won't be reading novels, no, not for some time, but poetry won't be the first thing we restore. In the ruins, the words we once knew will fail us too, and we'll be left scrawling again along the walls in some noble attempt at inventing a new language to capture all that we've seen."[25] Thus, he joins the asemic in the present, figured as a resistance to algorithmic writing, to a postapocalyptic future in which computational media are inoperative and humans must rely once again on their intrinsic cognitions, unaugmented by artificial media. Oddly resonant with the works discussed in chapter 4, this vision of the asemic nevertheless leaves out of account the one aspect that two literary projects discussed in this chapter share—a belief in the endless possibilities of the codex.

Books with and Without Computers

Until as recently as the twentieth century, books were arguably more influential in transmitting, interacting with, modifying, and shaping human cognitions than any invention ever created, save perhaps language itself. They also have a fair claim to be among the most resilient and versatile of technologies. In these pages, we have encountered them as vertical bundles of reeds, rolls of papyrus, sheep skins sown together, pages printed by spinning photographic discs, mass-produced paperbacks, print-on-demand objects rolling off the back of a DocuTech, projected images flashed on a computer screen, books with words and without, books that only humans can read, and others that only computers can parse. Were all of our computational media somehow to crash tonight, never to be resurrected, it is beyond imagination that books would crash too. I have no doubt that whatever the future brings for our species, books will continue to be inscribed, made, read, passed around, and appreciated. In this sense, becoming computational marks only the most recent of the book's instantiations and not necessarily the last.

While this moment lasts, one of its distinctive characteristics is the becoming computational of books and people together. A moment's thought could have predicted that one of our oldest and most pervasive cognitive technologies, the book, would of course interact with computational media, our newest and most powerful symbiont yet. It is fitting that this argument comes to you—how else?—in the form of a book written, designed, formatted, produced, distributed, sold (and perhaps read) with computational media. The postprint carrier of the information partakes of the information about postprint that it carries. This recursivity, as satisfying as it is inevitable, makes and marks the aesthetic of bookishness in the twenty-first century.[26]

Epilogue

Picturing the Asemic

One final anecdote. During my stay at Uppsala University in Sweden in 2018, my host, Danuta Fjellestad, organized a one-day symposium around my work. To enrich the experience, she included an art exhibit of photographs by Nick Sergeant, husband of a colleague. In a typically generous gesture, she offered to gift one of these photographs to me, asking me to choose my favorite. All were attractive, but because my lecture that day was based on the material I discuss in chapter 5, I was drawn to an image that seemed to suggest asemic writing: although it was not decipherable as language, something about its horizontal lines and looping figures suggested handwriting.

When I asked Nick about its provenance, he said that he had been passing an official-looking door when he noticed that on each side there were imprints of plaques that had been removed, leaving behind the glue marks used to affix them. The photograph, he explained, depicted one of those imprints; he also had an image of its companion, obviously similar in form but different in details. He suggested that I could have both and display them as a diptych.

As I look at these photographs framed in my study where I am typing these lines, aware that I am thereby enmeshed in selective asemiosis, I see the marks of a human hand intent upon

Epilogue: Picturing the Asemic

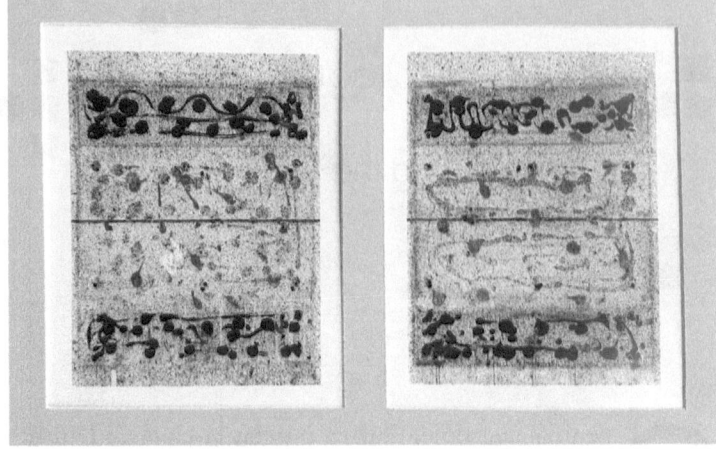

6.1 Nick Sergeant, "The Human Stain," 2018.

Source: From the collection of Katherine Hayles. Image courtesy of Nicholas Gessler.

its work of preparing the surface for an inscription that will be incised in letters and read by passersby to indicate a building's official functions. But underneath and unseen until circumstances drastically alter those functions is an ur-language that speaks no words but still conveys meaning through the gestural traces made by a human hand.

The images came from a wall and through several mediating and remediating processes now once again hang on a wall. But that is not the only place they are manifested; they are also imprinted on the pages of this book. I might end by citing the earlier quotation from Mirtha Dermisache: "It has to be inside a book, to be read." And so it is.

Notes

1. Introducing Postprint

1. For $37,500, you, too, can own this first edition; see https://www.abebooks .com/servlet/BookDetailsPL?bi=9075319536&searchurl=an%3Dwillia m%2Bfaulkner%26sortby%3D1%26tn%3Dsound%2Band%2Bfury&cm _sp=snippet-_-srp1-_-image1.
2. Alexander Starre, *Metamedia: American Book Fictions and Literary Print Culture After Digitization* (Iowa City: University of Iowa Press, 2015), 15.
3. Elizabeth J. Eisenstein, *The Printing Press as an Agent of Change* (Cambridge: Cambridge University Press, 1979); Adrian Johns, *The Nature of the Books: Print and Knowledge in the Making* (Chicago: University of Chicago Press, 1998).
4. Amaranth Borsuk, *The Book* (Cambridge, MA: MIT Press, 2018), 206, 11.
5. Jessica Pressman, "The Aesthetic of Bookishness in Twenty-First Century Literature: Steven Hall's *The Raw Shark Texts*," *Michigan Quarterly Review* 48, no. 4 (Fall 2009): not paginated.
6. N. Katherine Hayles and Jessica Pressman, eds., *Comparative Textual Media: Transforming the Humanities in the Postprint Era* (Minneapolis: University of Minnesota Press, 2013); Jeff Gomez, *Print Is Dead: Books in Our Digital Age* (London: Palgrave Macmillan, 2007); N. Katherine Hayles, *Writing Machines* (Cambridge, MA: MIT Press, 2002), 18–33.
7. Hayles, *Writing Machines*. Anne Burdick was the book's designer at MIT Press, not a coauthor, but her work was indeed a collaboration, and she deserves to have it recognized.
8. Borsuk, *The Book*, 40.
9. N. Katherine Hayles, *How We Became Posthuman: Virtual Bodies in Cybernetics, Literature, and Informatics* (Chicago: University of Chicago Press,

1. Introducing Postprint

1999); *My Mother Was a Computer: Digital Subjects and Literary Texts* (Chicago: University of Chicago Press, 2005); *How We Think: Digital Media and Contemporary Technogenesis* (Chicago: University of Chicago Press, 2012); *Unthought: The Power of the Cognitive Nonconscious* (Chicago: University of Chicago Press, 2017).

10. See, for example, Jesper Hoffmeyer, *Signs of Meaning in the Universe* (Bloomington: Indiana University Press, 1997); Terrence Deacon, *The Symbolic Species: The Co-evolution of Language and the Brain* (New York: Norton, 1998); and Wendy Wheeler, *Expecting the Earth: Life/Culture/Biosemiotics* (London: Lawrence and Wishart, 2016).
11. See Jacob Von Uexküll, *A Foray Into the Worlds of Animals and Humans: With a Theory of Meaning* (Minneapolis: University of Minnesota Press, 2010).
12. See N. Katherine Hayles, "Can Computers Create Meanings? A Cyber/Bio/Semiotic Perspective," *Critical Inquiry* 46, no. 1 (2019): 32–55.
13. IBM is developing a chip that works on synapses rather than on circuits—hence, the term *neuromorphic*. The acronym SyNAPSE stands for "Systems of Neuromorphic Adaptive Plastic Scalable Electronics." IBM bills this project as combining the brain's architecture and efficiency with the programmable properties of a chip (IBM, "The Brain's Architecture, Efficiency . . . on a Chip," *IBM Research Blog*, December 19, 2016, https://www.ibm.com/blogs/research/2016/12/the-brains-architecture-efficiency-on-a-chip/).
14. To see the robots in action, check out "Boston Dynamics Robot Can Stack Boxes with Amazing Ease," YouTube video, March 30, 2019, https://www.youtube.com/watch?v=uuO6oeOo-ts.
15. See Bruno Latour, *Reassembling the Social: An Introduction to Actor-Network-Theory* (Oxford: Oxford University Press, 2007), 63–86.
16. Gilles Deleuze and Felix Guattari, *A Thousand Plateaus: Capitalism and Schizophrenia*, trans. Brian Massumi (Minneapolis: University of Minnesota Press, 1987), 39–75.
17. See, for example, Gilbert Simondon, *On the Mode of Existence of Technical Objects*, trans. Cecile Malaspina and John Rogove (Minneapolis: University of Minnesota Press, 2017), and Alfred North Whitehead, *Process and Reality* (New York: Free Press, 1979).
18. See, for example, Jennifer Gabrys, *Program Earth* (Minneapolis: University of Minnesota Press, 2016).
19. Johanna Drucker, *SpecLab: Digital Aesthetics and Projects in Speculative Computing* (Chicago: University of Chicago Press, 2009); Matthew Kirschenbaum, *Track Changes: A Literary History of Word Processing*

1. Introducing Postprint

(Cambridge, MA: Belknap Press of Harvard University Press, 2016); Dennis Tenen, *Plain Text: The Poetics of Computation* (Stanford, CA: Stanford University Press, 2017); Borsuk, *The Book*.

20. I have been exploring the idea of cognitive assemblages in relation to literary texts and writing for some years. See the following essays to follow this line of thought: "Cognitive Assemblages: Technical Agency and Human Interactions," *Critical Inquiry* 43, no. 1 (Autumn 2016): 32–55; "Literary Texts as Cognitive Assemblages: The Case of Electronic Literature," *Electronic Book Review*, August 5, 2018, http://electronicbookreview.com/essay/literary-texts-as-cognitive-assemblages-the-case-of-electronic-literature/; "Writing//Posthuman: The Literary Text as Cognitive Assemblage," *Theoretical Studies in Literature and Art* 38, no. 3 (2018): 6–21.
21. Borsuk, *The Book*, 147.
22. Borsuk, *The Book*, 147, 247.
23. Amaranth Borsuk and Brad Bouse, *Between Page and Screen* (Denver: SpringGun, 2016).
24. Garrett Stewart, *Book Text Medium: Cross Sectional Reading for a Digital Age* (Cambridge: Cambridge University Press, forthcoming), 3. I am grateful to Garrett Stewart for generously providing me with a PDF version of his manuscript before its publication. The page numbers cited here refer to the manuscript PDF.
25. Garrett Stewart, *Bookwork: Medium to Object to Concept to Art* (Chicago: University of Chicago Press, 2011).
26. Stewart, *Book Text Medium*, 23.
27. Amy Hungerford, *Making Literature Now* (Stanford, CA: Stanford University Press, 2016).
28. Eli Horowitz, Matthew Derby, and Kevin Moffett, *The Silent History* (New York: Farrar, Straus and Giroux, 2014); J. J. Abrams and Doug Dorst, *Ship of Theseus* (New York: Mulholland, 2013).
29. Hungerford, *Making Literature Now*, 110.
30. Jay David Bolter, *Writing Space: The Computer, Hypertext, and the History of Writing* (1990; reprint, New York: Routledge, 2001), 3, quoted in Ted Striphas, *The Late Age of Print: Everyday Book Culture from Consumerism to Control* (New York: Columbia University Press, 2009), 3.
31. Striphas, *The Late Age of Print*, 3.
32. Striphas, *The Late Age of Print*, 93–94.
33. Striphas, *The Late Age of Print*, 98.
34. Alexander Starre, *Metamedia: American Book Fictions and Literary Print Culture After Digitization* (Iowa City: University of Iowa Press, 2015), 8.

35. Mark Danielewski, *House of Leaves*, 2nd ed. (New York: Pantheon, 2000); Jonathan Safran Foer, *Extremely Loud and Incredibly Close* (New York: Houghton Mifflin, 2005), and *Tree of Codes* (London: Visual Editions, 2010).
36. Starre, *Metamedia*, 13.
37. Starre, *Metamedia*, 55.
38. Wolfgang Ernst, *Memory and the Digital Archive* (Minneapolis: University of Minnesota Press, 2012), 55.
39. Ian Bogost, *Alien Phenomenology, or What's It Like to Be a Thing* (Minneapolis: University of Minnesota Press, 2012), 65–66.
40. Ernst, *Memory and the Digital Archive*, 55.
41. Ernst, *Memory and the Digital Archive*, 56.
42. Jussi Parikka, *What Is Media Archaeology?* (London: Polity, 2012), 74.
43. Lori Emerson, *Reading Writing Interfaces: From the Digital to the Bookbound* (Minneapolis: University of Minnesota Press, 2014).
44. Simondon, *On the Mode of Existence of Technical Objects*, 2.
45. Friedrich A. Kittler, *Discourse Networks, 1800/1900*, trans. Michael Metteer (Stanford, CA: Stanford University Press, 1992).
46. Ernst, *Memory and the Digital Archive*, 45.
47. Bernhard Siegert, *Cultural Techniques: Grids, Filters, Doors, and Other Articulations of the Real*, trans. Geoffrey Winthrop-Young (New York: Fordham University Press, 2015), 11, also quoting Thomas Macho, "Zeit und Zahl: Kalender- und Zeitrechnung als Kurturtechniken," in *Bild-Schrift-Zahl*, ed. Sybille Krämer and Horst Bredekamp (Munich: Wilhelm Fink, 2003), 179.
48. In the "nothing new under the sun" department, I note that a similar debate raged in cultural anthropology during the 1980s and 1990s. Under the banner of "cultural materialism," anthropologists such as Marvin Harris urged anthropologists to study material culture (artifacts, everyday objects, cooking utensils, and so forth) and behavior rather than use the method of selecting a native informant and asking him questions, a practice that revolved almost entirely around beliefs and concepts rather than around practices. See, for example, Marvin Harris, *Cultural Materialism: The Struggle for a Science of Culture* (1979; reprint, Lanham, MD: AltaMira Press, 2001).
49. Siegert, *Cultural Techniques*, 9, 11, emphasis in original.
50. Siegert, *Cultural Techniques*, 14.
51. Mark B. N. Hanson, *Feed-Forward: On the Future of Twenty-First-Century Media* (Chicago: Chicago University Press, 2015); Erich Hörl, *General Ecology: The New Ecological Paradigm* (London: Bloomsbury Academic, 2017).

2. Print Into Postprint

52. For these examples and more, see Oguz Ali Acar and Jan van den Ende, "Knowledge Distance, Cognitive-Search Processes, and Creativity: The Making of Winning Solutions in Science Contests," *Psychological Science* 27, no. 5 (2016): 692–99.
53. Alena Graedon, *The Word Exchange* (New York: Anchor Books, 2014).
54. Vilém Flusser, *Does Writing Have a Future?*, trans. Nancy Ann Roth (Minneapolis: University of Minnesota Press, 2011), and *Into the Universe of Technical Images*, trans. Nancy Ann Roth (Minneapolis: University of Minnesota Press, 2011).

2. Print Into Postprint

I am grateful to Matthew Kirschenbaum and John W. Maxwell for comments and suggestions on a draft of this chapter. Their remarkable stores of knowledge certainly made the chapter more accurate; of course, any errors that remain are entirely my responsibility.

1. John Maxwell reminds me that Charles Babbage proposed a printing device that would connect to his Analytical Engine, although it was never actually built.
2. Mark Twain, memorandum, quoted in Albert Bigelow Paine, *Mark Twain: A Biography*, 4 vols. (New York: Harper, 1912), 2:chap. 174, https://www.gutenberg.org/files/2988/2988-h/2988-h.htm.
3. Paine, *Mark Twain*, 2:chap. 174.
4. How complex was the Paige Compositor? Wendell Oswald, an anthropologist, developed a quantitative measure for complexity by counting the number of *different* individual units in an artifact, which he called "techno-units" (*Anthropological Analysis of Food-Getting Technologies* [New York: Wiley-Interscience, 1976]); a hundred identical screws would thus count as one techno-unit. Although this approach works well for Paleolithic technologies (a bow, for example, is more complex than a flint), it becomes problematic in the electronic age. Does a computer chip count as one techno-unit, despite having hundreds of circuits inscribed on it? The problem is that as information technologies have proliferated, their complexity has to do rather with their ability to manipulate flows of information, which correlates with the complexity of their software architectures rather than with the number of mechanical parts. These are the kinds of complexities that Oswald's scheme does not capture. In 2012, a team of anthropologists from UCLA expanded Oswald's method to "procedural units," which they defined as "mutually exclusive manufacturing steps that make a distinct contribution to the finished form of a technology" (Charles Perreault, Jeffrey Brantingham, Steven L. Kuhn,

Sarah Wurz, and Xing Goa, "Measuring the Complexity of Lithic Technology," *Current Anthropology* 54, supplement 8 [December 2013]: S397). This transition from parts to processes perhaps provides for a better understanding of contemporary complexity, although by focusing on *manufacturing* steps, it still is not adequate for grasping the complexities of informational media. It is an interesting question which machine would count as more complex, the Paige Compositor or the DocuTech discussed at the end of this chapter. Is a line of code a techno-unit? If so, then the DocuTech beats the Compositor hands down because it had well more than a million lines of code (in addition to all its mechanical parts).

5. Cornell University also had a Paige Compositor but donated it for iron scrap during World War II.
6. Paine, *Mark Twain*, 2:911; Mark Twain, quoted in "Notes on Typesetter," n.d., Mark Twain Museum Archives, Hartford, CT.
7. Mergenthaler Linotype Company, *Linotype Machine Principles* (New York: Mergenthaler Linotype Company, 1940), 1–39.
8. John M. Maxwell, private e-mail to the author, April 16, 2018.
9. Matthew Kirschenbaum, *Track Changes: A Literary History of Word Processing* (Cambridge, MA: Belknap Press of Harvard University Press, 2016).
10. Matthew Kirschenbaum, private e-mail to the author, January 8, 2018.
11. An exception is Kirschenbaum's discussion of how in 1972–1973 Peter Weiner, having previously worked with Alvin Eisenman to connect a Mergenthaler Super-Quick phototypesetting machine to the PDPII mainframe computer at Yale University, then enlisted creative writer and essayist John Hersey to produce his latest book using editing software called the Yale Editor. As Kirschenbaum makes clear, the Yale Editor not only used a cathode ray tube interface to input the text but also created "an actual computational model of text that it instantiated" (*Track Changes*, 134). That is, rather than encoding the text as a linear string of alphanumeric symbols, it treated the display as one quadrant of a two-dimensional sheet of paper. In this sense, it anticipated the full-page description software developed by John Warnock and Charles Geschke at Adobe in the early 1980s.
12. Frank Romano, *History of the Phototypesetting Era* (San Luis Obispo: California Polytechnic State University, 2014), 77.
13. Romano, *History of the Phototypesetting Era*, vii.
14. Louis Moyroud, MIT seminar, c. 1970s, transcript printed in Romano, *History of the Phototypesetting Era*, 65.

2. Print Into Postprint

15. Moyroud seminar, in Romano, *History of the Phototypesetting Era*, 66.
16. The electronic photocomposition system invented by Fairchild Semiconductor in the 1960s, for example, used a Fairchild keyboard without a display. The typist was required to check the accuracy of a line by typing it a second time. If the two lines matched, then a bell rang, and the machine produced a punched paper tape, which was then fed into a photosetting device. If the lines failed to match, then the typist had to start over from the beginning—a nightmare for someone like me, who makes frequent typing mistakes.
17. Moyroud seminar, in Romano, *History of the Phototypesetting Era*, 67.
18. Moyroud seminar, in Romano, *History of the Phototypesetting Era*, 68.
19. Romano, *History of the Phototypesetting Era*, 73.
20. Romano, *History of the Phototypesetting Era*, 72.
21. Moyroud seminar, in Romano, *History of the Phototypesetting Era*, 68.
22. Graphic Arts Research Foundation, *Report to the Subscribers* (Reston, VA: Graphic Arts Research Foundation, 1952), quoted in Romano, *History of the Phototypesetting Era*, 76.
23. John Maxwell notes that the Interface Photosetter used "photographic negatives in the middle" of the brass negatives and that the Linofilm, a second-generation phototypesetter by Mergenthaler, also used photographic techniques (private communication, May 16, 2018). However, it was the Lumitype that initiated this line of development.
24. Examination of the C/A/T fiber bundle under a microscope revealed more than ten thousand square bundles, in each of which were additional thousands of fibers.
25. Here is Nicholas Gessler's description of the fiber-optic cable shown in figure 2.9: "This flexible coherent fiber optic bundle has image input and output windows measuring 8.0 by 10.5mm. In the finished window an array of approximately 140 by 180 square mini-bundles may be seen with a low power microscope. These, in turn, contain mini-mini-bundles of individual fibers. Assuming a typical fiber size of 10u, the finished window has an image area of 840,000 fibers, or pixels, a megapixel being sufficient resolution for a letter of print" (private e-mail to the author, July 7, 2017).
26. Schott North America, *An Introduction to Fiber Optic Imaging*, 2nd ed. (Southridge, MA: Schott North America, 2007), 8, 48. Thanks to Nicholas Gessler for drawing this source to my attention.
27. For details, see on YouTube the "Computerphile" videos by Professor Tim Brailsford—for example, "Printing and Typesetting History," December 15, 2013, https://www.youtube.com/watch?v=HdModNEH_1U.

2. Print Into Postprint

28. Dennis Tenen, *Plain Text: The Poetics of Computation* (Stanford, CA: Stanford University Press, 2017), 117.
29. Romano, *History of the Phototypesetting Era*, 3.
30. Albro Gaul, *The Wonderful World of Insects* (New York: Rinehart, 1953), n.p., end of book.
31. Edward Webster, *Print Unchained: Fifty Years of Digital Printing: 1950–2000 and Beyond* (Burlington VT: DRA of Vermont Inc., 2001), 109.
32. John Warnock, quoted in Webster, *Print Unchained*, 162.
33. Dick Hackborn, interview, n.d., reprinted in Webster, *Print Unchained*, 164, emphasis in original. I wondered about the name "LaserJet" because laser technology was in fact sharply distinguished from ink jet technology, and the two methods were pursued through different lines of development within HP. Hackborn clears up the mystery when he tells Webster a "fun story." He comments that the HP ink jet printer was marketed as "Think Jet," its name a condensation of *thermal* and *ink*. When the new laser printer was ready, some of the marketing people suggested "LaserJet" by analogy. Hackborn recounts that "we engineers all said, 'No, there's no "jet" in this machine. It is lying to the market! The market won't go for it!'" (quoted in Webster, *Print Unchained*, 173). History shows how little factuality matters when it comes to deciding on a successful marketing name.
34. Webster, *Print Unchained*, 164–65.
35. Chip Holt, the manager who masterminded the DocuTech, defines *print-on-demand* as "the ability to print current/variable data at the place and time of need" (interview by Edward Webster, 1999, in Webster, *Print Unchained*, 190).
36. Holt interview, in Webster, *Print Unchained*, 188–89.
37. Holt interview, in Webster, *Print Unchained*, 191, 187.
38. Holt interview, in Webster, *Print Unchained*, 189.
39. Holt interview, in Webster, *Print Unchained*, 190.
40. Sarah Spiekermann, *Ethical IT Innovation: A Value-Based System Design Approach* (Boca Raton, FL: Auerbach, Taylor & Francis, 2015), 43.
41. Spiekermann, *Ethical IT Innovation*, 11.
42. Spiekermann, *Ethical IT Innovation*, 13, 10, 12, emphasis in original.
43. Efforts to combat this problem include the development of open-access software and open-access publishing; the latter issue is discussed at length in chapter 3.
44. I use the term *e-book* to refer to the digital file displayed on an e-reader; in contrast, I use *e-reader* to refer to the device.

2. Print Into Postprint

45. The iPad recognizes these gestures specifically: tap and double tap, drag, flick, swipe, pinch, touch and hold, shake, and multifinger press.
46. It is worth mentioning here the work of the Institute for the Future of the Book, Bob Stein's brainchild, and its efforts to develop Sophie as an easy-to-use software tool that enables collaborative authoring and reading in rich multimedia environments. The webpage on Sophie 2.0 states, "Sophie is intended to redefine the 'book' as we know it, and to provide mechanisms for reader feedback and interactive conversation" ("About Sophie 2.0," December 15, 2008, http://sophie2.org/trac/wiki/AboutPage).
47. Ted Striphas, *The Late Age of Print: Everyday Book Culture from Consumerism to Control* (New York: Columbia University Press, 2009), 27, 29. See also John B. Thompson, *Books in the Digital Age: The Transformation of Academic and Higher Education Publishing in Britain and the United States* (Cambridge: Polity Press, 2005).
48. The original Bernays campaign and its aftershocks succeeded so well, in fact, that Amy Hungerford complains about a surfeit of contemporary fiction, noting that the "number of new novels published in the United States alone each year has risen from less than 10,000 in 1990 (a level that had been sustained since the 1940s) to upward of 55,000 in 2010" (*Making Literature Now* [Stanford, CA: Stanford University Press, 2016], 14).
49. Edward L. Bernays, quoted in Striphas, *The Late Age of Print*, 35.
50. Striphas, *The Late Age of Print*, 37, 38.
51. Mike Masnick, "Another Reminder That You Don't Own Your eBooks: Amazon Removing More eBooks You 'Bought' from Archives," *Techdirt*, December 15, 2010, https://www.techdirt.com/articles/20101215/02571612282/another-reminder-that-you-dont-own-your-ebooks-amazon-removing-more-ebooks-you-bought-archives.shtml.
52. N. Katherine Hayles, *How We Became Posthuman: Virtual Bodies in Cybernetics, Literature, and Informatics* (Chicago: University of Chicago Press, 1999).
53. Tenen, *Plain Text*, 3, 39, 129.
54. Mireille Hildebrandt, *Smart Technologies and the End(s) of Law* (Cheltenham, U.K.: Edward Edgar, 2015), 137–58; Tenen, *Plain Text*, 129.
55. Tenen, *Plain Text*, 4.
56. Tenen, *Plain Text*, 91.
57. Tenen, *Plain Text*, 89, 26, 36, 164.
58. Tenen, *Plain Text*, 40.

3. The Mixed Ecologies of University Presses

1. These examples are given in Edward Webster, *Print Unchained: Fifty Years of Digital Printing: 1950–2000 and Beyond* (Burlington, VT: DRA of Vermont Inc., 2001), 133.
2. Dennis Tenen, *Plain Text: The Poetics of Computation* (Stanford, CA: Stanford University Press, 2017), 7.
3. John B. Thompson, *Books in the Digital Age: The Transformation of Academic and Higher Education Publishing in Britain and the United States* (Cambridge: Polity Press, 2005), 93–107.
4. Tenen, *Plain Text*, 4.
5. In the interest of full disclosure, here are my ties to these university presses: I am currently writing this book under contract to Columbia University Press and have in process a proposal for another book with it. University of Chicago Press has been my publisher for more than twenty years, and I have worked closely with Alan Thomas, the editor there. I codirect the Electronic Mediations series with the University of Minnesota Press. I have also served on the Editorial Board of Duke University Press and was a faculty member at Duke University for ten years. Although not officially allied with the University of California Press, I hold the position of Distinguished Research Professor at the University of California, Los Angeles, where I spent fifteen years on the faculty.

    My readers should know that I sent copies of the relevant interview material to each participant quoted here, and each was allowed to modify, delete, or otherwise revise their comments as desired. Some chose to excise candid or gritty comments that I would have liked to keep, but I thought professional ethics dictated that I would publish only those comments that they approved of when given time for reflection and thought.
6. Examples of such premature closure are legion, from Adobe's decision no longer to support Flash, the favored software for electronic literature in the new millennium, to Google Earth's decision no longer to support certain mapping functionalities, a move that dealt a death blow to projects such as Todd Presner's HyperCities initiative.
7. Jennifer Crewe, interview by the author, Columbia University Press, New York, May 18, 2017; all statements by Crewe come from this interview except where noted.
8. Thompson, *Books in the Digital Age*, 93–94.
9. Jennifer Crewe, "The Future of the University Press: How Should the University Press Role in Hiring and Promotion Change?" *Chronicle of Higher Education*, June 4, 2017.

3. The Mixed Ecologies of University Presses

10. Michael Haskell, interview by the author, Columbia University Press, New York, May 18, 2017.
11. Philip Leventhal, interview by the author, Columbia University Press, New York, May 18, 2017.
12. Garrett Kiely, interview by the author, Chicago University Press, July 24, 2017.
13. Alan Thomas, interview by the author, Chicago University Press, July 24, 2017.
14. Dean Blobaum, interview by the author, Chicago University Press, July 24, 2017.
15. Krista Coulson, interview by the author, Chicago University Press, July 24, 2017.
16. Alan Thomas, private e-mail to the author, January 16, 2018.
17. Steve Cohn, interview by the author, Duke University Press, Durham, NC, November 8, 2017.
18. Kenneth Wissoker, Duke University Press, Durham, NC, phone interview by the author, November 7, 2017.
19. Aimee Meredith Cox, *Shapeshifters: Black Girls and the Choreography of Citizenship* (Durham, NC: Duke University Press, 2015).
20. Kathleen Fitzpatrick, Michigan State University, East Lansing, phone interview by the author, June 5, 2017; Christopher Kelty, interview by the author, University of California, Los Angeles, June 8, 2017; Todd Presner, interview by the author, University of California, Los Angeles, June 19, 2017. All quotations from Fitzpatrick, Kelty, and Presner are from these interviews unless otherwise noted.
21. Nancy L. Maron, Christine Mulhern, Daniel Rossman, and Kimberly Schmelzinger, "The Costs of Publishing Monographs: Toward a Transparent Methodology," *JEP: Journal of Electronic Publishing* 19, no. 1 (February 5, 2016), https://quod.lib.umich.edu/j/jep/3336451.0019.103?view=text;rgn=main.
22. Christopher Kelty, in an e-mail dated January 6, 2018, offered this comment on the economics of monograph publishing: "The reality is that most of the scholarly presses in existence rely on a kind of 'blockbuster' model, where 9 of 10 books lose money, and one of them sells 10 or 20K copies and covers the losses on the others. But those 9 books remain inaccessible rather than open, in the hopes that eventually, over the long run, they will recoup the $35K it cost to produce them. This is largely an accounting problem, not an economic one: do you measure your costs in aggregate or per unit? If a press succeeds with 1 out of every 10 books, and that keeps them above water, what justifies keeping the other 9

3. The Mixed Ecologies of University Presses

locked up?" Kelty is correct about the "blockbuster" aspect, which Jennifer Crewe called the "right mix" approach. However, what his comment does not capture is that the nine other books (I am not sure if that proportion is accurate) do bring in some income, even though they may lose money overall, and this income would be lost if a press were to go entirely to an open-access format.

23. Kathleen Fitzpatrick, *Planned Obsolescence: Publishing, Technology, and the Future of the Academy* (New York: New York University Press, 2011).
24. Christopher Kelty, *Two Bits: The Cultural Significance of Free Software* (Durham, NC: Duke University Press, 2008).
25. Todd Presner, David Shepard, and Yoh Kawano, *HyperCities: Thick Mapping in the Digital Humanities* (Cambridge, MA: Harvard University Press, 2014).
26. Todd Presner, "Mapping Jewish Los Angeles," 2017, http://www.mappingjewishla.org/.
27. See Christopher Johanson and Diane Favro, "Death in Motion: Funeral Processions in the Roman Forum," *Journal of the Society of Architectural History* 69, no. 1 (2010): 12–37.
28. John Unsworth, "The Humanist: 'Dances with Wolves' or 'Bowls Alone'?," paper presented at the Association of Research Libraries conference "Scholarly Tribes and Tribulations: How Tradition and Technology Are Driving Disciplinary Change," Washington, DC, 2003, http://www.arl.org/wp-content/uploads/2007/07/scholarly-tribes-unsworth-17oct03.pdf.
29. Todd Presner, private e-mail to the author, January 25, 2018.
30. Douglas Armato, University of Minnesota Press, Minneapolis, phone interview by the author, August 7, 2017.
31. John Hartigan, *Social Theory for Nonhumans*, Manifold ed. (Minneapolis: University of Minnesota Press, 2018), https://manifold.umn.edu/project/social-theory-for-nonhumans; Grant Wythoff, *The Perversity of Things: Hugo Gernsback on Media, Tinkering, and Scientifiction*, Manifold ed. (Minneapolis: University of Minnesota Press, 2017), https://manifold.umn.edu/project/the-perversity-of-things; Stephanie Boluk and Patrick Lemieux, *Metagaming: Playing, Competing, Spectating, Cheating, Trading, and Making and Breaking Videogames*, Manifold ed. (Minneapolis: University of Minnesota Press, 2017), https://manifold.umn.edu/project/metagaming.
32. Grant Wythoff, *The Perversity of Things: Hugo Gernsback on Media, Tinkering, and Scientifiction* (Minneapolis: University of Minnesota Press,

4. Postprint and Cognitive Contagion

2016); Stephanie Boluk and Patrick Lemieux, *Metagaming: Playing, Competing, Spectating, Cheating, Trading, and Making and Breaking Videogames* (Minneapolis: University of Minnesota Press, 2017).

33. Stanford University Press, "Publishing Digital Scholarship," n.d., https://www.sup.org/digital/.
34. Mark Amerika, *Remixthebook* (Minneapolis: University of Minnesota Press, 2011).
35. See Tom Mitchell et al., "NELL: Never Ending Language Learning," Read the Web, Carnegie Mellon University, n.d., http://rtw.ml.cmu.edu/rtw/; DeepMind, "AlphaGoZero: Learning from Scratch," October 18, 2017, https://deepmind.com/blog/alphago-zero-learning-scratch/.
36. Tenen, *Plain Text*, 93.
37. See N. Katherine Hayles, *How We Think: Contemporary Technogenesis and Digital Media* (Chicago: University of Chicago Press, 2012).

4. Postprint and Cognitive Contagion

1. See, for example, Terrence Deacon, *The Symbolic Species: The Co-evolution of Language and the Brain* (New York: Norton, 1998).
2. N. Katherine Hayles, *How We Think: Contemporary Technogenesis and Digital Media* (Chicago: University of Chicago Press, 2012).
3. N. Katherine Hayles, "How We Read: Close, Hyper, Machine," *ADE Bulletin* 150 (2011), http://www.ade.org/bulletin/.
4. See Nicholas Carr, *The Shallows: What the Internet Is Doing to Our Brain* (New York: Norton, 2011); Bernard Stiegler, *Taking Care of Youth and the Generations* (Stanford, CA: Stanford University Press, 2010); Thomas H. Davenport and John C. Beck, *The Attention Economy: Understanding the New Currency of Business*, rev. ed. (Cambridge, MA: Harvard Business Review Press, 2002).
5. Dennis Tenen, *Plain Text: The Poetics of Computation* (Stanford, CA: Stanford University Press, 2017), 156.
6. Tenen, *Plain Text*, 123, 2, 4.
7. To be fair to Thoreau, I recognize that his stance toward language, as distinct from the unsayable, is considerably more complex than I represent here.
8. Amy Hungerford, *Making Literature Now* (Stanford, CA: Stanford University Press, 2016), 106–7.
9. Matthew Derby, "Visual Essay Series: An Interview with Matthew Derby," interview by Sarah Minor, *Essay Daily*, February 2016, https://www.essaydaily.org/2016/02/visual-essay-series-interview-with.html.

10. Eli Horowitz, Matthew Derby, and Kevin Moffett, *The Silent History* (New York: Farrar, Straus and Giroux, 2014), 9.
11. Derby, "Visual Essay Series."
12. Hungerford, *Making Literature Now*, 110.
13. Derby, "Visual Essay Series."
14. Hungerford, *Making Literature Now*, 118.
15. Derby, "Visual Essay Series."
16. Horowitz, Derby, and Moffett, *The Silent History*, 352, 46, 209.
17. Horowitz, Derby, and Moffett, *The Silent History*, 51, 8; ellipses indicate omitted text unless otherwise noted.
18. Horowitz, Derby, and Moffett, *The Silent History*, 82.
19. In the app version, it is Theodore who invents the implant, a development that makes him an even more compromised figure than he is in the codex, where the app invention is a collaborative effort between Burnham and a minor character, Prashant Nuregesan.
20. Horowitz, Derby, and Moffett, *The Silent History*, 99, 101, ellipses in original.
21. Horowitz, Derby, and Moffett, *The Silent History*, 68, 41.
22. Horowitz, Derby, and Moffett, *The Silent History*, 347, 288.
23. Horowitz, Derby, and Moffett, *The Silent History*, 350–52.
24. Horowitz, Derby, and Moffett, *The Silent History*, 395.
25. Horowitz, Derby, and Moffett, *The Silent History*, 410.
26. Horowitz, Derby, and Moffett, *The Silent History*, 418.
27. Horowitz, Derby, and Moffett, *The Silent History*, 455, 463–64.
28. Horowitz, Derby, and Moffett, *The Silent History*, 464–65, emphasis in original.
29. Curious about how the authors contrived to make Slash's intervention even remotely plausible, considering that the mediating PhonCom network had crashed, I found a sentence buried back in the part where Calvin is wearing the calibration helmet the night the servers are bombed. He offhandedly remarks, "The helmet ran on a local dev branch that had its own language bank so it could operate independently from PhonCom" (Horowitz, Derby, and Moffett, *The Silent History*, 351). A Band-Aid attempting to cover the narrative gap, to be sure, but maybe it's better than nothing.
30. Horowitz, Derby, and Moffett, *The Silent History*, 481.
31. Horowitz, Derby, and Moffett, *The Silent History*, 503.
32. See Octavia Butler's story "Speech Sounds," in *Bloodchild and Other Stories* (New York: Seven Stories/Penguin, 2005), 87–110, for a harsher and

4. Postprint and Cognitive Contagion

undoubtedly more realistic vision of what humans without language would be like.
33. Horowitz, Derby, and Moffett, *The Silent History*, 512.
34. Horowitz, Derby, and Moffett, *The Silent History*, 513.
35. These lines were written before the novel coronavirus pandemic, and they are even more true now in the era of social distancing and economic lockdown.
36. Hayles, "How We Read."
37. Tenen, *Plain Text*, 4.
38. Alena Graedon, *The Word Exchange* (New York: Anchor Books, 2014), 48.
39. Graedon, *The Word Exchange*, 67, 70, 75; ellipses indicate omitted text in all instances.
40. Alan Lui, *The Laws of Cool: Knowledge Work and the Culture of Information* (Chicago: University of Chicago Press, 2004).
41. Since the "Meme" is mentioned in *The Silent History* as the digital device used to record the Testimonials, the use of this name in *The Word Exchange* may be Graedon's homage to that work. Although the print version of *The Silent History* was published the same year as Graedon's novel, it is possible that it was available earlier or that she had read the iPhone app version.
42. Graedon, *The Word Exchange*, 12, 85.
43. Graedon, *The Word Exchange*, 106.
44. Graedon, *The Word Exchange*, 107–8; see also Neal Stephenson, *Snow Crash* (New York: Del Rey, 2000). In chapter 2, we saw that the name "LaserJet" was a (technically inaccurate) play on *inkjet*. Graedon takes this liberty one step further with *biojet*, which ironically is more technically accurate in the sense that the device injects itself into the user's cognitive functioning.
45. Graedon, *The Word Exchange*, 194.
46. Stiegler, *Taking Care of Youth and the Generations*, 202, 78, 96, 98, 147.
47. Graedon, *The Word Exchange*, 90.
48. Graedon, *The Word Exchange*, 84, 289.
49. Graedon, *The Word Exchange*, 188.
50. Graedon, *The Word Exchange*, 103–4.
51. Graedon, *The Word Exchange*, 194–95, emphasis in original.
52. Claire Luchette, "Q&A: Alena Graedon on 'The Word Exchange': The Influence and Influenza of Words," *Bustle*, April 24, 2014, https://www.bustle.com/articles/21163-qa-alena-graedon-on-the-word-exchange-the-influence-and-influenza-of-words.

4. Postprint and Cognitive Contagion

53. Graedon, *The Word Exchange*, 145.
54. Graedon, *The Word Exchange*, 41.
55. Another way in which this text anticipates the coronavirus pandemic, although without the linguistic reverberations that echo through *The Word Exchange*.
56. Stiegler, *Taking Care of Youth and the Generations*, 16.
57. Stiegler, *Taking Care of Youth and the Generations*; Mark B. N. Hansen, *Feed-Forward: On the Future of Twenty-First-Century Media* (Chicago: Chicago University Press, 2015); David Rambo, "Technics Before Time: Experiencing Rationalism and the Techno-aesthetics of Speculation," PhD diss., Duke University, 2018; Andy Clark, *Natural-Born Cyborgs: Minds, Technologies, and the Future of Human Intelligence* (Oxford: Oxford University Press, 2004), and *Supersizing the Mind: Embodiment, Action, and Cognitive Extension* (Oxford: Oxford University Press, 2010); Hayles, *How We Think*.
58. Hansen, *Feed-Forward*, 274.
59. N. Katherine Hayles, *Unthought: The Power of the Cognitive Nonconscious* (Chicago: University of Chicago Press, 2017).

5. Bookishness at the Limits: Resiting the Human

1. Jessica Pressman, "The Aesthetic of Bookishness in Twenty-First Century Literature: Steven Hall's *The Raw Shark Texts*," *Michigan Quarterly Review* 48, no. 4 (Fall 2009): not paginated.
2. I prefer this formulation for its homophonic pun connecting orality with inscription—"resiting/reciting." In computational media, both speech and text exist as binary strings, a connection that, as we have seen, is important in the works discussed in chapter 4 as well as for the unspeakability of the works discussed here.
3. This is easier said than done. The system is very sensitive to the exact placement of the page; even a centimeter displacement will cause the word images to disperse and become unreadable, the words appearing to flash apart and disappear from the screen.
4. Andrew Whiteacre and Amaranth Borsuk, "Podcast: Amaranth Borsuk, 'Between Page and Screen': Digital, Visual, and Material Poetics," Comparative Media Studies, MIT, April 14, 2011, https://cmsw.mit.edu/amaranth-borsuk-between-page-and-screen/; N. Katherine Hayles, *Writing Machines* (Cambridge, MA: MIT Press, 2002).
5. Garrett Stewart, *Book Text Medium: Cross Sectional Reading for a Digital Age* (Cambridge: Cambridge University Press, forthcoming).

5. Bookishness at the Limits: Resiting the Human

6. Amaranth Borsuk and Brad Bouse, *Between Page and Screen* (Denver: SpringGun, 2016). Page numbers for quotations from *Between Page and Screen* are not given because the pages have no numbers.
7. In addition to Flash, a variety of other software packages were used. The website for the book says, *"Between Page and Screen* uses the FLARToolkit to project animations in an augmented-reality. The application also uses the Robot Legs framework, Papervision 3D engine, BetweenAS-3animation engine, and Jiglis physics engine" ("About," https://www.betweenpageandscreen.com/). Of course, the more commercial software a project uses, the more vulnerable it is to obsolescence in the vicious trade-off between sophistication and durability.
8. Michael Jacobson, "On Asemic Writing," interview by Sample Kanon, *Asymptote*, 2013, https://www.asymptotejournaom/visual/michael-jacobson-on-asemic-writing.
9. Johanna Drucker, *A Century of Artists' Books*, 2nd rev. ed. (New York: Granary Books, 2004); Garrett Stewart, *Bookwork: Medium to Object to Concept to Art* (Chicago: University of Chicago Press, 2011); Kiene Brillingburg Wurth, "Diffraction, Handwriting, and Intramediality in Louise Paillé's *Livres-livres*," *Parallax* 20, no. 3 (2014): 258–73. Brillingburg Wurth is expanding her reading of Paillé into an intramedial methodology in her book in progress "Literature and the Future of Alphabetic Writing."
10. Mirtha Dermisache, *Selected Writings*, ed. Daniel Owen and Lisa Pearson (New York: Siglio/Ugly Duckling Press, 2017).
11. Will Fenstermaker, "Mirtha Dermisache and the Limits of Language," *Paris Review*, January 30, 2018, https://www.theparisreview.org/blog/2018/01/30/mirtha-dermisache-limits-language/.
12. Mirtha Dermisache, quoted in Fenstermaker, "Mirtha Dermisache and the Limits of Language."
13. Fenstermaker, "Mirtha Dermisache and the Limits of Language."
14. Dermisache, quoted in Fenstermaker, "Mirtha Dermisache and the Limits of Language."
15. Dermisache, quoted in Fenstermaker, "Mirtha Dermisache and the Limits of Language."
16. Peter Schwenger, "Language Will Eat Your Brain," in *Technologies of the Gothic in Literature and Culture: Technogothics*, ed. Justin D. Edwards (New York: Routledge, 2017), 180.
17. William S. Burroughs, *The Ticket That Exploded* (New York: Grove, 1994), 49. See also Tony Burgess, *Pontypool Changes Everything* (Toronto: ECW, 2009), and Ben Marcus, *The Flame Alphabet* (New York: Vintage, 2012).

18. Indeed, the art of creating jingles relies precisely on this replicating quality of language, as anyone who has ever heard "It's a Small World" can testify.
19. Vilém Flusser, *Does Writing Have a Future?*, trans. Nancy Ann Roth (Minneapolis: University of Minnesota Press, 2011), and *Into the Universe of Technical Images*, trans. Nancy Ann Roth (Minneapolis: University of Minnesota Press, 2011).
20. Rita Raley, "The Asemic at the End of the World," presentation at the Modern Language Association Convention, Philadelphia, January 7, 2017, 12.
21. Jacobson, "On Asemic Writing."
22. Franco Bernardi, "Emancipation of the Sign: Poetry and Finance During the Twentieth Century," reprinted in *eflux* 30 (2012), http://www.e-flux.com/journal/emancipation-of-the-sign-poetry-and-finance-during-the-twentieth-century/.
23. Martin Ford, *The Rise of the Robots: Technology and the Threat of a Jobless Future* (New York: Basic Books, 2015), 83–128.
24. The GPT-2 program was deemed so effective that OpenAI refrained from publishing the fully trained program and released only a partial version lest it be used for malicious purposes. With a slimmed-down version put on the web by Adam King, users can input text, and the program will continue in a similar style (Adam King, "Talk to Transformer," n.d., talktotransformer.com). Finding the challenge irresistible, I spent a few hours trying it out. My favorite was the program's response to a modified Shakespeare quotation, "Life is a tale full of sound and fury, signifying nothing." It answered, "This is not true. On the contrary, on a regular, and not unimportant level, we are trying to maintain the balance. The reason we have to keep reminding ourselves to refrain from shouting is because it will not prevent us from shouting and therefore, from saying the truth. We are in a way trying to prevent the voice from interfering with the truth. There is no substitute for the truth." I was struck by its forthright disagreement ("This is not true") as well as by the sophisticated double negative ("not unimportant"), the equivocation ("in a way"), the leap from "sound and fury" to "shouting," and the logical illogic of reminding ourselves not to shout because it won't prevent us from shouting or from the "voice interfering with the truth," an observation expanded into an essay by no less a writer than George Saunders in "The Braindead Megaphone" (in *The Braindead Megaphone: Essays* [New York: Riverhead Books/Penguin, 2007], 1–20). Perhaps most of all, I was struck by the leap from "full of" to the inference that "full"

5. Bookishness at the Limits: Resiting the Human

means there is no room left—and room for what? The algorithm evidently decided "truth," perhaps in opposition to "signifying nothing." Hence, the program begins by denying the truth of the sentence ("This is not true") to make the necessary space for another kind of "truth," as in "there is no substitute for"—an idea that we are very much in need of in this era of "alternative facts."

25. Fenstermaker, "Mirtha Dermisache and the Limits of Language."
26. In *Metamedia: American Book Fictions and Literary Print Culture After Digitization* (Iowa City: University of Iowa Press, 2015), Alexander Starre argues that this kind of recursivity is a hallmark of the contemporary novel.

Bibliography

Abrams, J. J., and Doug Dorst. *Ship of Theseus*. New York: Mulholland, 2013.
Acar, Oguz Ali, and Jan van den Ende. "Knowledge Distance, Cognitive-Search Processes, and Creativity: The Making of Winning Solutions in Science Contests." *Psychological Science* 27, no. 5 (2016): 692–99.
Amerika, Mark. *Remixthebook*. Minneapolis: University of Minnesota Press, 2011.
Armato, Douglas. University of Minnesota Press, Minneapolis. Phone interview by N. Katherine Hayles, August 7, 2017.
Bernardi, Franco. "Emancipation of the Sign: Poetry and Finance During the Twentieth Century." Reprinted in *eflux* 30 (2012). http://www.e-flux.com/journal/emancipation-of-the-sign-poetry-and-finance-during-the-twentieth-century/.
Blobaum, Dean. Interview by N. Katherine Hayles. Chicago University Press, July 24, 2017.
Bogost, Ian. *Alien Phenomenology, or What's It Like to Be a Thing*. Minneapolis: University of Minnesota Press, 2012.
Bolter, Jay David. *Writing Space: The Computer, Hypertext, and the History of Writing*. 1990. Reprint. New York: Routledge, 2001.
Boluk, Stephanie, and Patrick Lemieux. *Metagaming: Playing, Competing, Spectating, Cheating, Trading, and Making and Breaking Videogames*. Minneapolis: University of Minnesota Press, 2017.
———. *Metagaming: Playing, Competing, Spectating, Cheating, Trading, and Making and Breaking Videogames*. Manifold ed. Minneapolis: University of Minnesota Press, 2017. https://manifold.umn.edu/project/metagaming.
Borsuk, Amaranth. *The Book*. Cambridge, MA: MIT Press, 2018.
Borsuk, Amaranth, and Brad Bouse. *Between Page and Screen*. Denver: SpringGun, 2016.

Bibliography

"Boston Dynamics Robot Can Stack Boxes with Amazing Eaze." YouTube video, March 30, 2019. https://www.youtube.com/watch?v=uuO6oeOo-ts.

Brailsford, Tim. "Printing and Typesetting History." YouTube video, December 15, 2013. https://www.youtube.com/watch?v=HdModNEH_1U .

Brillenburg Wurth, Kiene. "Diffraction, Handwriting, and Intra-mediality in Louise Paillé's *Livres-livres*." *Parallax* 20, no. 3 (2014): 258–73.

Burgess, Tony. *Pontypool Changes Everything*. Toronto: ECW, 2009.

Burroughs, William S. *The Ticket That Exploded*. New York: Grove, 1994.

Butler, Octavia E. "Speech Sounds." In *Bloodchild and Other Stories*, 87–110. New York: Seven Stories/Penguin, 2005.

Carr, Nicholas. *The Shallows: What the Internet Is Doing to Our Brain*. New York: Norton, 2011.

Clark, Andy. *Natural-Born Cyborgs: Minds, Technologies, and the Future of Human Intelligence*. Oxford: Oxford University Press, 2004.

———. *Supersizing the Mind: Embodiment, Action, and Cognitive Extension*. Oxford: Oxford University Press, 2010.

Cohn, Steve. Interview by N. Katherine Hayles. Duke University Press, Durham, NC, November 8, 2017.

Coulson, Krista. Interview by N. Katherine Hayles. Chicago University Press, July 24, 2017.

Cox, Aimee Meredith. *Shapeshifters: Black Girls and the Choreography of Citizenship*. Durham, NC: Duke University Press, 2015.

Crewe, Jennifer. "The Future of the University Press: How Should the University Press Role in Hiring and Promotion Change?" *Chronicle of Higher Education*, June 4, 2017.

———. Interview by N. Katherine Hayles. Columbia University Press, New York, May 18, 2017.

Danielewski, Mark. *House of Leaves*. 2nd ed. New York: Pantheon, 2000.

Davenport, Thomas H., and John C. Beck. *The Attention Economy: Understanding the New Currency of Business*. Rev. ed. Cambridge, MA: Harvard Business Review Press, 2002.

Deacon, Terrence W. *The Symbolic Species: The Co-evolution of Language and the Brain*. New York: Norton, 1998.

DeepMind. "AlphaGoZero: Learning from Scratch." October 18, 2017. https://deepmind.com/blog/alphago-zero-learning-scratch/.

Deleuze, Gilles, and Felix Guattari. *A Thousand Plateaus: Capitalism and Schizophrenia*. Trans. Brian Massumi. Minneapolis: University of Minnesota Press, 1987.

Derby, Matthew. "Visual Essay Series: An Interview with Matthew Derby." Interview by Sarah Minor. *Essay Daily*, February 2016. https://www.essaydaily.org/2016/02/visual-essay-series-interview-with.html.

Bibliography

Dermisache, Mirtha. *Selected Writings*. Ed. Daniel Owen and Lisa Pearson. New York: Siglio/Ugly Duckling Press, 2017.

Drucker, Joanna. *A Century of Artists' Books*. 2nd rev. ed. New York: Granary Books, 2004.

———. *SpecLab: Digital Aesthetics and Projects in Speculative Computing*. Chicago: University of Chicago Press, 2009.

Eisenstein, Elizabeth J. *The Printing Press as an Agent of Change*. Cambridge: Cambridge University Press, 1979.

Emerson, Lori. *Reading Writing Interfaces: From the Digital to the Bookbound*. Minneapolis: University of Minnesota Press, 2014.

Ernst, Wolfgang. *Memory and the Digital Archive*. Minneapolis: University of Minnesota Press, 2012.

Fenstermaker, Will. "Mirtha Dermisache and the Limits of Language." *Paris Review*, January 30, 2018. https://www.theparisreview.org/blog/2018/01/30/mirtha-dermisache-limits-language/.

Fitzpatrick, Kathleen. Michigan State University, East Lansing. Phone interview by N. Katherine Hayles, June 5, 2017.

———. *Planned Obsolescence: Publishing, Technology, and the Future of the Academy*. New York: New York University Press, 2011.

Flusser, Vilém. *Does Writing Have a Future?* Trans. Nancy Ann Roth. Minneapolis: University of Minnesota Press, 2011.

———. *Into the Universe of Technical Images*. Trans. Nancy Ann Roth. Minneapolis: University of Minnesota Press, 2011.

Foer, Jonathan Safran Foer. *Extremely Loud and Incredibly Close*. New York: Houghton Mifflin, 2005.

———. *Tree of Codes*. London: Visual Editions, 2010.

Ford, Martin. *The Rise of the Robots: Technology and the Threat of a Jobless Future*. New York: Basic Books, 2015.

Gabrys, Jennifer. *Program Earth*. Minneapolis: University of Minnesota Press, 2016.

Gaul, Albro. *The Wonderful World of Insects*. New York: Rinehart, 1953.

Gessler, Nicholas. Private e-mail to N. Katherine Hayles, July 7, 2017.

Gomez, Jeff. *Print Is Dead: Books in Our Digital Age*. London: Palgrave Macmillan, 2007.

Graedon, Alena. *The Word Exchange*. New York: Anchor Books, 2014.

Graphic Arts Research Foundation. *Report to the Subscribers*. Reston, VA: Graphic Arts Research Foundation, 1952.

Hansen, Mark B. N. *Feed-Forward: On the Future of Twenty-First-Century Media*. Chicago: Chicago University Press, 2015.

Harris, Marvin. *Cultural Materialism: The Struggle for a Science of Culture*. 1979. Reprint. Lanham, MD: AltaMira Press, 2001.

Bibliography

Hartigan, John. *Social Theory for Nonhumans.* Manifold ed. Minneapolis: University of Minnesota Press, 2018. https://manifold.umn.edu/project/social-theory-for-nonhumans.

Haskell, Michael. Interview by N. Katherine Hayles. Columbia University Press, New York, May 18, 2017.

Hayles, N. Katherine. "Can Computers Create Meanings? A Cyber/Bio/Semiotic Perspective." *Critical Inquiry* 46, no. 1 (2019): 32–55.

———. "Cognitive Assemblages: Technical Agency and Human Interactions." *Critical Inquiry* 43, no. 1 (Autumn 2016): 32–55.

———. *How We Became Posthuman: Virtual Bodies in Cybernetics, Literature, and Informatics.* Chicago: University of Chicago Press, 1999.

———. "How We Read: Close, Hyper, Machine." *ADE Bulletin* 150 (2011). http://www.ade.org/bulletin/.

———. *How We Think: Contemporary Technogenesis and Digital Media.* Chicago: University of Chicago Press, 2012.

———. "Literary Texts as Cognitive Assemblages: The Case of Electronic Literature." *Electronic Book Review*, August 5, 2018. http://electronicbookreview.com/essay/literary-texts-as-cognitive-assemblages-the-case-of-electronic-literature/.

———. *My Mother Was a Computer: Digital Subjects and Literary Texts.* Chicago: University of Chicago Press, 2005.

———. *Unthought: The Power of the Cognitive Nonconscious.* Chicago: University of Chicago Press, 2017.

———. *Writing Machines.* Cambridge, MA: MIT Press, 2002.

———. "Writing//Posthuman: The Literary Text as Cognitive Assemblage." *Theoretical Studies in Literature and Art* 38, no. 3 (2018): 6–21.

Hayles, N. Katherine, and Jessica Pressman, eds. *Comparative Textual Media: Transforming the Humanities in the Postprint Era.* Minneapolis: University of Minnesota Press, 2013.

Hildebrandt, Mireille. *Smart Technologies and the End(s) of Law: Novel Entanglements of Law and Technology.* Cheltenham, U.K.: Edward Edgar, 2015.

Hoffmeyer, Jesper. *Signs of Meaning in the Universe.* Bloomington: Indiana University Press, 1997.

Hörl, Erich. *General Ecology: The New Ecological Paradigm.* London: Bloomsbury Academic, 2017.

Horowitz, Eli, Matthew Derby, and Kevin Moffett. *The Silent History.* New York: Farrar, Straus and Giroux, 2014.

Hungerford, Amy. *Making Literature Now.* Stanford, CA: Stanford University Press, 2016.

Bibliography

IBM. "The Brain's Architecture, Efficiency . . . on a Chip." *IBM Research Blog*, December 19, 2016. https://www.ibm.com/blogs/research/2016/12/the-brains-architecture-efficiency-on-a-chip/.

Jacobson, Michael. "On Asemic Writing." Interview by Sample Kanon. *Asymptote*, 2013. https://www.asymptotejournal.com/visual/michael-jacobson-on-asemic-writing.

Johanson, Christopher, and Diane Favro. "Death in Motion: Funeral Processions in the Roman Forum." *Journal of the Society of Architectural History* 69, no. 1 (2010): 12–37.

Johns, Adrian. *The Nature of the Book: Print and Knowledge in the Making*. Chicago: University of Chicago Press, 1998.

Kelty, Christopher. Interview by N. Katherine Hayles. University of California, Los Angeles, June 8, 2017.

——. Private e-mail to N. Katherine Hayles, January 6, 2018,

——. *Two Bits: The Cultural Significance of Free Software*. Durham, NC: Duke University Press, 2008.

Kiely, Garrett. Interview by N. Katherine Hayles. Chicago University Press, July 24, 2017.

King, Adam. "Talk to Transformer." N.d. Talktotransformer.com.

Kirschenbaum, Matthew. Private e-mail to N. Katherine Hayles, January 8, 2018.

——. *Track Changes: A Literary History of Word Processing*. Cambridge, MA: Belknap Press of Harvard University Press, 2016.

Kittler, Friedrich A. *Discourse Networks, 1800/1900*. Trans. Michael Metteer. Stanford, CA: Stanford University Press, 1992.

Latour, Bruno. *Reassembling the Social: An Introduction to Actor-Network-Theory*. Oxford: Oxford University Press, 2007.

Leventhal, Philip. Interview by N. Katherine Hayles. Columbia University Press, New York, May 18, 2017.

Livre de prières. Lyons, France: n.p., 1883.

Luchette, Claire. "Q&A: Alena Graedon on 'The Word Exchange': The Influence and Influenza of Words." *Bustle*, April 24, 2014. https://www.bustle.com/articles/21163-qa-alena-graedon-on-the-word-exchange-the-influence-and-influenza-of-words.

Lui, Alan. *The Laws of Cool: Knowledge Work and the Culture of Information*. Chicago: University of Chicago Press, 2004.

"A Machine with 18,000 Elements." *Scientific American*, March 9, 1901.

Macho, Thomas. "Zeit und Zahl: Kalender- und Zeitrechnung als Kurturtechniken." In *Bild-Schrift-Zahl*, ed. Sybille Krämer and Horst Bredekamp, pages unavailable. Munich: Wilhelm Fink, 2003.

Bibliography

Marcus, Ben. *The Flame Alphabet*. New York: Vintage, 2012.
Maron, Nancy L., Christine Mulhern, Daniel Rossman, and Kimberly Schmelzinger. "The Costs of Publishing Monographs: Toward a Transparent Methodology." *JEP: Journal of Electronic Publishing* 19, no. 1 (February 5, 2016). https://quod.lib.umich.edu/j/jep/3336451.0019.103?view=text;rgn=main.
Masnick, Mike. "Another Reminder That You Don't Own Your eBooks: Amazon Removing More eBooks You 'Bought' from Archives." *Techdirt*, December 15, 2010. https://www.techdirt.com/articles/20101215/02571612282/another-reminder-that-you-dont-own-your-ebooks-amazon-removing-more-ebooks-you-bought-archives.shtml.
Maxwell, John W. Private e-mails to N. Katherine Hayles, April 15 and 16, 2018.
Mergenthaler Linotype Company. *Linotype Machine Principles*. New York: Mergenthaler Linotype Company, 1940.
Mitchell, Tom, et al. "NELL: Never Ending Language Learning." Read the Web, Carnegie Mellon University, n.d. http://rtw.ml.cmu.edu/rtw/.
"Notes on Typesetter." N.d. Mark Twain Museum Archives, Hartford, CT.
Oswald, Wendall. *Anthropological Analysis of Food-Getting Technologies*. New York: Wiley-Interscience, 1976.
Paine, Albert Bigelow. *Mark Twain: A Biography*. 4 vols. New York: Harper, 1912. https://www.gutenberg.org/files/2988/2988-h/2988-h.htm.
Parikka, Jussi. *What Is Media Archaeology*? London: Polity, 2012.
Perrault, Charles, P. Jeffrey Brantingham, Steven L. Kuhn, Sarah Wurz, and Xing Goa. "Measuring the Complexity of Lithic Technology." *Current Anthropology* 54, supplement 8 (December 2013): S397–S406.
Presner, Todd. Interview by N. Katherine Hayles. University of California, Los Angeles, June 19, 2017.
——. "Mapping Jewish Los Angeles." 2017. http://www.mappingjewishla.org/.
——. Private e-mail to N. Katherine Hayles, January 25, 2018.
Presner, Todd, David Shepard, and Yoh Kawano. *HyperCities: Thick Mapping in the Digital Humanities*. Cambridge, MA: Harvard University Press, 2014.
Pressman, Jessica. "The Aesthetic of Bookishness in Twenty-First Century Literature: Steven Hall's *The Raw Shark Texts*." *Michigan Quarterly Review* 48, no. 4 (Fall 2009): not paginated.
Raley, Rita. "The Asemic at the End of the World," Presentation at the Modern Language Association Convention, Philadelphia, January 7, 2017.
Rambo, David. "Technics Before Time: Experiencing Rationalism and the Techno-aesthetics of Speculation." PhD diss., Duke University, 2018.
Romano, Frank. *History of the Phototypesetting Era*. San Luis Obispo: California Polytechnic State University, 2014.

Bibliography

Saunders, George. "The Braindead Megaphone." In *The Braindead Megaphone: Essays*, 1–20. New York: Riverhead Books/Penguin, 2007.
Schott North America. *An Introduction to Fiber Optic Imaging*. 2nd ed. Southridge, MA: Schott North America, 2007. http://www.us.schott.com/d/lightingimaging/7aab7d6d-b1db-4ef6-8694-cbcb27ab5529/1.0/fo.book.pdf.
Schwenger, Peter. "Language Will Eat Your Brain." In *Technologies of the Gothic in Literature and Culture: Technogothics*, ed. Justin D. Edwards, 179–86. New York: Routledge, 2017.
Siegert, Bernhard. *Cultural Techniques: Grids, Filters, Doors, and Other Articulations of the Real*. Trans. Geoffrey Winthrop-Young. New York: Fordham University Press, 2015.
Simondon, Gilbert. *On the Mode of Existence of Technical Objects*. Trans. Cecile Malaspina and John Rogove. Minneapolis: University of Minnesota Press, 2017.
Spiekermann, Sarah. *Ethical IT Innovation: A Value-Based System Design Approach*. Boca Raton, FL: Auerbach, Taylor & Francis, 2015.
Stanford University Press. "Publishing Digital Scholarship." N.d. https://www.sup.org/digital/.
Starre, Alexander. *Metamedia: American Book Fictions and Literary Print Culture After Digitization*. Iowa City: University of Iowa Press, 2015.
Stephenson, Neal. *Snow Crash*. New York: Del Rey, 2000.
Stewart, Garrett. *Book Text Medium: Cross Sectional Reading for a Digital Age*. Cambridge: Cambridge University Press, forthcoming.
———. *Bookwork: Medium to Object to Concept to Art*. Chicago: University of Chicago Press, 2011.
Stiegler, Bernard. *Taking Care of Youth and the Generations*. Stanford, CA: Stanford University Press, 2010.
Striphas, Ted. *The Late Age of Print: Everyday Book Culture from Consumerism to Control*. New York: Columbia University Press, 2009.
Tenen, Dennis. *Plain Text: The Poetics of Computation*. Stanford, CA: Stanford University Press, 2017.
Thomas, Alan. Interview by N. Katherine Hayles. Chicago University Press, July 24, 2017.
———. Private e-mail to N. Katherine Hayles, January 16, 2018.
Thompson, John B. *Books in the Digital Age: The Transformation of Academic and Higher Education Publishing in Britain and the United States*. Cambridge: Polity Press, 2005.
Unsworth, John. "The Humanist: 'Dances with Wolves' or 'Bowls Alone'?" Paper presented at the Association of Research Libraries conference "Scholarly

Bibliography

Tribes and Tribulations: How Tradition and Technology Are Driving Disciplinary Change," Washington, DC, 2003. http://www.arl.org/wp-content/uploads/2007/07/scholarly-tribes-unsworth-17oct03.pdf.

Von Uexküll, Jacob. *A Foray Into the Worlds of Animals and Humans: With a Theory of Meaning*. Minneapolis: University of Minnesota Press, 2010.

Webster, Edward. *Print Unchained: Fifty Years of Digital Printing: 1950–2000 and Beyond*. Burlington, VT: DRA of Vermont Inc., 2001.

Wheeler, Wendy. *Expecting the Earth: Life/Culture/Biosemiotics*. London: Lawrence and Wishart, 2016.

Whiteacre, Andrew, and Amaranth Borsuk. "Podcast: Amaranth Borsuk, 'Between Page and Screen': Digital, Visual, and Material Poetics." Comparative Media Studies, MIT, April 14, 2011. https://cmsw.mit.edu/amaranth-borsuk-between-page-and-screen/.

Whitehead, Alfred North. *Process and Reality*. New York: Free Press, 1979.

Wissoker, Kenneth. Duke University Press, Durham, NC. Phone interview by N. Katherine Hayles, November 7, 2017.

Wythoff, Grant. *The Perversity of Things: Hugo Gernsback on Media, Tinkering, and Scientifiction*. Minneapolis: University of Minnesota Press, 2016.

———. *The Perversity of Things: Hugo Gernsback on Media, Tinkering, and Scientifiction*. Manifold ed. Minneapolis: University of Minnesota Press, 2017. https://manifold.umn.edu/project/the-perversity-of-things.

Index

Abrams, J. J., 23–24, 142
access: for digital print, 103; license as, in e-books, 81–82; in postprint era, 80–85. *See also* open access publishing
actor-network theory, 32
adaptability: of cognition, 8; of cognitive technology, 11
Adobe software: Flash programming and, support for, 172, *173*, 178, 200n6; licensing ethics of, 88; page description format and, 67, 88, 108; in personal computers, 67
aesthetic of bookishness, 4–5, 171
agencement, 13
Amazon Kindle, 77
Amerika, Mark, 127
Animal Farm (Orwell), 82
animals. *See* nonhumans
anxiety themes: in asemic writing, 186; in *The Silent History*, 141
Apple iPad, 77, 199n45
Apple Macintosh, 67–68
Armato, Douglas, 121–22
ASCII symbols, *4*, 77–78

asemic writing, 38–39, 178–80, *181*, 182–83, *184–85*, 186–87, 189–90; communication desires through, 182; techno-anxiety in, 186
asemiosis, 154; mediated, 140; selective, 135, *136*, 137, 141, 158, 160, 167, 177, 179, 189
assemblages, 13
Autotune, 36
Avery, Matt, 108

Babbage, Charles, 195n1
becoming, 13
Bernardi, Franco, 186
Bernays, Edward, 80–81
Between Page and Screen (Borsuk and Bouse), 21–22, 38, 171–79; code for, *173*, 177–78; computer initialization for access to, 172, 174–78; as coscript, 177; cover images, *173*; Flash programming and, 172, *173*, 178, 207n7; materialist poetics in, 174; text projections, *173*, 174, *176*
Bewilderment (Ferry), 101
binary code: of sentences, *4*; speech and text as, 206n2

Index

binary system, in Lumitype machine, 57
biological cognition, 6; evolution of, 10
biosemiotics, 6–7
Blobaum, Dean, 106–7
Bogost, Ian, 29
Bolter, Jay David, 25
Boluk, Stephanie, 121
Book, The (Borsuk), 17, 20
book and publishing industry: authors and editors in, relationship between, 105–6; corporate booksellers, 26; desktop printers and, 68; EAN International and, 26; expansion of, 25–26; ISBN and, 25–27; open access publishing, 103, 105, 198n43
Book of Prayers. See *Livre de prières*
Book Text Medium (Stewart), 21–22
Bookwork (Stewart), 22, 179
Borsuk, Amaranth, 3, 17, 20–22, 38, 171–79. See also *Between Page and Screen*
Bouse, Brad, 21–22, 38, 171–79. See also *Between Page and Screen*
Buell, Dwight, 44
Burdick, Anne, 5, 27, 174
Burgess, Tony, 183
Burroughs, William, 183

Caldwell, Samuel, 57
capitalism: creative destruction through, 159–60; semiocapitalism, 168; in *The Word Exchange*, 158–67
captcha technology, 186–87
Carr, Nicholas, 134, 179
Castell, Manuel, 35

C/A/T. *See* Computer Assisted Typewriter
celebrity writers, 23
Century of Artists' Books, A (Drucker), 179
chromolithography, 2
Chronicle of Higher Education, 95–96
Citation Index, 128
Clark, Andy, 167
code, coding and: alphabetic writing and, decline of, 39; binary, 4, 206n2; development of, 39; for DocuTech, development of, 70; for e-books, 108; for e-readers, 79; for *Between Page and Screen*, 173, 177–78
cognition, 5–12, 18; adaptability of, 8; artificial revolution for, 10; biological, 6; evolution of, 10; central processors in, 24; computational media and, 6, 8; definition of, 6; distribution of capabilities, 17; as embodied, 8; in e-readers, capacity, 76–80; evolvability of, 8; flexibility of, 8; in *Homo sapiens*, 8; human to machine cognition, 42–53 (*see also specific devices*; *specific machines*); interjection of code into textuality, 5–6; interpretation and, 6–7; inversions of, 10–11; literature on, 6; machine cognition as influence on, 10; meaning and, 6–7; nonconscious, 13; in nonhumans, 8, 49; Paige Compositor and, 36, 47–48; in phototypesetting, 54–55; reconceptualization of, 6; symbolic reasoning and, 10.

Index

See also cognitive technology; human to machine cognition

cognitive assemblages: abstract flows in, 13; applications for, 9–10; cognitive devices and, 33–34; computational media and, 9, 14–15; conceptual development of, 13–14; cultural techniques and, 28–34; cybersymbiosis and, 14; in DocuTech, 69; in e-readers, 80; framework of, 9, 12–13, 25, 39; literary texts and, 193n20; materialities of individuals in, 13; media archaeology and, 28–34; Mergenthaler Linotype machine, 15; networked books as, 130–31; through nonconscious cognition, 13; Paige Compositor and, 15, 41; participants in, 13; postprint and, 15–18; scope of, 8–9; in *The Silent History*, 140–41; transporter networks and, 9–10; university presses and, 92–93, 130–31; XML code and, *16*

cognitive devices: cognitive assemblages and, 33–34; media archaeology and, 29. *See also specific devices*

cognitive redistribution, 66

cognitive technology: adaptability of, 11; in developed societies, applications of, 12; evolvability of, 11; flexibility of, 11; university presses and, 129–30. *See also specific technologies*

Cohn, Steve, 109–11

Columbia University Press, 93–100

Comparative Textual Media, 4–5

computational media: cognition and, 6, 8; cognitive assemblages and, 9, 14–15; consciousness of, 7; evolution of, 14–15; in *The Silent History*, 154–55; speech and text as binary strings, 206n2

computational poetics, 85

Computer Assisted Typewriter (C/A/T), 43, 60–63; fiber-optic bundles and, 61–62, *63*; Graphic Systems International and, 43, 60, 62; UNIX operating system in, 62

computers: book studies and, 18–19; cathode ray tubes in, 60; external milieus for, 7–8; internal milieus for, 7–8; phototypesetting and, 53–59; software in, development of, 60, 62. *See also* computational media; personal computers; software

conceptual art, 22

concurrency concept, 72

consciousness, of computational media, 7

copyright protections, for e-books, 83

coscripts, 177

Coulson, Krista, 107–9, 123–24

Cox, Aimee Meredith, 112

CreateSpace, 1, 100

Crewe, Jennifer, 93–100, 201n22; on digital technologies, influence of, 93–94; on monograph publishing, future of, 93. *See also* monograph publishing

cultural materialism, 194n48

Cultural Techniques (Siegert), 31–34

cultural techniques approach, 28–34; German media theory and, 31–34; media archaeology and, 32

cybersymbiosis, 18; cognitive assemblages and, 14

221

Index

Danielewski, Mark, 27
Deacon, Terrence, 7, 133
deep attention, 134
Deleuze, Gilles, 13–14
Derby, Matthew, 23–24, 38, 133–34, 137–56, 205n41. *See also Silent History, The*
Dermisache, Mirtha, 38, 171–72, 179–80, *181*, *184–85*, 190; graphemes, 182. *See also* asemic writing
desktop printers, 66–68; DocuTech, 37, *69*, 69–73; Hewlett-Packard and, 68; LaserJet printers, 68, 198n33; LaserWriter printer, 67–68; nonimpact technologies in, 67; print-on-demand market as result of, 72–73; publishing with, 68
Digital Millennium Copyright Act, U.S. (1998), 83
digital print: computational transformation as result of, 3–4; cost-savings from, 102; Crewe on, 93–94; declines in library sales and, 103; fake journal requests, 103; monograph publishing influenced by, 99; open access for, 103; piracy issues with, 103; print books' decline as result of, 20; repurposing of material with, 103; of *The Silent History*, 138–39. *See also* e-books
digital publishing platforms: CreateSpace, 1, 100. *See also* e-books
Discourse Networks 1899/1900 (Kittler), 31
DocuTech, 37, *69*, 195n4; code development for, 70; cognitive assemblages in, 69; concurrency concept and, 72; Holt and, 70; human to machine cognition in, 71–72; multitasking capabilities of, 71; Paige Compositor and, 70–71; positive-feedback loop, 72; in print-on-demand market, domination of, 73; productivity of, 71
Dorst, Doug, 23–24, 142
Drucker, Johanna, 17, 179
Duke University Press, 104, 109–12; donation of royalties, 111; e-book revenues, 111

EAN International. *See* European Article Number International
e-books: coding for, 108; as content-specific, by audience, 84; copyright protections for, 83; definition of, 198n44; Duke University Press and, 111; flexibility of, 108–9; human to machine cognition and, 43; in libraries, 82; license for access to, 81–82; materiality and text, relationship between, 3; print books and, similarity to, 84–85; printed books and, 104; reflow design of, 108; for scholarly writing, criticisms of, 108
Eisenman, Alvin, 196n11
Eisenstein, Elizabeth, 3
Ely, Timothy, 183
embodied, as concept, cognition as, 8, 49
Emerson, Lori, 30
Endo, Ichiro, 87
e-readers: Amazon Kindle, 77; Apple iPad, 77; ASCII strings and symbols in, 77–78; coding

Index

for, 79; cognitive assemblages in, 80; cognitive capacities of, 76–80; computational poetics, 85; definition of, 198n44; development of, 35; functionality of, 78; human readers and, relationship between, 76–77; human to machine cognition and, 43; interpretation and, figures available for, 85; media archaeology and, 77; surveillance issues with, 78, 80. *See also* e-books

Ernst, Wolfgang, 28–31
error correction, in Lumitype machine, 57
Ethical IT Innovation (Spiekermann), 73–76
ethics: of Adobe PDF software licensing, 88; in information technology, 73–76
European Article Number (EAN) International, 26
evolution, 18
evolvability: of cognition, 8; of cognitive technology, 11
Extremely Loud and Incredibly Close (Foer), 27

fake journal requests, 103
Faulkner, William, 1
Feed-Forward (Hansen), 35, 168
Fenstermaker, Will, 180, 182–83
Ferry, David, 101
fiber-optic bundles, 60–63, 197n25; composition of, 60; Computer Assisted Typewriter and, 61–62, 63; flexible, 61, 63; manufacture of, 60–61; mono-fibers, 61; troff software for, 62
Field Reports, 138–39

Fitzpatrick, Kathleen, 112, 114, 116–17, 127
Fjellestad, Danuta, 189
Flame Alphabet, The (Marcus), 183
Flash programming, 172, *173*, 178, 207n7
flexibility: of cognition, 8; of cognitive technology, 11
flexible fiber-optic bundles, 61, *63*
Flusser, Vilém, 39, 183, 187
Foer, Jonathan Safran, 27

Garth, W. E., 57
Gaul, Albro, 64–66
General Ecology (Hörl), 35
German media theory, cultural techniques and, 31–34
Gernsback, Hugo, 121–24
Geschke, Charles, 67, 196n11
Gessler, Nicholas, 197n25
Global Positioning System (GPS), 24
Gomez, Jeff, 5
GPS. *See* Global Positioning System
Graedon, Alena, 38, 133–34, 156, 158–67, 205n41, 205n44. *See also* *Word Exchange, The*
Graphic Systems International (GSI), 43, 60, 62. *See also* Computer Assisted Typewriter
GSI. *See* Graphic Systems International
Guattari, Félix, 13–14
Gutenberg, Johannes, 1–3

Hackborn, Dick, 68, 198n33
Hansen, Mark, 35
Harris, Marvin, 194n48
Hartigan, John, 121–22
Harvard University Press, 95–96

Index

Haskell, Michael, 96, 98
Hayles, N. Katherine, 49, 108, 168–69
Hersey, John, 196n11
Hewlett-Packard (HP): desktop printers and, 68; planned obsolescence of printers as corporate strategy, 66–68, 76
Hidebrand, Harold, 36
Higonnet, René, 36, 54–59. *See also* Lumitype machine
Hildebrandt, Mireille, 83
Hoffmeyer, Jesper, 7
Holt, Chip, 70, 87–88, 198n35
Homo sapiens (humans), 8; symbolic reasoning and, 10
Hörl, Erich, 35
Horowitz, Eli, 23–24, 38, 133–34, 137–56, 137–1156, 205n41. *See also Silent History, The*
hot-metal casting, in Linotype machine, 52
House of Leaves (Danielewski), 27
Howard, Robert, 87
HP. *See* Hewlett-Packard
HTML code. *See* hypertext markup language code
humanities scholarship, 124–30
humans: embodied cognition for, 49; thinking connected with, 49. *See also Homo sapiens*
Human Stain, The (Sergeant), *190*
human to machine cognition: Computer Assisted Typewriter, 43; in DocuTech, 71–72; e-books and, 43; e-readers and, 43; Linotype machine, 50–53; Lumitype machine, 42, 50–51; nodal points of, 42–43; Paige Compositor and, 42–53;
reprographic technologies, 43; shift from, 44; in typesetting machines, 44–53
Hungerford, Amy, 23, 139, 199n48
hyperattention, 134
HyperCities (Presner), 117
HyperCities project, 117–18, 126, 200n6
hypertext markup language (HTML) code, 97; in *The Silent History, 155*

illiteracy: new, 134–38; partial, 38
information technology (IT): design processes for, 73–74; ethics in, 73–76; innovation in, 73–76; radio-frequency identification, 74; sustainability of, 75; values in, as element of design process, 73–74; venture-capital funding for, 74
innovation: in costs of university presses, 112–21; in information technology, 73–76
International Standard Book Number (ISBN), 25–27
interpretation, as concept: cognition and, 6–7; e-reader content and, 85
iPad. *See* Apple iPad
ISBN. *See* International Standard Book Number
IT. *See* information technology

Jacobson, Michael, 178–79, 186
Jacquard, Joseph Marie, 44
Jacquard cards, *45*
Jacquard loom, 44
Jobs, Steve, 67
Johanson, Christopher, 117
Johns, Adrian, 3

Index

Kelty, Christopher, 112–13, 116–17, 201n22
Kernighen, Brian, 62
Kerns, David, 71, 87–88
Kiely, Garrett, 100–104, 127; on cost-savings from digital publishing, 102. *See also* monograph publishing
Kindle. *See* Amazon Kindle
King, Adam, 208n24
Kirschenbaum, Matthew, 17, 53–54
Kittler, Friedrich A., 31

language-processing programs, 129
language therapy, 164–67
LaserJet printers, 68, 198n33
LaserWriter printer, 67–68
late age of print, 25
Late Age of Print, The (Striphas), 24–25
Latour, Bruno, 13; actor-network theory of, 32
LeMieux, Patrick, 121
Leventhal, Philip, 98–99
libraries: digital print as influence on, 103; e-books in, 82
Libro No. 1 (Dermisache), 179–80
Linofilm, 197n23
Linotype machine, 15; early commercial use of, 51–52; hot-metal casting in, 52; human to machine cognition in, 50–53; mold methods in, 52; Paige Compositor compared to, 52–53
lithography, as technological advancement, 2
Livre de prières (Book of Prayers), 44, *46*
Lui, Alan, 159
Luminos initiative, 112–21; Author Waiver Fund, 113–14; failure of, 115; open-access platforms, 113–16; peer-review practices, 113

Lumitype machine, 36–37, 54; binary system in, 57; commercial introduction of, 58–59, *59*; early exhibitions of, 58–59; early prototypes, 57; error correction in, 57; Garth as investor in, 57; human to machine cognition and, 42, 50–51; justification calculations by, 56–57; mechanical memory in, 57; preproduction model, 58–59; processes of, 55–56; spacing mechanisms, 57; type disc, *56*

machine cognition. *See* human to machine cognition
Macho, Thomas, 31
Macintosh personal computer. *See* Apple Macintosh
Making Literature Now (Hungerford), 23
Manifold project, 34, 121–24
Marcus, Ben, 183
Mark Twain (Paine), 44–45
Marx, Karl, 159
materialist poetics, 174
materialities of individuals, in cognitive assemblages, 13
matrix printers, development of, 87
Maxwell, John M., 52, 195n1, 197n23
meaning: cognition and, 6–7; of medium, 21–22
mechanical memory, in Lumitype machine, 57
media archaeology, 28–34; cognitive devices and, 29; cultural techniques and, 32; discursive surfaces and, 29; e-readers and, 77; Ernst on, 28–31; focus of, 29;

225

media archaeology (*continued*)
human subjectivity and, 29–30; narrative as distinct from, 29; nondiscursive elements in, 31; Parikka on, 30; promotion as purpose of, 29–30; technical capabilities of, 30; techno-epistemological configurations, 29
media ecologies: humanist values in, 88–89; Tenen on, 88–89. *See also* university presses
mediated asemiosis, 140
mediated language, in *The Silent History*, 146–48
media theory. *See* German media theory
medium, meaning of, 21–22
Mergenthaler, Otto, 15, 50–51, 55. *See also* Linotype machine
Metagaming (Boluk and LeMieux), 121
metamedia, 27–28
Michaux, Henri, 183
Mitchell, Tom, 129
Moffitt, Kevin, 23–24, 38, 133–34, 137–56, 205n41. *See also Silent History, The*
mold methods, in Linotype machine, 52
mono-fiber optic bundles, 61
monograph publishing: costs of, 94–95; Crewe on, 93; declining sales for, 104–5; digital technologies as influence on, 99; disadvantages of, 109–12; economics of, 201n22; financial viability of, 96; future of, 93–100; HTML code, 97; of literary criticism, 96; online discourse as influence on, 99;

print-on-demand and, 95; revenues of, 94–95; scholarship in, 106–7; short-run digital printing and, 95; template sample, 97; university presses and, 90–91, 93–100
moveable type: invention of, 1–3. *See also specific devices*
Moyraud, Louis, 36, 54–59. *See also* Lumitype machine

narrative approach, media archaeology as distinct from, 29, 31
natural-language learning, 129
NELL. *See* Never Ending Language Learning
networked books, as cognitive assemblage, 130–31
networked model of scholarship, 91
networks, cognitive assemblages and, 13
Network Society, 35
neural nets, 11
neuromorphic chips, 11, 192n13
Never Ending Language Learning (NELL), 129
new illiteracy, 134–38; Tenen on, 135–36
1984 (Orwell), 82, 148
nonconscious cognition, 13
nonhumans, cognition in, 8, 49
nonimpact technologies, in desktop printers, 67

obsolescence. *See* planned obsolescence
offset printing, 2; print-on-demand and, differences between, 101

Index

On the Mode of Existence of Technical Objects (Simondon), 30–31
open access publishing, 105, 198n43; for digital print, 103
Orwell, George, 82, 148
Ossanna, Joe F., 62
Oswald, Wendell, 195n4
ownership, in postprint era, 80–85

page description format (PDF), 67, 88; coding for, 108
page description language (PDL), 67
Paige, James, 42, 44, 46–47. *See also* Paige Compositor
Paige Compositor: cognitive abilities of, 36, 47–48; cognitive assemblages and, 15, 41; complexity of, 195n4; dead matter redistribution by, 49, 52; demise of, 50–53; DocuTech and, 70–71; human to machine cognition and, 42–53; Linotype machine compared to, 52–53; patent applications for, 50, *51*; perfectionism of, 46; Twain and, 42, 44–47, 50; views of, *47–48*
Paillé, Louise, 179
Paine, Albert Bigelow, 44–47
paradox themes, 159–60
Parikka, Jussi, 30
partial illiteracy. *See* illiteracy
PDF. *See* page description format
PDL. *See* page description language
Perkins, Maxwell, 105–6
personal computers: Adobe software and, 67; Apple Macintosh, 67–68; historic development of, 67–68; page description format and, 67; page description language and, 67

photocomposition systems, 197n16
phototypesetting: cognitive advances in, 54–55; cognitive redistribution and, 66; computation and, 53–59; decline of, 64–66; materiality differences in, 54; peak period of use for, 64; *The Wonderful World of Insects*, 64–66. *See also* Linotype machine; Lumitype machine
piracy, of digital print, 103
Plain Text (Tenen), 17, 62, 83–85
Planned Obsolescence (Fitzpatrick), 116
planned obsolescence, as corporate strategy, 66–68, 76
POD. *See* print-on-demand
Pontypool Changes Everything (Burgess), 183
positive-feedback loop, in DocuTech, 72
postprint: cognitive assemblages and, 15–18; continuities as element of, 25; definition of, 2; development of, as popular term, 5; as equivocal figure, 18–19; partial illiteracy, 38; print as distinct from, 3; ruptures as element of, 25; scholarship on, 19–28. *See also specific works*; scope of, 25; *The Silent History* and, 141–56; as verbal cue, 19
Presner, Todd, 113, 127; HyperCities project, 117–18, 126, 200n6
Pressman, Jessica, 4–5, 171
print: computational transformation of, through digital text, 3–4; postprint as distinct from, 3. *See also* printing industry

227

Index

print books: accessibility of, 125; contradictory perceptions of, 1–2; definition of, 2; digital text and, 20; early history of, 35; e-books and, 104; as rentals, 110; *The Silent History* as, 142; transformation of, 2; X-ray versions of, 3–4

printers. *See* desktop printers; matrix printers

printing industry: chromolithography, 2; lithography, 2; offset printing, 2; rotary presses, 2; technological advancements in, 2. *See also* moveable type

Print is Dead (Gomez), 5

print-on-demand (POD): book publishers and booksellers and, 101–2; cost savings with, 102; DocuTech domination of, 73; limitations of, 101; monograph publishing and, 95; offset printing and, differences between, 101; University of Chicago Press and, 100–103, 109

processual philosophy, 14

proprietary software, 135, *136*

Publishing Digital Scholarship, 122–23

publishing industry. *See* book and publishing industry

Quinn, Russell, 141

radio-frequency identification (RFID), 74

Raley, Rita, 183, 186

Rambo, Dave, 167

reasoning. *See* symbolic reasoning

remixthebook (Amerika), 127

rentals, print books as, 110

reprographic technologies, 43

RFID. *See* radio-frequency identification

Roman Forum model, 117–18, 126–27

Romano, Frank, 54, 58, 64

rotary presses, 2

Schrödinger, Erwin, 36

Schumpeter, Joseph, 159

Schwenger, Peter, 183

selective asemiosis, 135, *136*, 137, 141, 158, 160, 167, 177, 179, 189

Selectric, 66

self-publishing, 105

semiocapitalism, 168

Sergeant, Nick, 189, *190*

Shapeshifters (Cox), 112

Ship of Theseus project, 23–24, 142

short-run digital printing, 95

Siegert, Bernhard, 31–34, 180–81

Silent History, The (Derby, Horowitz, and Moffitt), 23–24, 38, 133–34, 137–56, 205n41; as codex, 156–58; cognitive assemblages in, 140–41; computational media in, 154–55; cultural anxiety themes in, 141; digital version of, 138–39; Field Reports and, 138–39; HTML code in, *155*; humans without language as theme in, 151–56; mediated language in, 146–48; narrative texts in, 139–40, 143, 156–58; as postprint production, 141–56; as print book, 142; selective asemiosis in, 160; surveillance themes in, 147–48

Simondon, Gilbert, 13, 30–31

Snow Crash (Stephenson), 161

Index

Social Theory for Nonhumans (Hartigan), 121–22
software, for computers: Adobe software, 67, 88; development of, 60; proprietary, 135, *136*; troff software, 62
Sound and the Fury, The (Faulkner), 1
spacing mechanisms, in Lumitype machine, 57
SpecLab (Drucker), 17
Spiekermann, Sarah, 73–76
Stanford University Press, 129–30
Starre, Alexander, 1–2; on metamedia, 27–28; on technotext, 27–28
Stein, Bob, 199n46
Stephenson, Neal, 161
Stewart, Garrett, 21–22, 174, 179, 193n24
Stiegler, Bernard, 134, 161–65, 167, 179
Striphas, Ted, 24–25, 80–81
subsistence writers, 23
surveillance issues: with e-readers, 78, 80; in postprint era, 80–85; in *The Silent History*, 147–48
sustainability, of information technology, 75
symbolic reasoning, 10

Taking Care of Youth and the Generations (Graedon), 161
techno-epistemological configurations, 29
technotext, 27–28; technological bias of, 27
Tenen, Dennis, 17, 62, 83–85, 129, 179; on Adobe PDF software, licensing ethics of, 88; computational poetics, 85; on laminate text, 135; on media ecologies, 88–89; on new illiteracy, 135–36; on partial illiteracy, postprint and, 38
text-generation programs, 129
thinking, being human and, 49
Thomas, Alan, 104–5, 108, 115; on self-publishing, 105
Thoreau, Henry David, 137
Ticket That Exploded, The (Burroughs), 183
Track Changes (Kirschenbaum), 17, 53–54
transindividuation movements, 14
Tree of Codes (Foer), 27
Turing, Alan, 58
Twain, Mark, 42, 44–47, 50
Two Bits (Kelty), 116–17
type disc, in Lumitype machine, 56
typesetting machines: machine cognition in, 44–53. *See also* Lumitype; Paige Compositor. *See also* Computer Assisted Typewriter

Uexküll, Jacob von, 7
Umwelten, 7
United States (U.S.), Digital Millennium Copyright Act in, 83
University of California Press, 104; evaluation models, 120; HyperCities project, 117–18, 126; Luminos initiative, 112–21; Roman Forum model, 117–18, 126–27
University of Chicago Press, 100–109; declines in library sales, 103; income accountability and, by book type, 102–3; piracy issues, 103; print-on-demand and, 100–103, 109; sustainability of, 105

229

Index

University of Minnesota Press, 121–24
university presses: accessibility of books, 125; *Citation Index*, 128; cognitive assemblages in, framework for, 92–93, 130–31; cognitive capacities of computational media and, 91–92; cognitive technologies as coauthors and collaborators, 129–30; Columbia University Press, 93–100; curation in, 127; Duke University Press, 104, 109–12; future ecology for, 124–30; Harvard University Press, 95–96; humanities scholarship, 124–30; innovating costs for, 112–21; interconnections in, 126–27; interoperability in, 126–27; language-processing programs and, 129; legacy of, 130–31; limitations of, 90–93; Manifold project, 34, 121–24; methodological approach to, 90–91; monograph publishing and, 90–91, 93–100; natural-language learning and, 129; networked books as cognitive assemblage, 130–31; networked model of scholarship and, 91; participants in cognitive assemblages, 92–93; protocols for, 90–93; Publishing Digital Scholarship, 122–23; remixing in, 127; scholarly evaluation criteria, 127–29; scholarship and, 89–90; speed of publication for, 126; Stanford University Press, 129–30; text-generation programs, 129; University of California Press, 104, 112–21; University of Chicago Press, 100–109; University of Minnesota Press, 121–24
Unsworth, John, 119
Unthought (Hayles), 49, 108, 168–69
U.S. *See* United States

von Neumann, 11

Wang, An, 87
Warnock, John, 67, 196n11
Waters, Lindsay, 95–96
Weiner, Peter, 196n11
What is Life? (Schrödinger), 36
Wheeler, Wendy, 7
Whitehead, Alfred North, 14
Wissoker, Kenneth, 111–12
Wonderful World of Insects, The (Gaul), 64–66, *65*
Word Exchange, The (Graedon), 38, 133–34, 156, 205n41, 205n44; capitalism as theme in, 158–67; language therapy as theme in, 164–67; paradox as theme in, 159–60
word processing: historical development of, 53–59; Word Star, 53. *See also* phototypesetting
Word Star, 53
work of words, 22
writers: celebrity, 23; subsistence, 23
Writing Machines (Burdick), 5, 27, 174
Wurth, Kiene Brillingburg, 179
Wythoff, Grant, 121

Xerox, 37, *69*, 69–73, 195n4. *See also* DocuTech
XML code, cognitive assemblages and, *16*

PREVIOUSLY PUBLISHED WELLEK LIBRARY LECTURES

The Breaking of the Vessels (1983)
Harold Bloom

In the Tracks of Historical Materialism (1984)
Perry Anderson

Forms of Attention (1985)
Frank Kermode

Memoires for Paul de Man (1986)
Jacques Derrida

The Ethics of Reading (1987)
J. Hillis Miller

Peregrinations: Law, Form, Event (1988)
Jean-François Lyotard

A Reopening of Closure: Organicism Against Itself (1989)
Murray Krieger

Musical Elaborations (1991)
Edward W. Said

Three Steps on the Ladder of Writing (1993)
Hélène Cixous

The Seeds of Time (1994)
Fredric Jameson

Refiguring Life: Metaphors of Twentieth-Century Biology (1995)
Evelyn Fox Keller

The Fateful Question of Culture (1997)
Geoffrey Hartman

The Range of Interpretation (2000)
Wolfgang Iser

History's Disquiet: Modernity, Cultural Practice, and the Question of Everyday Life (2000)
Harry Harootunian

Antigone's Claim: Kinship Between Life and Death (2000)
Judith Butler

The Vital Illusion (2000)
Jean Baudrillard

Death of a Discipline (2003)
Gayatri Chakravorty Spivak

Postcolonial Melancholia (2005)
Paul Gilroy

On Suicide Bombing (2007)
Talal Asad

Cosmopolitanism and the Geographies of Freedom (2009)
David Harvey

Hiroshima After Iraq: Three Studies in Art and War (2009)
Rosalyn Deutsche

Globalectics: Theory and the Politics of Knowing (2012)
Ngugi wa Thiong'o

Violence and Civility: On the Limits of Political Philosophy (2015)
Étienne Balibar

Dark Ecology: For a Logic of Future Coexistence (2016)
Timothy Morton

Knowledge, Power, and Academic Freedom (2019)
Joan Wallach Scott

Morphing Intelligence: From IQ Measurement to Artificial Brains (2019)
Catherine Malabou

In the Ruins of Neoliberalism: The Rise of Antidemocratic Politics in the West (2019)
Wendy Brown

GPSR Authorized Representative: Easy Access System Europe, Mustamäe tee 50, 10621 Tallinn, Estonia, gpsr.requests@easproject.com

www.ingramcontent.com/pod-product-compliance
Lightning Source LLC
Chambersburg PA
CBHW021942290426
44108CB00012B/930